MW00331383

GET OFF MY NECK

GET OFF MY NECK

Black Lives, White Justice, and a Former Prosecutor's Quest for Reform

DEBBIE HINES

The MIT Press
Cambridge, Massachusetts
London, England

© 2024 Debbie Hines

All rights reserved. No part of this book may be used to train artificial intelligence systems or reproduced in any form by any electronic or mechanical means (including photocopying, recording, or information storage and retrieval) without permission in writing from the publisher.

The MIT Press would like to thank the anonymous peer reviewers who provided comments on drafts of this book. The generous work of academic experts is essential for establishing the authority and quality of our publications. We acknowledge with gratitude the contributions of these otherwise uncredited readers.

This book was set in Adobe Garamond Pro by New Best-set Typesetters Ltd. Printed and bound in the United States of America.

Library of Congress Cataloging-in-Publication Data

Names: Hines, Debbie, author.
Title: Get off my neck : Black lives, white justice, and a former prosecutor's quest for
  reform / Debbie Hines.
Description: Cambridge, Massachusetts : The MIT Press, [2024] | Includes bibliographical
  references and index.
Identifiers: LCCN 2023028010 (print) | LCCN 2023028011 (ebook) |
  ISBN 9780262048910 (hardcover) | ISBN 9780262378154 (epub) |
  ISBN 9780262378147 (pdf)
Subjects: LCSH: Discrimination in criminal justice administration—United States. |
  Crime and race—United States.
Classification: LCC HV9950 .H54 2024 (print) | LCC HV9950 (ebook) |
  DDC 364.089—dc23/eng/20231115
LC record available at https://lccn.loc.gov/2023028010
LC ebook record available at https://lccn.loc.gov/2023028011

10 9 8 7 6 5 4 3 2 1

To my mother

Contents

INTRODUCTION

There but for the grace of God, go I.
—A paraphrase from 1 Corinthians 15:8–10

On an icy cold late December afternoon in 2022, I sat in a vehicle driven by Sam, a naturalized citizen who came to the United States as an immigrant from Pakistan and now owns a car service company. As we engaged in conversation, Sam talked about how America is a country where everyone has the same opportunities to advance. He talked about how he came to this country with few resources and now owns a fleet of vehicles. Sam said that he believes that in the United States, every person regardless of race can dream and work to turn those dreams into a reality.

As Sam told his personal story of success, I remained silent. It was Christmas Eve and hardly a good time for a challenging discussion, but I strongly disagreed with him. On another day, I might have told Sam how his experiences differ from those of many African Americans.

I wish I could have told Sam about my experiences as a former prosecutor and the experiences of my family, neighbors, and clients charged with crimes whose lives were upended due to a racially biased prosecutorial system. I would have explained to Sam how, by design, the power of the prosecutor perpetrates racial disparities against African Americans in the criminal justice system.

Often overlooked in the conversation about reforming the justice system is the pressing need to reform state prosecutorial offices, the most powerful institution in the criminal justice system. Prosecutors control all aspects of a criminal case. Very little happens in the criminal justice system without the prosecutor, whose hand is felt in every aspect of the system. The prosecutor decides whether to take a case before a grand jury for indictment; decides on a plea bargain offer, whether to go to trial, or use another means to end a case; and recommends whether to release an individual before trial on bail. The prosecutor prosecutes a case to obtain the desired goal of conviction, recommends the length of a prison sentence or probation, and participates in all posttrial conviction proceedings. Prosecutors are front and center in all aspects of a criminal case, and judges often rubberstamp their recommendations.

As a Baltimore prosecutor in my twenties and early thirties, I observed that criminal courtrooms were so filled with Black men that it appeared as though white people did not commit crimes. And now, as a trial attorney in private practice for over three decades, I still see the same racial disparities.

The United States has the largest criminal justice system in the world.[1] Within this system, disproportionate numbers of Black children and youth are arrested, charged, and sentenced to prison every day before they are old enough to drive. At age sixteen, my cousin was charged with a crime, was convicted, and later served five years in an adult prison, losing his freedom and constitutional rights. One of every three Black boys born in 2001 can expect to be imprisoned in their lifetime, compared to one in seventeen white boys.[2] Some states have no minimum age for charging a child with a crime.

A Black person is nearly six times as likely to be incarcerated as a white person.[3] For people detained in jail pending a trial date, prosecutors disproportionately deny bail to Black people, despite the US system's presumption of innocence until proven guilty. Black people represent 43 percent of the people in jail waiting for a trial to be held, while Black people make up only 13.4 percent of the US population.[4] I still recall a Black client who sat in a jail for months during the pandemic, including on Christmas, on a misdemeanor charge a few years ago because a prosecutor refused to recommend a bail amount. With an arrest or charge, even without a conviction, comes reduced potential for opportunities, including career, housing, and educational advancement.

Police arrest Black people ten times more frequently than they arrest white people.[5] On a national level, police search the vehicles of Black people more often than they search white people's vehicles, despite the fact that white people are more likely to have unregistered weapons or illegal drugs.[6]

Unarmed Black people who present with minimal to no threat to police are killed three times more often than whites, even though Black Americans are less likely than any other race to resist the police.[7] Rarely do prosecutors charge police officers for killing unarmed Black people.

The most atrocious sentences are imposed by the death penalty. Forty-four percent of all people on death row since 1976 are Black people.[8]

The "colorblind" justice system in America is actually color coded. And contrary to popular belief, the most powerful component of the criminal justice system (made up of law enforcement, courts, and corrections) is not the police: it is the prosecutor, who is part of the court system. Policing in the United States is conducted in a way that keeps the prosecutor's pipeline full for convictions. The police make the arrests. The prosecutor does the rest.

The local and state prosecutors' offices, not federal prosecutors, handle the bulk of criminal cases in the United States. They have huge daily court dockets of defendants charged with crimes, minimal prosecutor training, and fewer staff resources and staff than federal prosecutors, and they rely on local police departments to investigate cases. These factors often result in a rush to prosecutions and convictions that systemically target Black Americans. Unlike the US Attorney's Offices at the federal level, which process approximately eighty thousand cases each year, local and state prosecutors' offices handle thirteen million new cases annually at the misdemeanor level alone.[9] Depending on location, elected state and local prosecutors are referred to as attorneys general, chief prosecutors, county attorneys, district attorneys, prosecuting attorneys, and state's attorneys.

The purpose of this book is to provide a context for understanding the history of racial inequities in our prosecutorial system, describe how the 2,400 elected state and local nonfederal prosecutors (of which 95 percent are white) drive these racial inequities, and examine how our prosecutorial system adversely impacts African Americans by design.[10] Finally, this book provides a pathway to accomplishing transformational change within the US carceral prosecution system.

The US prosecutorial system will not change unless and until we reform the policies and procedures that run the state and local elected prosecutorial offices. We need prosecutors to lead with fairness and compassion instead of convictions and corruption. Reforms must include restorative justice measures conducted outside of the criminal justice system and prosecutor's office to overhaul the US carceral system. *Get Off My Neck* provides strategies and a blueprint for prosecutors, community activists, racial justice organizations, lawmakers, and all people who desire to transform local and state prosecutorial offices so that they serve justice and racial equity. It will take a concerted effort with all hands on deck through education and firsthand experiences. While there are currently some reform-minded prosecutors—and that number is growing—we cannot leave all the work to these elected prosecutors to transform a system that prosecutors created.

To take the necessary next steps, we must first understand a crucial point of context—the historical significance of the present moment. Racism is encoded in the DNA of the United States. Its history holds hundreds of years of programming and messaging that have conditioned Americans to see Black people as violent, dangerous, and without value. These messages are embedded in the psyche of America and all its systems, working like the DNA of our bodies to pass down from one generation to the next the illness of racism and infect its culture, morals, policies, and enforcement (or lack thereof) of laws. With this coding of racism, prosecutors have created a system to degrade and devalue Black lives, and this was done by design. That DNA continues to affect us, and we cannot ignore how it affects prosecutors in their racially systemic treatment of Black people. We must face it head on. As James Baldwin stated in his book *The Price of the Ticket*, "the great force of history comes from the fact that we carry it within us, are unconsciously controlled by it in many ways, and history is literally present in all that we do."[11]

For many years, a few friends told me that I should write a book on this topic. I thought it was a good idea, but like many things in life, I placed it on the back burner to pursue at a later time. During the pandemic in 2020, as I sat at home and watched Reverend Al Sharpton deliver the eulogy for George Floyd, Sharpton's eulogy deeply resonated with me as it probably did for many other Black Americans. He spoke to the racial injustice experiences I encountered as a prosecutor and private trial attorney. He stated: "George Floyd's story has been the story of Black folks. . . . The reason we could never be who we wanted and dreamed of being is you kept your knee on our neck. . . . Like George, we couldn't breathe. . . . You wouldn't take your knee off our neck."[12]

Get Off My Neck is told through my lens as a Black woman, the daughter of hardworking parents of modest means, and a descendant of enslaved Black people. The personal recollections that I share as a former prosecutor may differ from those of my fellow prosecutors—particularly my white colleagues—but that makes them no less true.

My parents left school after ninth grade, and my mother worked as a sharecropper, domestic worker, and health/nurse's aide, while my father worked as a laborer in the local steel mill. They were young when they moved to Baltimore to escape the atrocities of the Jim Crow South, following the route traveled by many Black people who migrated to northern cities. My parents raised me to be compassionate. There was a saying often quoted in my household that "There but for the grace of God, go I"—meaning that if things were different, I might face the same bad consequences or unfortunate situations as another person experienced. I've embraced that belief throughout my life.

My brother and I were the first people in our family to attend and graduate from college, and I went on to graduate from law school. Of all attorneys in the United States, only 4.5 percent are Black attorneys, and even fewer have been prosecutors.[13] When I graduated from law school, I had no lawyer mentors. I knew only that I wanted to be a trial lawyer who worked in a courtroom. After all, that's what I had seen on TV shows and in the movies.

My first job was as an assistant attorney general in the Consumer Protection Division of the Maryland Office of the Attorney General. There I investigated unfair and deceptive trade practices, including false and deceptive advertising committed by businesses against consumers. I rarely left my desk. When a job opportunity arose at the Office of the State's Attorney for

Baltimore City, I jumped at the chance to work as an assistant state's attorney. I saw it as an opportunity to gain courtroom experience with jury trials and at the same time help Black people who became ensnarled with the prosecutor's office and charged with crimes.

Growing up in the Park Heights neighborhood of Baltimore, a lower socioeconomic Black community, I watched as my neighbors, friends, and relatives were impacted by crime or charged with crimes. I felt that my family background and my knowledge of my neighborhood would allow me to help people. I expected to be able to perform my job with fairness, compassion, and justice. But I learned almost immediately that the work done in a prosecutor's office bears little resemblance to justice or compassion. The prosecutor's main goal is conviction for anyone charged with a crime—even in a flawed case or where the evidence shows that no crime occurred.

This book doesn't cover all areas of injustices in the prosecutorial system (there are far too many to cover here) but paints with a broad brush to provide a framework for learning and moving toward action. Entire books have been devoted to only a single topic, such as juvenile justice, probation, plea bargains, sentencing, reform prosecutors, policing, or prisons. I provide information on the subject areas that I deem most relevant in the context of race, the prosecutor's office, and prosecutorial reforms. In this book, I set aside discussions of intersectionality of class and gender. Those discussions are important, but my research and experience are focused on race alone.

Over the years, many people have asked me why I became a prosecutor. In the beginning, I thought I knew the answer. I became a prosecutor to make a positive impact in people's lives and gain trial experience. I accomplished the goal of attaining trial experience, but my goal to help people charged with crimes was not achievable in my role as a line prosecutor. This book shows how we can change those outcomes and make the prosecutor's office a place where the people working there can help people.

Throughout the book, I use the terms *African American* and *Black American* interchangeably, as those terms are how I define myself. Given shared history and culture, I capitalize Black to reflect the collective experiences and sense of community among Black people in America. In describing stories of my personal experiences and as a prosecutor and private attorney, I've

changed the names of individuals and altered facts related to specific inci-
dences. For some stories, I drew on my memory, and for others, I relied on
the assistance of public records. No stories related here were told by clients
or through client communications.

My mother always told my brother and me that "Knowledge is key."
My hope is that, armed with knowledge of how prosecutors work, everyone
who seeks racial justice and prosecutorial reform will act to make transformative changes that lead to a noncarceral prosecutorial system that is just
and compassionate.

I WHITE JUSTICE: THE HISTORY

1 JUSTICE AND BLACK REALITY

History, despite its wrenching pain, cannot be unlived, but if faced with courage, need not be lived again.
—Maya Angelou, "On the Pulse of Morning"

Many people in the United States think of slavery as a historical era, something that happened so long ago that it has nothing to do with our present-day experiences as individuals or collectively as a nation. But the reality is that slavery endured until very recently, and its echoes are still being felt. My father's grandmother, Julia (née Wright) Hines, was born an enslaved child in the unincorporated small town of Wadley, Georgia, in 1858. For almost five years, until the Emancipation Proclamation was issued on January 1, 1863, she was legally identified as chattel. The law of this land did not consider her to be human.

In 2020, the results of a DNA test connected me with my paternal relatives, who had traced our family history all the way back to Julia's mother, Classie Smith, who was born an enslaved person in 1834. After marrying Simeon Hines and together raising what records show to be at least eighteen children, Julia lived a long life and died at the age of ninety-four in August 1952. She lived her entire life in Georgia—through slavery and the Jim Crow South. She never experienced full freedom. Anyone who is at least twenty years old most likely knows someone who was born in the early 1950s when Julia—someone who lived during the era of legalized enslavement of Black people—was still alive. This is living memory. History is not simply the study of past events. It is an inescapable link that connects these events across time, allowing us to understand and grow from them. The history of my family is the history of America, and that history permeates every aspect of current-day American life and culture, from clerking at a grocery store to the inner workings of a prosecutor's office.

When I began my career as a prosecutor in the Office of the State's Attorney for Baltimore City in my twenties, Black people in my childhood neighborhood often disparagingly told me, "You put Black people in jail for a living."

I eventually came to see why they felt that way.

The US justice system is in conflict with the purported American ideals of justice and freedom for all—but it is consistent with American history. Thomas Jefferson and the founding fathers defined the word "all" in a narrow sense. In 1776, the Declaration of Independence declared that "all men are created equal" with unalienable rights to life and liberty, but it did not apply these rights to enslaved Black people and women.[1] Just as the DNA of my family runs through my veins, connecting me to ancestors once unknown to me, the racial DNA of America runs through its veins, connecting it to its forgotten or ignored past. The disease of racism toward Black people took root in America's DNA when white colonizers enslaved the first African people in 1619. Today the justice system and prosecutor's office function in exactly the same way they were intended to work when they were founded centuries ago—to imprison and punish Black people.

HOW PROSECUTION WORKS

My initial goal as a prosecutor was to obtain trial experience and help victims of serious violent crimes. However, the realities of the prosecutor's office quickly exposed the naivete of those simple intentions. The rigid office policies I encountered often had little bearing on justice and sometimes were explicitly racist. Some senior white male prosecutors refused to speak to me, a Black woman prosecutor.

In my almost five-year tenure, I prosecuted thousands of defendants in Baltimore. Only two of them were white.

In the United States, the symbol of justice—a blindfolded woman holding balanced scales—represents the supposed impartiality of the justice system, a system that is said to be not only blind but also colorblind. But the belief that the criminal justice system treats every citizen the same, regardless of race, couldn't be further from the truth. The justice system in America is actually color coded, and anyone who touts colorblindness as a badge of equality is ignoring the realities of systemic racism in the prosecution of Black people.

The United States has the largest criminal justice system in the world, and it disproportionately impacts Black people.[2] In 2018, 2.8 million Black people were arrested.[3] Police arrest Black people ten times more frequently than they arrest white people, despite the fact that Black people do not commit ten times more crimes. One of every three Black boys born in 2001 can expect to be imprisoned in their lifetime, compared to one in seventeen white boys, according to the Sentencing Project's "Report to the United Nations on Racial Disparities in the US Criminal Justice System."[4] Overall, a Black person is nearly six times as likely to be incarcerated as a white person.[5]

In my first days as a prosecutor in the Office of the State's Attorney for Baltimore City, I was assigned a misdemeanor jury trial docket crammed with dozens of Black people, most of whom were arrested for petty theft, loitering, or other minor offenses. As a new prosecutor eager to do a good job, I went to my team captain for advice. He told me to be tough with my plea bargains. In other words, don't give anyone an easy out. I looked again at my docket full of minor crimes and wondered why we had to be so rigid. What purpose did it serve? Where was the justice or public safety in maximizing a plea bargain for a minor offense?

I entered that job with a set of expectations that were dramatically different from the reality I encountered. As I soon learned, justice and public safety were not the goals. Instead, the main outcome expected by the prosecutor's office was conviction. The defendant's guilt or innocence barely mattered. Often, we had no choice but to prosecute because the office instituted strict policies that prevented prosecutors from exercising discretion and considering more lenient treatment of defendants. That is the Black reality in a white justice system, and that reality is a holdover from a race-based system that was consciously designed to oppress Black people.

THE BEGINNING

Many people think that Abraham Lincoln's Emancipation Proclamation (1863) and the thirteenth amendment (1865) to the US Constitution ended perpetual servitude for enslaved Black people, but they simply prohibited slavery "except as punishment for crime." Consequently, as Reconstruction (1865–1877) began, Southern states wasted no time enacting laws designed to reenslave Black people, laws known today as Black Codes (1865–1866). Black Codes criminalized practices such as unemployment, loitering, and vagrancy, targeting Black people. In 1866, the year after the passage of the thirteenth amendment, lawmakers in Georgia, Mississippi, and Texas passed convict leasing laws, which allowed their white-controlled governments to lease the labor of imprisoned Black people to state-owned and private farms. So imprisoned Black people were sent back to work on plantations. As author Carol Anderson describes in her book *White Rage: The Unspoken Truth of Our Racial Divide*, in the year after the Civil War (1865), Black Americans who could provide no proof of employment were charged with vagrancy, put on an auction block, and sold to the highest bidder. Black Americans who showed any defiance or behaviors that white southerners deemed to be insulting or inappropriate could be whipped. Under the Black Codes, criminal courts transferred power over formerly enslaved Black people from enslavers to a carceral state.[6] Anderson states the passage of the thirteenth amendment in 1865 triggered white rage and that the trigger for white rage was Black advancement.[7] From the end of slavery to the present day, white rage has worked to disproportionately criminalize Black people.

When Reconstruction ended, Jim Crow laws began in 1877.[8] Jim Crow laws were state and local laws that enforced racial segregation and carried fines for breaking such laws, fines so steep that they often led to incarceration for Black people who defied them. Jim Crow laws lasted for nearly a hundred years until the passage of the Civil Rights Act of 1964 and the Voting Rights Act of 1965.[9]

RHYMING PROSECUTION PRACTICES

The criminal justice system became one of the central institutions for sustaining racial domination over Black people and continuing their economic exploitation. Today, it is unconstitutional to enact laws that penalize and criminalize Black people and exclude white people, but as a quote often attributed to Mark Twain states: "History doesn't repeat itself, but it often rhymes."[10]

Although the practice of convict leasing ended, we can find plenty of rhyming practices in today's society. Prison labor is still legal, with some prisoners working for no pay whatsoever and others receiving as little as sixty cents an hour. As of 2020, over 4,100 US corporations had used prison labor.[11] In one particularly rhyming example, inmates today at the Louisiana State Prison in Angola literally pick cotton.[12] In November 2022, voters in Alabama, Louisiana, Tennessee, Vermont, and Oregon responded to ballot initiatives to remove slavery language in their state constitutions, and all but Louisiana voted to remove the offensive language.[13] In a fitting parallel, Louisiana has the nation's highest incarceration rate.[14] Almost twenty state constitutions contain language that permit slavery and involuntary servitude for criminal punishment.[15]

The way that the justice system generates the convicts who do that labor also closely resembles historical precedent. Instead of explicit Black Codes or Jim Crow laws, we now have what I call "nuisance charges." These charges come from violating laws that criminalize normal day-to-day behavior (like a minor nonviolent infraction) or merely a police officer's whim. The most common nuisance charges are loitering, trespassing, disorderly conduct, and failure to obey police. On their own, these charges don't carry significant jail time, but they often initiate a person's involvement in the criminal justice system, which leads to more arrests and to jail time, especially if the defendant was arrested while serving probation. As a Baltimore prosecutor, I saw hundreds of Black people prosecuted for these minor crimes, but most defendants took a plea bargain, which meant that they avoided going to trial and risking jail time. The plea bargains for these minor charges usually resulted in fines or probation. However, a plea bargain requires a defendant to admit to guilt, which counts as a conviction and bolsters a prosecutor's conviction rate.

Defenders of the current system argue that these laws exist for good reason and that if someone is charged with violating them, they should face the consequences. However, when you look more closely at each category of nuisance charge, it becomes obvious how little their enforcement contributes to public safety. Take loitering and trespassing, for example. Maryland defines loitering as aimless lingering or obstructing the free flow of pedestrians or traffic in a public space. Trespassing, its close cousin, prohibits a person from trespassing on property where signs are prominently posted and carries a penalty of ninety days in jail and/or a fine of $500 and up to six months in jail for a subsequent violation.

As a Baltimore prosecutor, I reviewed hundreds of loitering or trespass cases. In many cases, the description of the "crime" consisted of people relaxing outdoors with friends and family in their neighborhood. Sweltering summers were prime months for loitering cases, as the police charged huge numbers of Black people who were sitting outside to escape the stifling heat of their homes. Sometimes, my loitering cases consisted of Black teens or young men who stood on street corners for lack of anywhere else to go. Many people were talking, listening to music, or singing a cappella when the police officers arrived to disburse the crowd, and if anyone failed to follow police orders to disperse, they were charged with either loitering, trespassing, or failure to obey a lawful police order.

Most of those accused weren't suspected of any genuine criminal activity, like selling drugs or possessing weapons. They landed in court for existing and relaxing with their friends, as if it were a crime for two or more Black people to stand together outside. And even though it was an open secret in the prosecutor's office that pursuing these cases did nothing to make Baltimore safer, I was instructed to prosecute them, which, as a young prosecutor, I did. One of my favorite judges dismissed almost any loitering case where the officer charged someone for merely standing in public, but he was in the minority. Most of the time, these cases were resolved with a plea bargain that rendered the accused guilty as charged.

In 2015, several decades after my tenure in the misdemeanor unit, Baltimore police arrested Freddie Gray, a twenty-five-year-old Black man, for possessing a knife, which the city's state's attorney later determined was a lawful knife under Maryland law.[16] The officers shackled Freddie, put him in the back of a police van without a seat belt, and sped around town, taking sharp turns. Gray, shackled and unable to balance, careened around the inside of the van and collided with the metal walls. Baltimore's Black residents had a name for this bit of wanton cruelty: they called it a "rough ride." This ride broke Freddie Gray's neck. He died a week later. In the wake of his death, the United States Department of Justice (DOJ) conducted an investigation that exposed the pervasive civil rights abuses of the Baltimore police and prosecutors.

Part of the DOJ report found that Baltimore police and, by extension, its prosecutors unconstitutionally used loitering and trespassing laws to target Black communities.[17] They described several cases that resembled what I had seen as a prosecutor, including one in which a police officer told an African American man and his four-year-old son playing near a park that they "couldn't just stand around" and "needed to move."[18]

While loitering and trespassing are often obviously sham charges, disorderly conduct, resisting arrest, and assault on a police officer seemingly have more legitimacy. After all, they seem like real crimes. Even the word *assault* sounds violent. But as a prosecutor, I overwhelmingly saw cases in which the details of these types of charges didn't resemble any criminal or unsafe behavior. Usually, the police charged a defendant with these crimes as retaliation against a Black person who either questioned the officer or expressed a concern about the situation. I viewed these arrests as a violation of a person's constitutional first amendment rights, so I often declined to prosecute. But as I reflect on those days, I see now that my efforts to dismiss doubtful cases against Black people did little to help them. With an arrest on their record, the harm had been done.

In any case, any attempts to thwart unjust prosecutions, futile as they may have been, were uncommon in my office. The majority of prosecutors sided with police officers on almost every assault on police charge, even when the circumstances did not warrant the charge.

Another area where America's present-day practices rhyme too clearly with the past are Pig Laws. Pig Laws, like Black Codes, first appeared after the Civil War and reemerged after the Reconstruction era ended in 1877.

Like Black Codes, they targeted Black people while ignoring the white population and operated through extremely harsh penalties for misdemeanors, such as stealing a pig or other farm animal. People often landed on my docket for shoplifting food or other basic necessities, and each time they did, it reminded me of Pig Laws. Most of them stole goods totaling less than $100, so they faced a petty theft charge with a maximum penalty of ninety days in jail and/or a $500 fine. It disheartened me to see so many Black people in court for exercising survival tactics. They were stealing to eat, not for profit. I came home each day exhausted and shaken. For me, to be a Black woman and a prosecutor meant living in a constant state of shock. I had no idea that I signed up to offer plea bargains to convict people who were simply trying to survive.

Fortunately, my office had no hard-and-fast rules or policies on shoplifting cases. That meant that I could use my discretion and either decline to prosecute or offer lenient plea bargains. However, we offered no real support that would help the person survive without committing the same theft another time. We made no recommendations to social service organizations. After almost every sentencing, the judges said, "Good luck to you." But these individuals needed more than luck. Luck on its own can't feed people or their children.

The real problem with shoplifting for basic necessities arose when the defendant committed the crime while on probation for another charge. In those instances, it was office policy not to offer a probationary period again, however minor the first offense was. Instead, the defendant received jail time, even for something as minor as stealing a tube of toothpaste. In those instances, the prosecutors in my office usually offered a plea bargain for time served. In other words, we let them plead guilty to the crime, and their full sentence was the time they'd spent in jail awaiting trial. Time-served pleas provide some relief, but they can still act as a massive interruption of a person's life. Scores of people regularly have to wait in jail for months before their trial or a hearing date, often due to defense or prosecution postponements, the unavailability of witnesses, large court dockets that result in few available trial times, or other reasons that a judge accepts for postponing a hearing or trial. In the pandemic year of 2020, the number of people in US jails without a conviction decreased to 445,000 from a high of 482,000 in 2017,[19] still an appallingly large number. Past data show Black people represent 43 percent of the US pretrial numbers, while Black people make up only 13.4 percent of the US population.[20] In a country where we presume that everyone is innocent until proven guilty, we lock up an awful lot of presumptively innocent people.

BAIL OR JAIL

Being detained in jail while awaiting trial, no matter how brief, can have sweeping and devastating consequences on a person's life. One Black defendant I knew died in jail due to a drug overdose and the failure of the jail staff to provide adequate medical attention. The bail amount that would have secured his release was less than $500. While pretrial release is often preferable to indefinite detention without bail, the way that pretrial release is administered is problematic. Maryland, like many jurisdictions, has a cash bail system. This means that people can secure their release if they pay their bail amount or a bail bond of 10 percent of their bail. In this system, defendants can also be held without bail or released on their own recognizance, with or without conditions. In Maryland, the initial bail recommendation isn't made by the prosecutor but instead by a pretrial services representative from the Division of Parole and Probation. Within twenty-four hours of an arrest, the representative interviews the defendant and generates a bail recommendation based on several factors, including the charges, verification of housing, employment, connection and ties to the community, and indication of flight risk or threat of harm to the community. That information is documented in a report and delivered to the prosecutor.

The defendant and a defense attorney review the report and appear at a bail hearing, where a judge makes the final bail determination. At these hearings, the prosecutor usually relies on the pretrial services report for making bail recommendations, unless the prosecutor has additional information that makes a more stringent bail necessary. Prosecutors rarely offer a lower bail or fewer conditions for release. The defense attorney usually argues for more lenient bail terms.

Judges can set bail at a higher or lower level than that recommended by the pretrial services report or prosecutor or even deny bail altogether at their discretion. If defendants cannot pay the initial bail, which often happens, they can request a bail review hearing in an attempt to lower the cost. Those bail reviews often fail, and people remain in jail. They often lose their jobs, their homes, and contact with their family. In the worst instances, they lose their lives in jail awaiting a trial. Between 2008 and 2019, 4,998 people died in US jails awaiting their trial or arraignment date on mostly minor charges.[21] Most died from unattended physical illness or mental health breakdowns.[22] One such individual was Larry Eugene Price. In August 2020, Larry Eugene Price, a six-foot two-inch tall, 185-pound, fifty-year-old developmentally disabled Arkansas Black man, was arrested during an acute mental health crisis. He was charged with "terroristic threatening in the first degree" due to his erratic behavior of yelling and cursing at police officers. Unable to make the $1,000 bail, he remained in jail pending his trial. Jail officials placed him in solitary confinement. Price didn't eat or drink for long periods of time due to his mental condition. He received no medical attention. One year later, on August 29, 2021, while still awaiting his trial, he died. At the time of his death, he had lost over half his initial body weight and weighed only 90 pounds. He died from acute dehydration and malnutrition in jail awaiting his court date.[23]

From 2008 to 2019, Black Americans made up 28 percent of the people who died in US jails while waiting for a trial date, a percentage more than twice the US Black population.[24] Alexis de Tocqueville wrote in 1835 that American criminal procedure has only two means of action—committal or bail: "The first act of a proceeding consists in obtaining bail from the defendant, or if he refuses, in incarcerating him; afterwards, one discusses the validity of the title or the gravity of the charges."[25]

A no-cash bail system is far more just. The District of Columbia, where I also practice, has had such a system since 1992. The District releases approximately 94 percent of people without using money as an incentive to return to court, and less than 2 percent are rearrested for a violent crime.[26] In the District of Columbia, the no-cash bail system does not result in an increase of danger to the public safety. In July 2023, the Illinois Supreme Court paved the way for Illinois to become the first state to eliminate cash bail.[27]

MANDATORY MINIMUMS, ENHANCED PENALTY, OR HABITUAL OFFENDER LAWS

As large as the numbers are, people held in jails before they are convicted account for only a small percentage of America's massive prison population. To fully understand how prosecutors have contributed to the exploding numbers of incarceration, we need to look at the Violent Crime Control and Law Enforcement Act of 1994 (the 1994 Crime Bill), which was passed during the Bill Clinton administration. One of the changes made by this sweeping piece of legislation was a mandatory sentencing law, which instituted a mandatory minimum sentence for a crime, regardless of the facts of the case. In the years after 1994, several states followed the federal government's lead and instituted their own minimum sentencing laws. The prosecutor stood at the forefront of this new legislation and the new laws that followed its enactment in states across the nation.

While prosecutors have no control over mandatory minimums, they do have control over what charge to bring against a defendant. As a former prosecutor, I saw firsthand how systemic racial disparities in the criminal justice system continued the historical practices of blatant racism against Black people through the subtle application of the law. For instance, the prosecutor makes the sole determination of whether to bring enhanced penalties, whether a case meets the most stringent criteria as a capital punishment case, and whether to seek the death penalty.

I'm still haunted by one mandatory minimum case. I prosecuted a Baltimore schoolteacher, a married Black man without a criminal record, who faced a misdemeanor charge for use of a handgun in the commission of a crime of violence and one felony count. After my review of the case and interview with the victim, I doubted the alleged victim's version of the incident. While I believed that a crime occurred, her story didn't ring entirely true. A prosecutor bears the burden of proving a case beyond a reasonable doubt—the highest standard of proof. In order to convict, all twelve members of the jury must unanimously agree. With no physical evidence, inconsistent statements by the victim, and no witnesses who could support the victim's story, it amounted to a weak case. When I discussed the case with the defense attorney, I offered a plea bargain to reduced misdemeanor charges of assault and possession of a handgun with probation before judgment, which meant the defendant would not receive a criminal record and could continue to teach in his job. The defendant accepted the terms, and the victim agreed to them as well.

In court, however, when I presented the plea to the judge, the victim had a change of heart. She vehemently spoke against the plea bargain. The law does not require that a victim give consent to a plea bargain, but after hearing her, the judge refused to accept the plea. Due to the inherent weaknesses of the case and the victim's sudden change of heart, I went to my supervisor and the deputy state's attorney for guidance. My supervisor ordered me to try the case before a jury and let the chips fall.

We seated a jury. The victim testified. The jury returned a guilty verdict. I was shocked, as were the defense attorney and the judge. Throughout the trial, the victim gave inconsistent testimony on key points, amounting to a serious lack of credibility. Nevertheless, use of a handgun in the commission of a crime of violence requires a mandatory minimum sentence of five years, with a maximum term of twenty-five years. The judge sentenced the defendant to five years, explaining that, regretfully, he was legally obliged to do so. The defendant was escorted out of the courtroom in handcuffs to serve his time.

Other mandatory sentencing laws that flourished after the crime bill focused on people convicted more than once for violent crimes. For each ensuing conviction of a violent crime, the minimum number of years that the defendant must serve increases. In Maryland, the mandatory minimums are ten years for a second conviction, twenty-five years for a third conviction, and life without parole for a fourth conviction for a crime of violence.

A related set of laws, known as enhanced penalties and habitual offender laws, add extra years to a sentence for people convicted more than once of the same or comparable offenses. Unlike mandatory minimums, however, a prosecutor makes the sole determination of whether to seek enhanced penalties or recommend a habitual offender penalty. Habitual offender laws, also known as "three-strikes laws," can have devastating effects on a person's life. Take, for example, the tragic case of Fair Wayne Bryant. Bryant was arrested in Louisiana for attempting to steal a pair of hedge clippers. He had three prior theft convictions and one robbery conviction, which made him eligible for habitual offender status. The prosecutor chose to seek the most severe sentence possible—life in prison without parole—for attempting to steal the hedge clippers.

Bryant was found guilty of the attempted theft and received a life sentence without parole. He served twenty-three years before being released, as Louisiana law allows for some people who have been sentenced to life without parole to be considered for parole under certain circumstances.[28] The sole African American judge on Louisiana's Supreme Court, Chief Justice Bernice Johnson, compared Bryant's life sentence and Louisiana's habitual offender laws to the historic Pig Laws and Black Codes.[29] Like Bryant, over 65 percent of US prisoners serving life without parole for a nonviolent offense are Black inmates.[30]

Enhancement penalties like habitual offender laws allow the prosecutor to seek additional prison or jail time for similar subsequent crimes committed. Proponents argue enhancement penalties serve to act as a deterrent for future crimes, but enhancement penalties can result in an illegal sentence if improperly calculated and then rubber-stamped by a judge. An illegal sentence occurs when a judge sentences a person to more time than the allowable maximum penalty under the law for the crime, including any enhancements. In my practice of law, I've encountered a defendant client who through his public defender appealed an enhancement penalty sentence that was wrongfully miscalculated. While he won on appeal, the harm was done at the sentencing.

The power of the prosecutor in these cases cannot be overstressed. While habitual offender laws and enhancement penalties vary from state to state, the prosecutor makes the sole determination of whether to recommend the enhanced sentence or the habitual offender sentence. The elected prosecutors who run their offices make rigid policies on whether to seek higher prison terms, and the facts of a particular case have little bearing on those policies. Because the prosecutors' primary goal is not truth-finding but conviction, they often upgrade charges and sentencing recommendations in an attempt to persuade a defendant to plead to a misdemeanor and avoid a trial. Ninety-five percent of those elected prosecutors are white. Nationwide, prosecutors are 50 percent more likely to file charges under habitual offender or three-strikes laws against Black people than against white people for committing the same crimes.[31]

LIFE OR DEATH

The prosecutor also bears the sole responsibility for determining whether a case meets the stringent criteria for a capital punishment case and, if so, whether the office will seek the death penalty, a present-day practice that rhymes with a gruesome part of American history—lynching. From 1877 to 1950, 4,084 Black people were lynched in twelve Southern states.[32] Lynching was an act of racial terror and a statement of white supremacy. Mobs justified and hailed lynching as a legal punishment for crimes. But it was race rather than any alleged offense that sealed a Black lynching victim's fate. In the South, 90 percent of lynchings were of Black people,[33] but lynchings were not confined to the South. In 2017, the Equal Justice Initiative documented more than three hundred lynchings from 1877 to 1950 in Illinois, Indiana, Kansas, Maryland, Missouri, Ohio, Oklahoma, and West Virginia.[34]

These heinous acts were meant to punish and terrorize Black people for alleged violations of Jim Crow laws and etiquette rules. Prosecutors rarely charged any perpetrators for lynching a person, even when an entire white community of ten thousand[35] attended as witnesses, including law enforcement officials. Over one century later, President Joe Biden signed the federal Emmett Till Anti-Lynching Act of 2022, making lynching a federal crime punishable by a maximum of thirty years in prison.[36]

Eight in ten lynching incidents from 1889 to 1918 were carried out in the South. And eight in ten executions since 1976 have occurred in the South.[37] As lynching decreased, state-perpetrated capital punishment rose to take its place, mainly in the form of the death penalty. Since 1976, 44 percent of all people on death row have been Black.[38] Countless individuals, often Black, have spent years on death row, only to be exonerated of their crimes through DNA evidence.[39] The Innocence Project reports that Black people make up 63 percent of people exonerated through DNA.[40] While we have made progress against the death penalty, as of 2022, it was still legal in twenty-four states, with three of those states on a moratorium.[41]

The death penalty was legal in Maryland at the time that I prosecuted cases. As I am opposed to the death penalty, I never worked on a death penalty case, but I did observe one in the office. In this case, the defendant, "Martin," robbed a fast-food restaurant in the neighborhood where I grew up and shot and killed the cashier. He faced the death penalty because he committed the murder while attempting to commit another felony, a charge known as felony murder. His attorney appealed the death sentence, and the Maryland appellate court sided with Martin. They overturned the sentence but not the convictions and ordered a new sentencing trial.

As part of our training, prosecutors are often instructed to watch more skilled and senior prosecutors in a trial. My office encouraged everyone to attend the closing arguments in Martin's trial. The prosecutor and the defense attorney handling that case were two of the best trial attorneys in Baltimore. It was a heavyweight legal bout. The small courtroom was packed with lawyers. I watched the lead prosecutor give his closing argument asking the jury to reimpose the sentence of death. When the prosecutor sat down, I expected to hear from the lead public defender, an eloquent attorney and strong advocate against the death penalty. Instead, Martin, the defendant himself, stood to give the closing argument.

It is the only time I've ever seen a defendant present his own closing argument. I can still recall his words. He recounted how, when the jury sentenced him to death the first time, his attorney laid his head on the trial table and cried, but Martin laughed. Martin explained that, at the time, he had no respect for his own life and therefore, no respect for the person whose life he took. Then he said he was no longer the person who took another person's life. That he respected and cherished his own life and the life of everyone else. And he begged them to grant him mercy and to spare him.

He gave one of the most passionate, intelligent, authentic, and artful closing arguments I have ever seen.

The jury deliberated on his fate. Once again, they sentenced him to death. This time, Martin did not laugh.

To my knowledge, Martin was never executed. Most defendants linger on death row for years or even decades, and Maryland abolished the death penalty in 2013. But that moment has stuck with me. The person who committed the heinous crime that took a life was long gone. In his place was a man who delivered a closing argument on his own behalf far better than most of the attorneys who sat in the courtroom could. The death penalty never fits the crime. It can't bring a slain victim back to life. But it always ends a life and, more often than not, a Black life.

After I resigned as a prosecutor, my knowledge of how police and prosecutors work proved invaluable, particularly on the morning my mother died peacefully in her sleep.

THE PERSONAL ACCOUNT

After months of lingering in impersonal medical facilities, my mother made it clear that one of her last wishes was to receive hospice care and eventually die at home. On July 14, 2006, I stood in the living room of my childhood home in the Park Heights area of Baltimore, a predominantly African American, mostly lower-income neighborhood. From there, I was to convey her body to Vaughn Greene Funeral Services, which was owned by my mother's friend and fellow church member. It had just turned 8:00 a.m. when I called the hospice facility to report her passing and arrange for her transport. However, because of my misunderstanding of the hospice administration process, my mother was not officially scheduled to be entered into the hospice system until ten o'clock, when a hospice employee would come to the house to finalize the insurance paperwork. Thus, the hospice had no official record of her and instructed me to call the police to arrange transport.

With my mother's nurse quietly consoling me, I called the police. When two officers responded, I told them that my mother was in home hospice care, and one of them asked for official papers verifying my story. Because

I didn't have the paperwork yet due to the hospice mix-up, the officer said that my mother would have to be moved to the city morgue. Confused by the officer's response, overwhelmed by the loss of my mother, and upset by the prospect of not being allowed to carry out her wish to have her body moved directly to her chosen funeral home, tears flooded my eyes and ran down my cheeks. I questioned the officer's authority to make such a demand, and in response, he threatened to arrest me, presumably for crying or talking because I had done nothing else. His partner remained silent.

I knew that the officers could arrest and charge me for "failure to obey a reasonable or lawful order." I also knew that if I continued to try to persuade the officer to allow my mother's body to go directly to a funeral home, the charge could rapidly escalate to resisting arrest. If he decided to handcuff me—even if I didn't hit or push the officer—an assault on a police officer charge would inevitably follow. Despite my position as a trial attorney, a former Baltimore prosecutor, and a former Maryland assistant attorney general, even I was not safe from the dynamics of racial disparities in our criminal justice system. Had I been arrested, I would have been charged, booked, and arraigned. A bail hearing would have been held. A prosecutor would have treated me the same as any other Black person in that position. My college pedigree and law licenses would not have shielded me.

The only reason none of the above happened was because I got lucky and also because I possessed knowledge most people don't: I knew how police and prosecutors operate with Black people. I forced myself to calm down enough to ask for permission to call my mother's physician, who explained the cause of death. The officers listened to the doctor and finally allowed the transport of my mother's body to the Vaughn Greene funeral home. I was able to keep my promise to my mother and narrowly avoid my own arrest.

In my experience as a prosecutor, the majority of resisting arrest or assault charges on an officer came from situations like mine. Whenever I saw charges like these on my docket, I rolled my eyes, knowing it would be a bumpy day. Unlike loitering and trespassing, assaulting an officer and failing to obey orders can carry serious penalties. Take Maryland's second-degree misdemeanor assault, defined as actual or attempted offensive or unwanted touching or threats to harm a person without the person's consent. That charge has a maximum penalty of ten years and/or a fine of $5,000.

Such a stiff maximum penalty would suggest that the offense is serious. Yet I saw defendants face second-degree assault charges for tugging or pulling away from the officer, turning away from being handcuffed, or any other threat the officer claimed to perceive, real or not. A person can bump into an officer in the course of an arrest and be charged with second-degree assault. Almost every second-degree assault charge against an officer came bundled with charges of resisting arrest and failing to obey a lawful order of an officer. The courts were flooded with Black people arrested on these charges, even though African Americans are the people less likely than whites to resist the police.[42] The arresting officers rarely needed medical treatment. And even though I recognized that the police often make trumped up charges, I had to proceed with caution. I regularly worked with these officers and needed their collaboration to do my job in cases that dealt with serious crimes. If I declined to prosecute when they claimed they'd been assaulted, it would amount to me calling them liars, and that would have jeopardized our working relationship.

Overwhelmingly, prosecutors place conviction over anything else. Prosecutors who did not meet those expectations were typically transferred to other units with fewer trials or no trials as punishment for such "failures." I was never told that my conviction rate met the expectations of the prosecutor's office, but I do recall that seemingly out of the blue, the deputy state's attorney once offered me an assignment to a smaller specialized felony sex offense unit, something like the unit in *Law & Order: Special Victims Unit*. After careful consideration, I declined the offer, and almost immediately thereafter, I was demoted. I went from the felony trial unit, where I prosecuted homicides and other serious violent crimes, to the grand jury unit, which requires minimal trial skills. In that unit, all I did was appear before a grand jury without any defense attorney present, recite the alleged facts, obtain an indictment, and later arraign defendants. Often, the arresting officers were the only witnesses. Shortly after that demotion, I resigned.

2 THE PROSECUTOR AND THE POLICE

There is no greater tyranny than that which is perpetrated under the shield of the law and in the name of justice.
—Charles-Louis de Secondat, baron de la Brède et de Montesquieu, *Spirit of the Laws* (1748)

In 2015, when I was in the Library of Congress researching the origins of racial inequities in prosecution, I came across the story of John Punch. In 1640, three of Hugh Gwyn's indentured servants—John Punch, a Black African man; James Gregory, a white Dutchman; and a man identified as Victor, a white Scotsman—ran away from the Virginia colony to the Maryland colony. At the time, indentured servants served for a specific number of years before they gained their freedom, and running away before a term was served was a crime. The three men were captured in Maryland soon after they fled. Hugh Gwyn petitioned the General Court of the Governor and Council to allow him to bring the three men back to Jamestown, Virginia, and on July 9, 1640, the court sentenced the two white servants to thirty lashes, one additional year of service to Gwyn when their original term of servitude ended, and an additional three years in service to the colony after their servitude to Gwyn ended. In the case captioned *In re: Negro John Punch*, the court also sentenced the Black servant, Punch, to a sentence of thirty lashes. But even though all three men committed the same crime at the same time, the court ordered Punch, a "negro," to serve his "master" or his assigns for the rest of his life in Virginia or elsewhere.[1] Punch became enslaved for the rest of his life.

POLICE, PROSECUTION, AND BLACK PEOPLE

To understand the overprosecution of Black people, we need to examine the history of policing, prosecution, and punishment in America. Most analyses of the overprosecution of Black people suggest that it began with the Violent Crime Control and Law Enforcement Act of 1994 (the 1994 Crime Bill), but the problem started much earlier. In 1704, slave patrols began in South Carolina and spread throughout the colonies. From their inception until 1865, members of these patrols (known as "slave catchers") searched for, apprehended, and beat runaway enslaved Black people.[2] The patrols acted as police and prosecutor. They often meted out the death penalty to runaways. In the rare cases when a slave patrol or plantation owner did not dispense punishment for serious crimes committed by an enslaved Black person, prosecutors brought capital cases in a court of law.[3] Colonial and state laws in Maryland (1717), North Carolina (1777), and Mississippi (1822) allowed enslaved Black people to testify in court, if needed, against another enslaved or freed Black person in a criminal case. Prosecutors allowed the testimony of enslaved Black people in trials, but only if their testimony was used to convict another Black person. I sometimes saw the continuation of this practice when prosecutors used the testimony of one Black defendant to convict another Black defendant.

My first murder case was one of those occasions. The defendant killed another Black man after midnight on the streets of East Baltimore. The only eyewitness was a Black woman who was selling drugs outside at the time. She knew the shooter only by his nickname, "Whirl." She testified at trial and identified Whirl as the shooter, and the jury found the defendant guilty of first-degree murder. Due to her cooperative and truthful testimony, the eyewitness's pending drug charge in an unrelated case was later either dismissed or plea bargained down to probation. Unfortunately, whenever a witness provides eyewitness testimony without any corroborated testimony or evidence and later receives a lesser penalty at sentencing or has charges dropped, the risk exists that the testimony may be tainted or obtained by overzealous prosecutors or police who want to secure a conviction.

Prosecutors and police usurped the legal rights of Black people immediately following slavery and throughout the twentieth century and have continued to do so today. White police officers have committed mass shootings, bombings, and massacres of unarmed Black people without facing prosecution. In June 1921, a violent white mob with law enforcement support massacred an estimated three hundred Black people in Tulsa, Oklahoma. Police officers deputized hundreds of white men who looted and burned Black-owned property over thirty-five square blocks. Following the one-day massacre, law enforcement personnel including the Oklahoma National Guard detained and jailed six thousand Black residents in makeshift holding cells throughout the city.[4] Despite the fact that white law enforcement officers engaged in criminal activities and recruited others to do the same, prosecutors convened an all-white grand jury that indicted fifty-six Black men for the massacre.[5] In the Tulsa massacre and others in cities such as Memphis, Chicago, and New Orleans, prosecutors failed to charge any white perpetrators. It wasn't until 2021, a full century later, that the United States officially recognized the Tulsa tragedy.[6]

Those who think a hundred years was a long time ago and that these police and prosecutorial acts are long past us need only look at what took place in Philadelphia in May 1985. Members of MOVE, a Black communal political, religious, and antigovernment organization founded in 1972, resided in a middle-class African American neighborhood in West Philadelphia. Neighbors frequently complained about nuisances caused by MOVE members, including trash piles, loud noise, profanity, and conflicts with neighborhood residents. Police obtained arrest warrants for several of MOVE's residents.[7] When MOVE members were evicted a few years earlier, in 1978, it had led to a stand-off that resulted in the death of an officer and the subsequent imprisonment of nine members. To avoid further violence, on the morning of May 13, 1985, police told neighbors to temporarily leave their homes due to anticipated police activity. They went door to door to ensure that neighbors were evacuated before an attempt to serve the warrants and order members of MOVE from their house.[8]

By evening, when police believed that everyone except MOVE members had evacuated, the Philadelphia Police Department gave orders to clear the building. According to neighbors' accounts, police officers fired tear gas and at least ten thousand rounds of ammunition into the house. Philadelphia's first Black mayor, W. Wilson Goode Sr., gave orders to "seize control of the house . . . by any means possible."[9] A police helicopter then dropped two bombs on the house. The fire department made no attempts to put out the fires caused by the bombing. In his later account of the event, Philadelphia Fire Commissioner William C. Richmond stated that Police Commissioner George Sambor instructed Richmond to let everything burn.[10]

The bomb and ensuing fire destroyed sixty-one homes in two city blocks, leaving mostly ashes. It displaced over 250 middle-class Black people, rendering them homeless. The police officers' actions killed eleven Black people, including five children, who resided in the MOVE house.[11] Despite two grand juries, prosecutors did not bring charges of murder or excessive force against the police.[12] All of this destruction occurred because police wanted to serve misdemeanor warrants on MOVE occupants.[13]

THE POLICE AND PROSECUTOR CONUNDRUM

Prosecutors and police officers work in tandem on a daily basis. One cannot exist without the other. And after spending almost five years as a prosecutor, I recall fewer than a handful of police officers whom I trusted to thoroughly investigate a case, discuss with me any flaws in or legal issues about a case, and accept my recommendations to dismiss a case if warranted without any pushback about my review. Most police officers that I encountered did not want to hear about any flaws in their work, any constitutional issues, or any other police errors or missteps. Like state's attorneys and district attorneys, police want to see convictions.

When I was a prosecutor, we were never trained in how to handle any police officers we suspected of misconduct, and there was no clear policy on or discussion of these matters. In fact, I had the displeasure of working with many cops that I viewed as dishonest. Given their prevalence in the system, it was unavoidable. The system in which I prosecuted did not allow any discussion of systemic police misconduct, whether in their testimony, investigations, or acts (or conduct).

I vividly remember the moment I first learned that a police officer had lied on a case. It was early in my career as a prosecutor, and I listened as the court clerk arraigned a defendant on drug charges, which stemmed from a search and seizure warrant served at the defendant's home. When the clerk read how much cash the officer had seized from the defendant's home, the defendant yelled, "Whoa, whoa! If I'm being charged with a crime, the cop should be charged with theft!" According to the defendant, the officer had seized much more than he noted in his sworn statement, in all likelihood pocketing the difference.

The arraignment continued as if nothing had occurred, and the bailiff told the defendant to remain silent except to enter his plea of not guilty or guilty. I don't know if the defendant ever filed an internal affairs complaint against the police officer, but years later, I learned that his claim certainly had merit. In January 2022, a five-hundred-page report commissioned by the Baltimore Police Department revealed that Victor Rivera, a former Baltimore police officer convicted of making false statements to a federal law enforcement agent regarding the sale of drugs taken during a drug raid, told investigators that for decades, many officers had been unlawfully pocketing money they had seized.[14] Similarly, a 2016 Department of Justice report on Baltimore police officers discovered an internal affairs police investigation report on a routine traffic stop during which an officer searched a Black man's vehicle for drugs without his consent in violation of his constitutional rights. A police officer who stops someone for a traffic violation may not search a vehicle for drugs without the person's consent unless a valid reason to suspect drugs exists. None existed in this case. After the officer failed to find any drugs in the vehicle, he ordered the man out of his car. The police officer then demanded that the man remove his pants and underwear, leaving him standing naked on the street. The officer then proceeded to search the Black man's genitals. After the officer found marijuana, he placed the suspect under arrest. He confiscated the marijuana but pocketed the man's $500, telling him he would get his money back if he provided information about serious crimes committed by other people, presumably Black people. The internal affairs unit reviewed the defendant's complaint, but then closed its review without taking any action. The man who was assaulted by the police officer—an officer who, unsurprisingly, had a long history of misconduct complaints—was not even interviewed.[15]

When I was in my former office, I don't recall a prosecutor ever investigating a police misconduct complaint for any potential crimes. At that time, body cams were not available. If they had been, scores of cases against Black defendants might have been dismissed due to an officer's misconduct as shown on video. I recall many times when defendants offered to take a polygraph test to prove their assertions of innocence, and a lie detector test may seem like a good option when there is a case of a police officer's word against a defendant's word with no other witnesses or evidence. But my team captains cautioned me that polygraphs were unreliable. My office never considered lie detector tests. And it's true: polygraphs prove nothing as they are inadmissible at trial. In every jury trial I participated in as a prosecutor, I said in my opening statement that we were on a fact-finding mission for truth and justice. And polygraphs can't participate in that mission. But information about officer misconduct in the current case and in past cases certainly ought to be a part of that fact-finding mission. How could I truly seek justice and truth without a complete evaluation of all the available information, including information about the officer's misconduct?

The arresting officer's record should be equally as important as the defendant's criminal record. In every case, I always reviewed a defendant's criminal record, including arrests without a conviction, but my case files did not include a police officer's administrative record of any misconduct complaints. When I reviewed cases that contained only police officers' sworn statements that they had arrested the defendant after witnessing a crime, I had no way to know if the officer had stolen money or planted drugs, guns, or other contraband to effectuate the arrest (not uncommon practices). I often experienced a cognitive dissonance between my responsibilities as a prosecutor and my intuition based on inconsistencies I observed in a case. Unfortunately, my office was not set up for prosecutors to submit their suspicions to a team captain, division chief, or state's attorney. Those in charge of my office wanted convictions. They did not want to hear my perceived excuses to grant a nolle prosequi (dismissal) or give a jury or judge an opportunity to acquit someone who might be innocent.

POLICE MISCONDUCT AND PROSECUTORIAL OBLIGATIONS

A prosecutor's legal obligation requires that any material evidence that may disprove a defendant's guilt, prove favorable to the accused, or show exculpatory evidence, including on the credibility of a witness, must be provided to the defendant. This obligation applies to all prosecutors and has done so since the US Supreme Court's ruling in *Brady v. Maryland* in 1963.[16] *Brady* generally applies to the case where a defendant faces charges. The disciplinary file of an officer's prior bad acts in other cases should be provided to defense lawyers by prosecutors, even if such reports, allegations, or officer statements are not admissible at trial. Prior misconduct acts in other cases may show an officer's propensity to act in a certain way as part of a pattern and practice. Previous acts may indicate the officer's racial animus or state of mind toward defendants—particularly Black defendants.

Derek Chauvin, the former Minneapolis police officer who in 2021 was convicted of murdering George Floyd in May 2020, had eighteen prior misconduct complaints against him during his nineteen years as a police officer. Only two incidents resulted in discipline.[17] On June 25, 2017, before Chauvin murdered George Floyd, he arrested Zoya Code, a Black woman, after her mother called the police and alleged that Code assaulted her and tried to strangle her with an extension cord. During the arrest and after a struggle with Code, Chauvin handcuffed her face down and held his knee on her back for four minutes and forty-one seconds, the same position he used on George Floyd.[18] Unlike George Floyd, Zoya Code survived, and a Minneapolis sergeant later approved Chauvin's use of force on her.[19] Zoya Code filed a complaint in federal court alleging that Chauvin used unreasonable force against her. On April 22, 2023, the Minneapolis city council voted to approve a $1.375 million settlement in her case.

Police departments in US cities and towns rarely sanction police misconduct with serious punishment or termination, so Chauvin's prior misconduct complaints are not surprising. One has to wonder if Minneapolis prosecutors ever received information from the police about those complaints. Based on my experience, I doubt it. It is important to note that, like Chauvin, most police officers in the United States are white, as white people make up nearly 88 percent of local police departments.[20]

As the prevalence of officers like Derek Chauvin has been recognized more widely, progressive prosecutors have begun to investigate systemic police failures. In 2022, the Cook County, Illinois, state's attorney, Kim Foxx, asked a Chicago judge to throw out a stunning total of 212 convictions related to illegal acts committed by a Black former police sergeant, Ronald Watts, and members of his tactical team.[21] Over a ten-year period, Watts and fellow officers planted drugs, extorted money, and filed bogus cases against innocent victims who resided in a public housing project on Chicago's South Side, effectively ruining their lives. Watts served thirty months in prison for his conviction of corruption. Black police officers engage in criminal acts and misconduct against Black people, like their fellow white officers.

Even in the relatively conservative jurisdiction of the Commonwealth of Virginia, changes are being made. In 2022, 146 law enforcement officers were stripped of their duties due in part to misconduct, use of excessive force, and lying.[22] Excessive force and lying were added to Virginia's list of offenses for decertification in the wake of George Floyd's murder. Before that, police officers in Virginia were decertified only if they failed a drug test, failed to stay current with police training, or were convicted of a felony, misdemeanor, or crime of moral turpitude.

Decertification in Virginia does not occur in all cases of impropriety, and there are certainly loopholes in the state's certification law. There is no guarantee that a rogue officer will not find work in another jurisdiction. Before his decertification could occur, Jonathan A. Freitag, a police officer in Fairfax County, Virginia, resigned in May 2020 after he was accused of stealing drugs, planting stolen drugs on innocent people, and committing other constitutional violations of people's rights. Based on accusations of Freitag's wrongdoing, Fairfax County prosecutors sought to toss out more than four hundred convictions. But none of these accusations stopped Freitag from obtaining further police work: he simply relocated to Florida. In August 2020, just three months after his Virginia resignation, he was hired by the Broward Sheriff's Office in Florida. To support his application, Freitag presented a letter from Fairfax County's human resources department that read in part: "You resigned from the position in good standing, your employment was entirely favorable, and you are eligible for re-hire."[23] When, eight months later, the Broward Sheriff's Office learned about the accusations made against Freitag in Virginia and the alleged criminal acts he committed there from the *Washington Post*, he was fired.[24] But major national newspapers can't write stories on every bad cop.

As bad as these misconduct examples are, they pale in comparison to the enormous number of state and local police officers charged with one or more crimes. Preeminent police expert Philip M. Stinson Sr., an attorney, a former police officer, and a professor of criminal justice at Bowling Green State University, has conducted extensive research on police crime and misconduct from 2005 to the present. His research data have been compiled in the Henry A. Wallace Police Crime Database, which is the only known database of its kind. It includes arrest information on state and local police officers and an analysis of data retrieved from various sources. There is only so much information Stinson can gather from the outside, however. The most reliable data should be uploaded for the public by law enforcement departments and other local and state governmental agencies, but no such government database exists.

Stinson's database includes over 18,000 criminal cases that involve the arrests of over 15,500 state and local law enforcement officers on one or more arrest charges from 2005 to 2021 in all fifty states and the District of Columbia. The database includes crimes committed while on duty, such as destroying evidence, falsifying records, stealing drugs from evidence rooms, planting evidence, illegal wiretapping, blackmail, committing civil rights violations, and official misconduct. Among other crimes were drug charges (selling, dealing, and trafficking drugs), sex crimes (including rape), robbery, fraud, theft, and grand larceny.[25] The database from 2005 to 2016 is publicly available online.[26]

Stinson's expansive work and database have led people to conclude that crimes committed by police officers are not, as some people might think, the work of a few bad apples but instead are part of a system that is ingrained with police misconduct.

PROSECUTORIAL RELIANCE ON POLICE

Although these charges of police misconduct are rarely pursued, most prosecutors side with police officers on almost every charge of assault on police, even when the circumstances do not warrant the charge. For instance, on August 30, 2015, the first weekend back to school after the summer break, my three college-student clients attended an on-campus party at the University of Maryland Eastern Shore, a historically Black college and university in Somerset County.[27] By this time, I was working as a private attorney. After a noise complaint was made to the campus police, officers arrived at the party and instructed the students to disburse.

As can be seen in a video taken by a student, an officer asked one of my clients for identification as he attempted to leave. The student showed his driver's license and turned to leave. After he walked past the police officers, another officer yelled, "Snatch his ass up!" In the video, the police can be seen arresting my client, though the reason for the arrest is not clear. My client's two friends attempted to intervene on his behalf, and ultimately campus police arrested them as well. Ultimately, all three students faced charges of assault on a police officer, disorderly conduct, failing to obey, interfering with a lawful arrest, and obstructing and hindering an arrest—and all faced jail time.

Despite the video evidence proving that my clients committed no disorderly conduct or assault, the prosecutor assigned to the case (a fellow Black woman) refused to dismiss the case. Fortunately, the judge did not believe that my clients' behavior warranted a conviction or jail time, but even without a conviction, she still sentenced them to probation before judgment and one hundred community service hours. In Maryland, to obtain probation without a judgment, a defendant must still plead guilty or enter an *Alford* plea, which allows a defendant to acknowledge the state has enough evidence to convict if the case is brought to trial. Even when defendants have not committed the crime they are accused of, defendants like my clients often prefer to take a plea bargain when faced with jail time and the testimony of white officers weighing against them, particularly in a conservative jurisdiction. After all, not even 120 years earlier, an angry white mob beat and lynched William Andrews, a seventeen-year-old Black teenager on the same Somerset County, Maryland, courthouse lawn where my three clients' cases were heard.[28]

Perhaps the most famous example of Baltimore police misconduct and policing is former homicide detective Donald Kincaid, with whom I had to work on multiple homicide cases. Kincaid and two collaborating officers, Josh Barrick and Bryn Joyce used false, coerced witness testimony to convict sixteen-year-old Alfred Chestnut, Andrew Stewart, and Ransom Watkins of the 1983 murder of Dewitt Ducker, a fourteen-year-old Harlem Park junior high school student. On top of the coerced testimony, the officers withheld evidence supporting the defendants' innocence.[29] Chestnut, Stewart, and Watkins received sentences of life in prison. Kincaid was the lead homicide investigator.

After a review in May 2019 by the Office of the State's Attorney for Baltimore City, along with an inquiry from an innocence project nonprofit, the prosecutor's office concluded that the three men were innocent. Thirty-six years after the three men were arrested as juveniles, they walked out of prison. The Baltimore state's attorney's office joined in a petition of actual innocence with defense counsel to support their release. The three men, known as the Harlem Park Three, served a combined 108 years in prison, believed to be the longest time served in US history for a wrongful conviction.[30]

Kincaid retired from the Baltimore police force and went on to receive notoriety as a character in the TV series *Homicide: Life on the Street* (1993–1999), a police drama about a fictional Baltimore homicide unit that is based on the book by David Simon. No criminal charges are pending against him, though in August 2020, Chestnut, Stewart, and Watkins filed a federal civil lawsuit against Kincaid, Barrick, Joyce, and the Baltimore Police Department, and over three years later that case is still in process.

From 1989 to 2022, twenty-five Baltimore men convicted of murder were exonerated due to police and prosecutors' failure to provide exculpatory evidence, police fabrication of evidence, and coercion of witnesses.[31] Several exonerated murder cases trace back to former homicide detectives Jerry Landsman and Gary Dunnigan, with whom I also worked with as a prosecutor. Landsman was glorified as a character in another David Simon–related

TV series, *The Wire* (2002–2008). I wonder, to this day, how many cases I prosecuted where Kincaid, Landsman, Dunnigan, and others like them provided false testimony, coerced witness testimony, or engaged in misconduct to obtain a conviction.

At least Alfred Chestnut, Andrew Stewart, and Ransom Watkins are now alive and free. A 2021 review of death penalty cases found 185 exonerations in twenty-nine states occurred due to police misconduct and police perjured testimony.[32] Exoneration means a convicted person is completely cleared of any wrongdoing and therefore innocent of the crime. From 1973 to 2021, multiple states executed 1,532 prisoners. Data shows that for approximately every 8.3 executions, a wrongfully accused and convicted death row person is exonerated.[33]

PROSECUTORIAL MISCONDUCT

The truth is that it's not just the police who engage in wrongful acts. Prosecutors also violate the law and participate in misconduct for which they may be held criminally accountable or civilly liable, though most often they are shielded by prosecutorial immunity. I knew prosecutors who vigorously sought convictions on scant evidence in order to achieve the highest possible conviction rates. High conviction rates mean that prosecutors can advance from lower-level juvenile divisions or misdemeanor trial units to a felony trial unit or the more specialized units of narcotics, homicide, and economic crimes. I did not know any prosecutors during my tenure who blatantly committed prosecutorial misconduct, but as a Black woman in a sea of white male prosecutors, I would have been the last person anyone would have confided in about unethical or illegal conduct.

Prosecutorial misconduct amounts to intentional acts committed by a prosecutor to break the law or engage in unethical behavior. The National Registry of Exonerations compiles all exonerations of wrongful convictions in the United States since 1989. Of 2,400 known exonerations from 1989 to 2019, 30 percent resulted from misconduct by prosecutors and police.[34]

Like the cases against former police officer Donald Kincaid and other police officers who commit criminal acts, prosecutors who coerce witnesses to give false testimony, withhold evidence favorable to a defendant, or engage in other illegal and unethical conduct are rarely found liable for prosecutorial misconduct. A 2020 study conducted by the Innocence Project, Resurrection After Exoneration, and the Veritas Initiative found 660 cases in five states where prosecutors committed misconduct over a period from 2004 to 2008. Similar to police misconduct, in all 660 cases, despite findings of prosecutorial misconduct, only one prosecutor was disciplined.[35]

It is rare, but not impossible, for a prosecutor to be charged and convicted for criminal wrongdoing in their duties. In 2005, Innocence Project attorneys who represented Michael Morton investigated the wrongdoing of Ken Anderson, a former prosecutor for William County, Texas, who later became a Texas district judge. Morton's attorneys alleged that in Morton's trial in 1987, Anderson withheld evidence that could have proven the innocence of the defendant, who was convicted of murdering his wife.[36] The information withheld by Anderson showed that another man was seen outside Morton's home before the murder occurred. In 2011, DNA testing did link another man, Mark Allen Norwood, to the crime, and the DNA evidence resulted in Morton's release and Norwood's conviction for the murder. Subsequent criminal contempt charges and attorney grievance proceedings for prosecutorial misconduct filed against Ken Anderson resulted in a ten-day jail sentence and the loss of his law license. Anderson served only five days of his sentence. Michael Morton served twenty-five years in prison before his release. To date, Ken Anderson is believed to be the only prosecutor sentenced in the United States to serve time for prosecutorial misconduct that resulted in a wrongful conviction.[37]

It is rarer still for a district attorney to be charged for misconduct, but it occurred after Jackie Johnson, a district attorney in Glynn County, Georgia, declined to bring charges against Gregory McMichael, his son Travis McMichael, and their neighbor William "Roddie" Bryan for killing Ahmaud Arbery, a twenty-five-year-old Black man who was jogging when the men attacked him on February 23, 2020. A 2021 investigation led by Chris Carr, Georgia's Republican attorney general, resulted in a grand jury indictment of one felony count and one misdemeanor count against Johnson for violating her oath of office and hindering a law enforcement officer by ordering the police to refrain from arresting then-suspect Travis McMichael.[38] Johnson had worked with Travis's father, Gregory McMichael, when he previously worked in the prosecutor's office as an investigator. Shortly after the shooting, Gregory left a voice message for Johnson in which he stated he needed her advice. Johnson was also indicted for showing favor toward Gregory McMichael. Her phone records showed that sixteen calls were made between her and Gregory McMichael.[39] Although the McMichaels remained free for two months following the murder of Arbery, Gregory McMichael, Travis McMichael, and William Bryan were later indicted and convicted. Johnson denied any wrongdoing. Three years after Arbery's murder, Jackie Johnson remained free with no court hearing or trial date scheduled.

POLICE WHITE SUPREMACY AND PROSECUTOR RACIAL BIAS

Our carceral system has racism woven into its very DNA. Police officers with documented white supremacist views continue to work closely with prosecutors on cases to convict people, with particularly egregious examples in Alabama, California, Connecticut, Florida, Illinois, Louisiana, Michigan, Nebraska, Oklahoma, Oregon, Texas, Virginia, Washington, and West Virginia.[40] Officers in forty states in over a hundred police departments have been shown to have sent racist emails and made racist comments in online groups or articles. One police chief in Oklahoma owned multiple white supremacist websites and appeared in a documentary about his views on white supremacy.[41] In following Freddie Gray's funeral in Baltimore and the protests it generated, one New York police officer posted online photos of Black protestors on top of a vehicle alongside a photo of baboons.[42]

I did not suspect any of my white colleagues of harboring white supremacist views, but I did observe that many of my white fellow prosecutors exhibited implicit racial bias due to a lack of involvement with Black Americans except mostly through the lens of prosecution. I doubt if many of my fellow white prosecutors had close Black friends, and I suspect their significant interactions with Black people outside of prosecution remained limited to our support staff, police officers, and the few Black prosecutors who worked with them. I recall a time when an unrepresented Black man asked to speak to a white prosecutor before court began. Before a judge sits on the bench to commence court, we generally take a roll call to ask any defendants in the room who are unrepresented by counsel to come forward. I remember this unrepresented man because he was known in the Black community as having once played as a professional basketball player. I stood nearby as the prosecutor and the defendant conversed. After the conversation ended, the white prosecutor asked me, "What did he say?" as if asking me to translate for someone who spoke a foreign language or with an accent.

Many white prosecutors rarely encounter socially and economically challenged Black people other than as defendants. Many live in mostly white neighborhoods. This lack of regular contact with Black people and those of limited financial resources means that white prosecutors often lack the skills that are necessary for evaluating the circumstances of a case, especially misdemeanor nonviolent cases occurring in Black neighborhoods. Two-thirds of states that elect their prosecutors have no Black prosecutors, despite an overrepresentation of Black defendants.[43]

Explicit and implicit racial bias is found in all segments of society. But when it is found in a police officer who is armed with a gun, it can prove deadly, and when it is empowered by white prosecutors in a court of law, it can result in injustice. In contemporary America, explicit and inherent implicit racial bias fuels police brutality and the overprosecution of Black people. From 2013 to 2017, unarmed Black people were 3.23 times more likely to be killed by police than were white people.[44] The statistics vary by location. In Chicago, African Americans are over 6.5 percent more likely to be killed by police than are white Americans.[45] Yet in the vast majority of these cases, prosecutors never even seek an indictment against the police officer.

This is hardly due to a lack of evidence. I know from my grand jury experience that it is usually relatively easy to obtain an indictment before grand jurors. Police brutality and many murders often occur in the open in front of witnesses, and some are photographed by police body cams or bystander video cameras. Yet a majority of prosecutors are reluctant to bring cases against police officer misconduct for a variety of reasons, including the difficulty of obtaining a successful prosecution, concerns about harming a productive work relationship with officers suspected of wrongdoing, the difficulty of countering an officer's stated defense of fear of imminent danger, and implicit racial bias toward the victim. All play a part in a prosecutor's decision of whether to bring charges against police. Instead of killings by police officers being investigated by an independent investigator or special prosecutor, local police often investigate their fellow police officers for lethal shootings and other killings. On the rare occasions that prosecutors bring charges before a grand jury, it is usually the same local prosecutors who work daily with the local police officer who committed the crime. It is rare that prosecutions (like that of former police officer Derek Chauvin by the Minneapolis attorney general's office) or disqualifications of a district attorney (like that of Mike Freeman, a county attorney, due to sloppy work) are pursued.[46]

The *Washington Post* maintains a database of fatal shootings committed by police officers in the line of duty from 2015 to 2023. No national government database exists. On average, a thousand people are fatally shot by police each year in the United States, with twice as many Black people shot and killed by police as white people.[47] From 2005 to 2021, out of over a thousand fatal police shootings occurring yearly, prosecutors charged only 155 officers.[48] In 2021, prosecutors charged 21 officers with either murder or manslaughter, the highest number of police officers charged in one year.[49] Of the total number of officers charged with a crime in a fatal shooting, prosecutors obtain a conviction in only a third of all cases.[50]

Looking at these cases in isolation, one might conclude that each offense is the work of a single rogue detective or one bad prosecutor. But when the behavior involves both the prosecutors who head the offices and set office policies and the elite detectives and officers who work closely with prosecutors, we are compelled to consider the systemic policies that allow such behavior to ruin lives. Even a brief reflection leads to the conclusion that this behavior is an indictment of the prosecutorial system and not the behavior of a few bad actors.

The lack of management of prosecutorial and police misconduct has allowed systemic racism to spread to the point that dishonest practices have fatally infected hundreds of prosecutors' offices and police departments and destroyed the lives of Black people in the process.

Hundreds of years of messaging have conditioned Americans to see the Black body as violent, dangerous, scary, aggressive, and without value.[51] These prejudices have infected our systems as well as our psyches. Prosecutors are not immune to this social script. Reform activists must understand the systemic racism embedded in our prosecutorial system in order to change it. Just as physicians ask their patients for a medical history to assess current medical conditions, we must understand prosecutorial history to assess our prosecutorial practice.

II   BLACK LIVES: DEGRADATION BY DESIGN

3 THE TEMPLATE AND THE TRUTH

Not everything that is faced can be changed; but nothing can be changed until it is faced.
—James Baldwin, "As Much Truth as One Can Bear," *New York Times*, January 14, 1962

As a prosecutor, every time I spoke the words "May it please the court," I was wielding enormous power over the lives of many Black people, though I didn't fully understand that power until I left the prosecutor's office.

My first job out of law school had provided me with very little courtroom experience, and so when I started work as an assistant state's attorney for Baltimore, I was thrilled by the thought of trying cases before juries and helping victims of crime. But my excitement did not last long. Like many young prosecutors, I was assigned to the misdemeanor unit. This division was (and still is) so overburdened by arrests of African Americans that I soon felt like an assembly-line worker, mindlessly moving defendants between the various stages of the criminal justice system—pretrial, bail hearings, arraignment, trial, and postconviction proceedings. The assembly line of justice starts with the police, who disproportionately arrest Black people. The line then moves defendants to the courts, where prosecutors charge them and judges sentence them pursuant to prosecutors' recommendations. And then it's off to jail, probation, or prison. At no point does anybody in the justice system consider the impact of these proceedings on Black lives. Why should they? Do Ford workers wonder what might happen to the cars they build? All that matters to prosecutors is efficiency and convictions.

BREAD AND BUTTER MISDEMEANORS

The misdemeanor unit is the bread and butter of a prosecutor's office. Eighty percent of all criminal cases are misdemeanors, which amounts to thirteen million cases per year in the United States.[1] Misdemeanor crimes vary from state to state, but are usually lower-level crimes and mostly nonviolent ones. Usually, people enter the judicial system through the misdemeanor courts, unless they are facing charges in juvenile courts.

The high caseload prevents prosecutors from fully examining each case, particularly in urban areas with large court dockets. They focus on obtaining convictions because convictions bring more taxpayer money to the office. The funding for prosecutor offices, while lower than funding for police departments, still comes mostly from taxpayer funds and a few grants in some cases.[2] Higher prosecution budgets correlate with higher conviction rates. For example, in Virginia, the funding of the prosecutor's office, as in other jurisdictions, is based on the number of convictions obtained in a year. So as more people are charged, prosecuted, and convicted, more money is received by the Virginia prosecutors' offices.[3] When I prosecuted, a conviction rate in the high 80 percent to 90 percent range was considered good—regardless of how many defendants were actually guilty.

In Maryland, misdemeanor crimes generally carry a maximum of ninety days to one year in jail and/or fines from $500 to $5,000, although a few offenses impose higher penalties. For example, misdemeanor second-degree assault carries a ten-year sentence. Misdemeanors include crimes like petty theft, shoplifting, illegal possession of guns, possession of drugs or drug paraphernalia in small quantities, assault, resisting arrest, trespassing, disorderly conduct, prostitution, criminal traffic matters (such as driving while intoxicated and reckless driving), domestic violence, and many other offenses.

My dockets consisted of 20 or 30 cases set for jury trial. My team captain scheduled me to appear in court an average of two days each week—more if any cases carried over from one day to another—and my heavy caseload was average for a prosecutor. A 2006 Harris County, Texas, prosecutor study found that its prosecutors handled up to 1,500 felony cases a year.[4] Cook County, Illinois, felony prosecutors handled 800 to 1,000 cases per year, and

Dallas/Fort Worth, Texas, misdemeanor prosecutors handled 1,200 to 1,500 misdemeanors.[5] Unless I had a jury trial, I spent roughly thirty minutes out of a forty-hour week on the preparation of each case.

Each time I appeared in misdemeanor court, I found the large Baltimore courtrooms filled, often to standing room only, with young Black men. I rarely saw a white person charged with a misdemeanor crime. Courtrooms in large cities across the United States feature the same racial disparities.

PLEA BARGAIN: DEAL OR NO DEAL

When I did have a misdemeanor jury trial, it was because defendants demanded their constitutional right to be tried by a jury of their peers. The TV show *Law and Order* would lead you to believe that every defendant gets a jury trial, but in real life, trials are more like the TV shows *Let's Make a Deal* or *Deal or No Deal*. Ninety-four percent of all state criminal trials end with a plea bargain.[6]

That assembly-line efficiency of the prosecutor's office rests solely with plea bargains. Without plea bargains, the entire prosecutorial system would fail. One misdemeanor jury trial takes on average two to two and a half hours depending on the offense charged, number of witnesses, time needed to select a jury, and time taken by opening and closing arguments. But most defendants do not choose to risk "rolling the dice," as lawyers term it, with a jury trial. The majority of defendants prefer to accept a plea bargain—even if they are innocent. US Supreme Court Justice Potter Stewart once said the prosecutor's job is to "persuade the defendant to forgo his right to plead not guilty."[7] Prosecutors have enormous power, and that power includes the ability to recommend a higher sentence if convicted by a jury. Simply put, a defendant will face harsher punishment if a jury convicts after a defendant rejects a plea offer. This is called a trial penalty. And even without a trial, if a defendant declines an earlier plea bargain and chooses to later plead guilty, a prosecutor won't offer the same deal. The terms of the plea will be worse, even if the defendant later accepts a plea deal without a jury trial.

Paul Lewis Hayes learned this lesson the hard way. Police arrested Hayes in 1977 for attempting to cash a bad check for $88.30 at a grocery store.

Prosecutors in Fayette County, Kentucky, charged him with forgery, which carried a penalty of two to ten years in prison. The prosecutor offered Hayes a plea bargain of five years in prison if he chose to plead guilty. Instead, Hayes rejected the plea deal and demanded his day in court before a jury. The prosecutor made clear that, due to Hayes's two prior felony convictions, Kentucky's Habitual Crime Act would be applied to his case if he was convicted, substantially increasing his penalty. Hayes still demanded his constitutional right to a jury trial, and the jury convicted him. He received a sentence of life in prison pursuant to the Habitual Crime Act. He appealed his case all the way to the US Supreme Court, and in *Bordenkircher v. Hayes* (1978), the Court sided with the prosecutor. It found that the prosecutor is constitutionally permitted to *threaten* to increase a recommended plea sentence if the defendant refuses to accept a plea bargain.[8] Since that decision, prosecutors have embraced their wide latitude and power to use plea bargains.

I had power to increase, reduce, or dismiss charges and to recommend probation, fines, community service, drug treatment, jail, or a prison sentence. If a defendant had no previous record of convictions and I had no restrictive office policy, I offered probation before judgment in most cases. Whenever possible, I tried to be lenient, but I also wanted to advance in the office. I walked a tightrope. And while I may have leaned toward more leniency, prosecutorial discretion resulted in a wide range of plea bargains offered for similar cases depending on the individual prosecutor assigned to a case.

US Supreme Court Justice Anthony Kennedy summed up plea bargaining when he stated that "it is the criminal justice system."[9] What Justice Kennedy did not say is that the plea bargain system, like the entire criminal justice system, is rife with racial disparities. A 2017 Wisconsin study of thirty thousand criminal cases conducted over seven years found that when defendants accepted a plea bargain, white defendants charged with similar misdemeanors who had no prior criminal history were 46 percent more likely than similar Black defendants to have all charges carrying a potential jail sentence dropped or reduced to charges that carry no potential imprisonment.[10] The evidence suggests that even when Black defendants had no prior criminal record, misdemeanor prosecutors still viewed Black defendants as potentially more dangerous or violent, which is how Black men have been viewed throughout history. The same study found that white misdemeanor defendants with the same charges in similar cases and with the same criminal record as Black defendants were 75 percent more likely than Black defendants to have all charges with potential imprisonment or jail time either dropped, dismissed, or reduced to a lesser charge or charges. And Wisconsin Black defendants were more likely to receive a sentence of imprisonment than their white counterparts in similar cases.[11] In the Manhattan district attorney's office, a larger two-year study of 200,000 defendants found that Black defendants with cases and criminal backgrounds that were similar to those of white defendants were more likely to receive a plea bargain of imprisonment and then receive imprisonment.[12] The Manhattan DA's study controlled for similar cases, prior record, charges, and even counsel (whether represented by a public defender or private counsel). In all similar cases, Black defendants received plea bargains that offered jail time 19 percent more times than white defendants did.[13] Studies suggest that in the South, the racial disparity among white and Black defendants in plea bargains is even greater.[14]

Armed with plea bargains, my misdemeanor dockets moved swiftly, despite the heavy volume, because everything in misdemeanor court moves like speedskating. Defense attorneys rushed to form a line to speak to me on their clients' behalf before the judge took the bench, and if they were lucky, they received one or two minutes of my time. There was no time for prolonged discussions about constitutional issues, legal defenses, alibis, innocence, diversion, or witness issues. With such a high volume of cases to process, speed was always the overriding factor, and that was true for the judges, too.

Toward the end of the day, the court called the defendants who were in the lock-up area, detained in jail and unable to make bail for their cases. I usually offered them a plea of time served, which would allow them to leave jail the same day. They usually jumped at the plea deal so that they could go home, even if they maintained their innocence, because otherwise, they would remain in jail for as long as it took to get through a trial.

Cases that I did not resolve by trial or guilty plea ended with a nolle prosequi (no prosecution), a stet (the case is set aside but technically can be reopened), or a defense or prosecution request for postponement. I entered a nolle prosequi or a stet when I found insufficient evidence or a negative laboratory report, when a witness, victim, or police officer was missing, or when witnesses or victims changed their statement or otherwise lacked credibility. Those were the lucky defendants—or so they thought. But that arrest remained forever on their criminal record unless expunged.

THE ANATOMY OF BALTIMORE'S MISDEMEANOR COURTS

Like many new misdemeanor prosecutors, I entered the job without any criminal trial training. My misdemeanor team captain was overstretched or unconcerned about the situation. He had to manage eight to ten prosecutors, each with a docket of twenty to thirty cases. He didn't review case specifics, and even when he had the time, he offered very little training or advice. In other words, the message we heard was "Do your best, but don't bother me." Overall, the office offered little training in substantive criminal law, procedure, or evidence. Office meetings and handouts recommended strict pleas for subsequent drunk driving offenses, drug offenses, gun crimes, and other crimes that were in the public eye.

On most days, my misdemeanor docket of twenty to thirty cases scheduled for court concluded by 12:30 pm. From that point, I might be free until I had to handle my next day's docket or was assigned to assist another line prosecutor with a heavier docket in the afternoon. I was asked to train another Black woman prosecutor, Sara, who was preparing for her first misdemeanor jury trial—though at that point I had completed only one myself. When the judge asked Sara for her opening statement, Sara whispered to me, "Do I have to give an opening statement?"

I whispered back, "Yes. I don't know what you should say, but you need to say something."

Most people probably think that prosecutors receive some training before they recommend a plea bargain or conduct a jury trial for the first time. I'm sure Ford Motors doesn't employ assembly-line workers to build cars without some job training. But our training was minimal at best. In state misdemeanor courtrooms, too many prosecutors lack sufficient training to evaluate cases for trial, and this deficiency can have cataclysmic effects on the lives of the people they are prosecuting. Many Black people's dreams die or their livelihoods suffer because they have been targeted by racist police officers, pulled into a racist system, and dropped into the lap of overburdened, undertrained prosecutors.

Think about prosecution as a gun. If you barely know how to shoot a gun but shoot it anyway, you can hurt plenty of people in the line of fire. My colleagues and I had to learn on the job, and we regularly made errors that likely landed many people in jail unjustly. Often these prosecutorial errors, while inexcusable, occurred because of the way justice is dispensed in the United States—in a hurry and with a focus on convictions.

The unspoken motto for misdemeanor prosecutors was "Sink or swim." I did not intend to sink, but in order to swim I needed to gain enough experience in misdemeanor jury trials to move up in the office, whether or not I knew what I was doing or had time to do it well. In misdemeanors, I usually took roughly thirty minutes to read the arresting officer's statement, interview the officer, interview witnesses, and discuss the case with the defense attorney. I didn't have time to go deeper. Often, if I couldn't reach a witness by phone, I had to interview them for the first time on the day of the defendant's trial. Then, I had to decide on the appropriate action—trial, plea bargain, or dismissal.

Nevertheless, even in the short windows I had for review, I was able to identify major flaws in many of my cases. An astonishing percentage of arrests lacked probable cause—meaning there had been no legally justifiable reason to stop the person. Many arrest reports were vague, and they all seemed eerily similar, as though the writers had copied their friends' homework but shifted around a few words. One Baltimore detective was infamous for parading hordes of arrested Black defendants into court, so many that a misdemeanor judge noticed, too. One day, after I finished questioning the detective, the judge asked him more questions and tossed the case out of court. The judge did not believe the detective could have seen what he said he had seen at night and at the distance from the alleged drug transaction. At that time, I couldn't tell whether police officers misunderstood and therefore misapplied the law or if they knew the law and failed to apply it correctly.

Regardless of the cause, the result was the same: more Black men than other people were arrested for petty crimes.

DOJ'S INVESTIGATION OF BALTIMORE POLICE

Today, I know that those police officers understood the law and that they intentionally arrested more Black men than white men. When the US Department of Justice (DOJ) investigated the Baltimore police, spurred by the arrest and death of Freddie Gray in 2015, it uncovered systemic, racially motivated police arrests of Black men. Its 163-page report found that police engaged in a pattern and practice of arresting Black people for insufficient legal reasons, lack of probable cause, or no reason at all. The DOJ report found that for every thousand Black residents, Baltimore police made over five hundred stops, compared to less than two hundred stops for one thousand white residents.[15] The DOJ also revealed that, to make these wildly disproportionate arrests more efficient, one shift commander created and distributed to police officers a template arrest report form with "Black male" already inserted in the identity box. All these practices add up to a staggering statistic: Baltimore police charged Black people for 86 percent of all crimes in a city with a 63 percent Black population.[16] This scathing report came as no surprise to me. It merely confirmed what I had begun to suspect while working in misdemeanor court.

The DOJ's report on Baltimore police evaluated criminal cases from January 2010 to May 2015. By 2021, Baltimore City had 576,498 residents, making it the twentieth largest city in the United States.[17] By comparison, the Baltimore Police Department was the eighth largest municipal police department in the country.[18] The DOJ report found that Baltimore police officers engaged in a pattern and practice of unlawful and unconstitutional acts in arresting Black people, and those arrests put many Black men on my misdemeanor dockets. Baltimore police targeted African Americans who lived in two of the least populated areas of the city, areas that represented only 12 percent of the total city's population but made up approximately 44 percent of the total stops and arrests between 2010 and 2014. Baltimore police went out of their way to target neighborhoods made up of 90 percent to 95 percent Black residents, many of whom lived in poverty. DOJ found that police arrested African Americans for drug possession—a misdemeanor—at five times the rate they arrested white people, even though Black people used drugs at the same rate as white people.[19] The DOJ report concluded that some police supervisors ordered officers to go out of their way to target Black people and arrest them.

Unsurprisingly, many Black residents had suspected for years that Baltimore police targeted and arrested large numbers of Black men for noncrimes. Baltimore police arrested Black people for 86 percent of the petty nonviolent misdemeanor crimes that I prosecuted. Black residents accounted for 84 percent to 91 percent of other misdemeanor arrests, particularly nonviolent misdemeanors. Overall, DOJ concluded that Baltimore police disproportionately arrested African Americans at higher rates that are unexplainable by crime rates, population, or other race-neutral factors.

STAFFING OF PROSECUTOR OFFICES

The difference between a manufacturing assembly line and the prosecutorial assembly line is that a manufacturing plant has quality controls to ensure that broken parts are not added to cars. The prosecutorial assembly line lacks quality controls, however, and mistakes often are not corrected. The office's overall concern is efficiency, which translates into speed and convictions. I usually had to work on my cases without much support. The office's lack of adequate support staff, supervisors, law clerks, and paralegals to assist prosecutors often led to problems. It meant the materials we were required to provide to defense attorneys during the discovery process were not always delivered before trial. The police often failed to provide me with items, and some missing items went unnoticed until shortly before or on the day of the trial.

Prosecutors rely on police officers to investigate cases and provide them with evidence. The most serious issue with overburdening misdemeanor prosecutors with heavy caseloads is the likelihood that they will fail to turn over to defense attorneys materials that may negate the guilt of defendants and might show innocence. When any serious legal issues arise, there is little time between preparing dockets to also perform legal research. When you are trying to keep your head above water, there is no time for research. My office had very few paralegals, and the few paralegals did no research. I don't recall any law clerks working there at the time. Many prosecutors in misdemeanors loathed the volume, but there was nothing we could do about it. At times in court during a trial, a judge asked a legal question and expected me to provide a specific analysis of the law. In those instances, I hoped for the best and answered, but mostly I would just shoot from the hip. My experience was no different from others in my office.

In 2006, four of the largest counties in Texas prosecuted 270,000 cases with fewer than thirty-five paralegals. In that same year, the Cook County State's Attorney's Office, which is the second largest in the country and represents Chicago and surrounding areas, prosecuted hundreds of thousands of cases with fewer than ten paralegals.[20] In 2021, Cook County handled 220,000 to 240,000 misdemeanor cases. The prosecutor's offices have large budgets, but they rarely hire a large support staff.

FELONY UNIT

My stay in the misdemeanor section lasted roughly eighteen months, after which I was promoted to the felony trial unit. There my case load lessened and became more manageable. For serious felonies, I often had a docket of four or five felony cases, fewer if I had been assigned a murder case. On average, I tried ten felony jury trials per year, which was considered acceptable. The felony unit, where I spent close to three years, worked less chaotically than misdemeanors. I had more time to devote to my cases. My team consisted of four other prosecutors, including a team captain, but we did not work together on cases. We simply were assigned to the same judge's courtroom. We worked independently of each other except in rare circumstances. I recall one occasion when my white male team captain asked me to try a murder case with him. The request came out of the blue, and I asked him why. He obviously did not need my help, and I had enough cases of my own. But then I learned the defense attorney was also a Black woman—a prominent attorney who appeared often on TV. My colleague did not need me; he just wanted me for window dressing.

Although prosecutors in the felony unit had more time to spend on our cases, we still did not have adequate support staff or much training. And with these cases—homicides, burglaries, robberies, narcotics, and sex offense crimes—the stakes were much higher. These serious types of cases had the most serious repercussions for those we convicted. As prosecutors, we relied on police detectives in the Criminal Investigation Divisions (CID) to investigate crimes of homicide, robbery, and narcotics. They investigated, located, and interviewed witnesses and obtained witness statements. CID units are small. I worked with many of the same detectives over and over again.

Plea bargains differed with felony cases, though they were still common. In felony court, we could not just pull a sentencing number off the top of our heads as in misdemeanors. Maryland law required that prosecutors with input from defense attorneys complete a Maryland Sentencing Guidelines worksheet to determine the proposed sentencing range for a felony case, regardless of whether it ended in a plea bargain or trial. The guidelines worksheet scored a sentencing range that depended on various factors, such as the type of crime, the seriousness of the crime, the defendant's prior record (including any juvenile delinquency record), parole or probation status at time of committing the crime, any victim injury, the special vulnerability of any victim (if younger than eleven or older than sixty-five), and other categories. Sentencing guidelines are intended to prevent disparities in sentencing, but that's not always the impact they have. For example, the guidelines may range from probation to jail time in a specific case. A judge must write on the guidelines worksheet an explanation or a reason for sentencing a defendant outside of the guidelines range for a case.

Like everything in the criminal justice system, Black men are sentenced more harshly than comparable white males within the same guidelines range.[21] Whenever there is a sentencing range between probation and incarceration, Black people are more likely than comparable white defendants to receive incarceration.[22] Black defendants also receive a harsher sentence when the victim is white versus a Black victim. The reverse is not true for white defendants when victims are white. These racial disparities help explain why Black Americans are incarcerated in state prisons at a rate of five times that of comparable white defendants.[23]

After a guidelines worksheet is prepared postconviction, a prosecutor makes a recommendation to the judge at the sentencing hearing. The same racial bias is both implicit and explicit in the minds of white prosecutors, and it determines the harsher sentencing recommendations for Black defendants. The Sentencing Project's 2021 report on state prisons reported that we must recognize the obvious fact that Black men are generally viewed as more dangerous and as a greater threat to public safety than their white counterparts are.[24] These misperceptions are behind the prosecutor's recommendations for a sentence within the guidelines. One thing that I saw in the misdemeanors unit remained the same in the felonies unit. If a person charged with a felony declined a plea offer by a prosecutor, took a case to a jury, and was convicted, the prosecutor's recommended sentence would be higher than the sentence offered in the pretrial plea deal. A five-year plea deal could easily double in years or more after a jury trial. In all my homicide and robbery cases that went to trial, I recommended a substantially higher sentence after trial, while staying within the Maryland sentencing guidelines. Just as in misdemeanor court, a judge would normally follow my sentencing recommendation. The trial penalty for Black people who proceed to trial rather than accept a plea bargain is higher than for white defendants.[25]

RACE AND JUSTICE

In 2022, decades after I prosecuted in Baltimore City, the University of Maryland published a report on racial justice in prosecution in Baltimore. It found that in a city whose population was 63 percent Black in 2017 and 2018, 88 percent of all Baltimore Circuit Court cases involved Black people and more than 80 percent of all felonies involved Black male defendants.[26] The prosecutorial experience in Baltimore is no different than that in New York City, Chicago, Miami, and other cities and towns across the country. In 2014, the killing of Michael Brown by a police officer in Ferguson, Missouri, and the failure of district attorney Robert McCullough to bring charges were catalysts for prosecutorial changes in that city. As in Baltimore, the US Department of Justice investigated the Ferguson Police Department after Brown's death and found uncannily similar police and prosecutorial practices. The March 4, 2015, DOJ report studied Ferguson court cases and police and prosecutorial practices from 2012 to 2014. Black residents represented 67 percent of Ferguson's population but represented 93 percent of all arrests made by the Ferguson police.[27] In Ferguson's municipal court, African Americans were 68 percent less likely to have their cases dismissed by prosecutors and more likely to have their cases continue with more appearances in court.[28] The DOJ found that these differences resulted from racial bias and stereotypes of Black people among police and court staff, including prosecutors. Ferguson police supervisors and court staff sent racist emails to each other that depicted Black people as criminals. One particularly inflammatory email made a joke that an abortion by a Black woman served as a means of crime control.[29]

Likewise, in Cook County, Illinois, a study conducted from 2000 to 2018 showed that Black people represented only 25 percent of the population of Cook County but over 60 percent of its three million criminal cases. In 2018, the percentage of Black defendants increased to 65 percent although the number of criminal cases decreased. A review of the jail population revealed that the incarceration rate of Black people is more than seventeen times that of white defendants. Although the number of cases decreased in Cook County after 2000, the racial disparity among Black people increased.[30]

Even in counties with low Black population, the racial disparity trend continues. The population of Alameda County, California, is only 10 percent Black residents, but Black defendants make up 43 percent of the county's jail population. Its population is 31 percent white, but white defendants make up 21 percent of the jail population.[31] Most people in jail are awaiting a trial or serving a short jail sentence as a result of a prosecutor's recommendation on bail or sentence. The ACLU of Florida cited similar racial disparities among Black defendants in the Miami-Dade County area in a report that looked at 200,000 defendants from 2010 to 2015.[32] The fifty-two-page report found that prosecutors are more likely to offer longer sentences to Black defendants while white defendants are more likely to be offered lesser terms or dismissals even though white defendants commit more serious crimes.[33]

The ACLU of Arizona's 2020 report revealed similar prosecutorial racial disparities. That report analyzed 51,000 criminal cases from 2013 to 2017 and found that prosecutors recommended longer incarceration terms for Black people compared to similar white defendants, Black people spent an average of eight months longer incarcerated than similar white defendants, and prosecutors dismiss the cases of white defendants more frequently than they dismissed the cases of people of any other race.[34] Prosecutors from these jurisdictions have the discretion to decide who is charged, whose charges are dismissed, who moves forward in the criminal system, and who goes to jail or prison and for how long. Nothing happens in the criminal justice system that the prosecutor doesn't have a hand in.

MY TRUTH AS A PROSECUTOR

As a Black woman prosecutor, I began my job expecting to do good for my city. My desire to help victims of crime and people in the criminal justice system was rooted in my upbringing. I grew up in Baltimore's Park Heights area, a Black neighborhood that is home to the famous Preakness horse race, brick rowhouses, and a sense of community. Over the years, it became shattered by poverty, drugs, and substantial crime. One of my homicide cases occurred just a block from my parents' home where I had grown up. A few of my neighborhood childhood friends ended up in the revolving door of the criminal justice system—locked up in Baltimore jails for mostly petty theft crimes due to drug use and alcohol abuse. I knew firsthand that close family and friends who were defendants in the criminal justice system had squared off against Baltimore prosecutors.

I thought my knowledge and background would help me help them, but I quickly learned that my office had no place for prosecutors who thought about the justice system with compassion. My expectations had to be revised as they encountered my office's policies. The truth is that a line prosecutor is almost powerless to do anything other than toe the line. My prosecutorial discretion was often limited to what the office required under certain circumstances, leaving my hands tied. When I could, I tried to use my position through my lens as a product of Park Heights, but the office had power over me, just as I had power over the defendants in the courtroom. A line prose-cutor's power to make positive changes is severely restricted by the policies of the state's attorney or district attorney. In a military operation, the general decides the war's strategy, and the foot soldiers perform the day-to-day oper-ations. In the prosecutor's office, the foot soldiers are the line prosecutors. The generals are the DAs and state's attorneys.

LIFE AFTER PROSECUTION

When I left the Office of the State's Attorney for Baltimore City and became a private attorney, I saw a different side of the prosecutorial system. In 2021, Baltimore police arrested my client, a middle-aged divorced Black man and father of two young children. He was charged with second-degree assault, a misdemeanor. According to the police report, during an argument with his former girlfriend, my client struck the woman several times, which caused a cut on her forehead and a swollen lip. After he voluntarily turned himself in on his arrest warrant, he appeared before the judge for his initial bail hearing, where the prosecutor recommended no bail. This meant that my client would remain in jail until his trial.

Traditionally, bail considerations are made based on whether the defen-dant poses a further threat to society and will appear for future court dates. I have seen bail set for persons accused of gun offenses, drug trafficking, sexual assault cases of minors, and murder. Even Derek Chauvin, the white police officer who murdered George Floyd, remained free on bail until his conviction. I argued for my client's release on monitored home detention, which would have allowed him to work, attend any doctor's appointments, and meet with me, his attorney, if necessary. In my opinion, my client, who had no criminal record for the past three decades, posed no flight risk or danger to society.

However, the prosecutor's office had a strict policy on domestic violence cases that uniformly argued against bail. Prosecutorial discretion flies out the window once the state's attorney sets a strict policy. There is no way around it. Therefore, in this hearing, as in most others, the judge sided with the prosecution, despite the facts that supported my argument for release on bail.

At trial six weeks later, I discovered the prosecutor had failed to interview the victim before the trial date. Had the young white male prosecutor interviewed the victim earlier, he would have discovered that she did not want to pursue charges. The prosecutor provided me with three forty-five-minute videos two days before the trial date, but he did not have time to watch them himself. He wanted to request a postponement to review the videos before he offered a plea bargain to my client. He wanted my client to remain in jail longer due to his own ineptness. My client had already spent over one month in jail.

Fortunately, after a little persuasion and argument on my part, the prosecutor's heavy docket demands, and the victim's reluctance to prosecute, he decided to dismiss the case—after my client had remained in jail for almost six weeks. If the prosecutor had requested a postponement on the day of trial, the judge would have allowed the postponement request. Most judges will allow the prosecutor and defense attorney at least one postponement—usually more. And due to the court's Covid-19 policy at the time, a postponement would have meant that my client would remain in jail for another several months or longer. But even those six weeks spent in jail awaiting his trial were long enough for my client to lose his job of eleven years.

The power to radically alter the course of Black lives rests with prosecutors. While line prosecutors can make their own choices about how to handle cases, they ultimately must adhere to the office policies and practices set by the elected district attorneys or state's attorneys. The DAs and state's attorneys are the ultimate sources of authority. I found that their office policies, protocols, and practices severely affected the most vulnerable members of society—children, teens, and emerging adults—in the most profound ways.

4 JUVENILES, JURIES, AND JUSTICE

The way to right wrongs is to turn the light of truth upon them.
—Ida B. Wells, journalist, in an 1892 speech

My cousin Edward was convicted of manslaughter when he was sixteen years old. Edward and another boy fought over a girl after a party, and during the fight, Edward accidentally stabbed the other teenager, who later died. Maryland law requires that certain serious crimes, even if committed by a minor, must automatically begin in adult court. So even though my cousin was a minor and had no prior involvement in the criminal justice system, the prosecutor charged his case in the adult criminal court—and then opposed Edward's request for a transfer to juvenile court. The judge agreed, and sixteen-year-old Edward's case stayed in adult court, a decision that affected the rest of Edward's life.

Edward, a high school student with mostly good grades who had just started his junior year, felt that he had been defending himself against the other teen in the altercation. A prosecutor disagreed. If Edward had been tried in juvenile court, he could have been sent to a juvenile detention facility until he turned twenty-one or received probation with counseling, rehabilitation, and other terms and conditions. Courts would have sealed his juvenile disposition to the public once he turned twenty-one. Instead, Edward was convicted of a felony. Faced with a maximum penalty of ten years in prison, Edward accepted the prosecutor's plea bargain and received a sentence of five years.

Edward served his time in a Maryland adult prison and walked free at twenty-one years old—still too young to rent a car. After his release, he obtained his GED certificate and worked at the General Motors plant in Baltimore for almost twenty years. He married his high school sweetheart, had two children, and owned his own home. By all accounts, he lived as a model citizen until his death at age fifty-two from a rare illness. Yet, for his entire life, Edward could neither vote nor serve on a jury. Was justice accomplished?

THE YOUTH FACTOR IN PROSECUTION

Every day prosecutors have a hand in the 48,000 youth under the age of eighteen held daily in juvenile detention centers or adult prisons, some still awaiting a trial or juvenile hearing in court,[1] though happily that number is actually decreasing: it was 60 percent higher in 2000.[2] Edward's case resembles many recent cases that involve Black youth, who in 2017 represented 15 percent of the total youth population but 54 percent of youth prosecuted in adult criminal court.[3]

In 2017, Howard Jimmy Davis was sixteen years old when he and two other males participated in an armed home invasion in Baltimore County. Before the home invasion, Davis had three other minor brushes with the juvenile justice system. During the armed invasion, Davis shot one of the three residents of the home. The bullet grazed the victim and did no serious harm. Prosecutors indicted Davis on multiple counts of attempted murder, as well as first-degree assault, which required that his case automatically be brought in adult court. Once a youth enters adult jurisdiction due to automatic transfer, Maryland law requires judges to consider several factors—the crime, public safety, and the defendant's age, physical and mental condition, and willingness to participate in treatment in a juvenile program or facility—to determine if a juvenile should be transferred to juvenile court.

While awaiting trial in a juvenile facility, Davis spent time in individual and group therapy. A psychologist testified before the trial judge that Davis was "our best student" and amenable to continued therapy and counseling, which he could continue to receive in the juvenile justice system.[4] Davis through his lawyer argued for a transfer to juvenile court. Had a judge granted Davis's request, he would have been able to continue counseling and other services available in the Maryland juvenile system with his same-age peers to assist with lowering his recidivism. Most important, he would have avoided an adult felony conviction.

A prosecutor disagreed with the request of Davis's lawyer, and the judge denied it. Ultimately, Davis pleaded guilty but reserved the right to argue on appeal for a juvenile transfer. A plea bargain resulted in a sentence of ten years in prison, five to be served without parole.

In 2020, the Maryland Court of Appeals sided with Davis and ordered his case back to the trial court judge for reconsideration of his juvenile transfer request. The court's primary concern was the likelihood of a reduction of recidivism and Davis's willingness to participate in treatment. The appeals court opinion opened the door for Davis (and other youth like him) to avoid adult prison terms. The help might have been a little too late for Davis because by then he had spent three years in an adult prison with adult male prisoners, some with lengthy sentences and records. Held in an adult prison for three years with hardened criminals, Davis was no longer the sixteen-year-old teen who entered the system. Now age twenty, he had only one more year to remain in juvenile detention, if the trial judge granted his request.

RACE AND JUVENILE COURTS

According to research conducted by the Sentencing Project, 90 percent of our nation's youth who are sent to adult court are Black and youth of color,[5] and in 2019, Maryland had the second highest number (behind Alabama) of juvenile transfers to adult court in the United States.[6] The Maryland Governor's Office of Crime Prevention, Youth, and Victim Services reports that between 2013 and 2020, Maryland prosecutors charged 7,800 youth in adult court; 80 percent were Black youth, and of that number 91 percent were Black males.[7] In 2021, 31.4 percent of Maryland's population was Black residents, according to US Census data,[8] and 31.6 percent of Maryland's population ages five to seventeen was Black youth for three years ending in 2019.[9]

And Maryland is by no means the worst-case scenario. Curtis Nelson, a former Louisiana juvenile prosecutor and assistant secretary for the Louisiana Office of Juvenile Justice, has argued that Louisiana prosecutors do not send enough kids to adult court.[10] He believes that prosecutors should consider charging more youth with adult crimes to increase public safety. Courts transfer 54 percent of Black youth cases to adult court versus 31 percent of white youth cases. The perception of the public and of many prosecutors is that Black youth are more dangerous to public safety than white youth, commit more serious felonies, and therefore belong in jail for their crimes.

Reality does not match that perception. Despite the high percentage of Black youth transfers to adult courts, white youth make up a greater percentage of delinquency cases, at 44 percent versus 35 percent for Black youth.[11] Of youth of color detained in Maryland in 2019, the Department of Juvenile Services reports that only 9.6 percent of all arrests were felony arrests. The vast majority, almost 70 percent, of all cases committed by youth of color were misdemeanor arrests,[12] and Black youth were arrested by police on mostly misdemeanors in more than 90 percent of all Maryland juvenile cases. The prosecutor holds the discretionary power to side with defense attorneys to transfer youth to juvenile court when they are automatically transferred or to refrain from a transfer recommendation to adult court in the first place, but they rarely do so. Again, the power of line prosecutors relies on the office policies of the state's attorneys and district attorneys who head the offices, and so even if individual line prosecutors would prefer to operate differently, it is difficult if not impossible for them to do so. When the issue arose, I often remained silent on my own position to implicitly signal to the judge that I took no position and therefore did not oppose a transfer to juvenile court. But that accomplished very little.

Later, as private counsel, I represented a Black high school student after his case was transferred to adult court. His school friends had asked him to hide a gun, and he complied with their request without question or hesitation, hiding the gun on school property. Law enforcement authorities discovered his act when they investigated a crime that involved his friends and the use of the gun in a crime. His decision at sixteen to help his classmates resulted in a criminal charge and expulsion from high school. Maryland law prohibits anyone to possess a deadly weapon on public school grounds, and if convicted, my client faced three years in prison and fines for his act. He had not committed a crime of violence and had not committed any prior crimes. The juvenile prosecutor assigned to his case recommended that his case be transferred to adult court, and based on that recommendation and the involvement of a gun, a juvenile judge transferred his case. Once there, the prosecutor in adult court refused to agree to my request for a reverse waiver to transfer his case back to juvenile court, even though my client had no prior involvement with the law. Four witnesses, including his pastor and a community organization representative, testified about his good character and remorse for his act. His parents told the judge about their decision to enroll him in an out-of-state school with a different environment. Fortunately for my client, he received probation—still a huge stain on his adult criminal record at only sixteen years of age.

Black teens are nine times as likely than white teens to receive an adult sentence.[13] In Maryland and many other states, minors who are convicted once in adult court are not eligible to have any new case heard in juvenile court. This is known as the "once an adult, always an adult" rule.

The high rate of transfers to adult court is rooted in a falsehood—that some kids are not amenable to rehabilitation. That description often applies to Black youth, who are viewed as dangerous. Multiple studies show that when prosecutors recommend and send juveniles to adult courts and then prisons, they are setting these young people on a path to more crime. There is more recidivism with youth tried in adult courts than with youth who are tried in juvenile court, and it happens sooner and more frequently.[14] In that regard, prosecutors do nothing to increase public safety.

PROSECUTION IN THE JUVENILE SYSTEM

The prosecution of youths charged with crimes in the juvenile court system differs substantially from their treatment in adult court. In Maryland, anyone who is under the age of eighteen, is charged with a crime, and enters the juvenile system may be offered diversion without prosecution. With diversion, youth are referred to a Maryland Department of Juvenile Services program for counseling and other recommended treatment or services. A prosecutor would not even receive the case unless the prosecutor intervenes, reverses the agency's decision, and pursues formal court processing. In serious cases, a referral can be made to the State's Attorney's Office in the county or city where the alleged crime occurred. The decision by the Department of Juvenile Services to refer a juvenile's case to a prosecutor is not based on any particular criteria, but two are the seriousness of the crime and the juvenile's prior involvement with the criminal justice system. Youth who have had multiple involvements with law enforcement may be more likely to be referred to the prosecutor's office.

When a prosecutor assigned to the juvenile division of a prosecutor's office receives the youth's case, the prosecutor prepares a petition that alleges the youth is delinquent, and a judge makes a determination based on the prosecutor's evidence. The standard used is delinquent or not delinquent with a finding by a judge. A youth is considered delinquent if a prosecutor proves that the alleged act would be a crime if committed by an adult. If the prosecutor or police believe the youth is a danger to the public or himself or a flight risk, a prosecutor or an arresting police officer may recommend to the court that the juvenile be detained—taken away from the parents' home and placed in a juvenile detention facility pending a hearing. As with adults in adult court held pending bail, the law requires that a hearing before a judge be held within twenty-four hours to determine if the juvenile should remain in detention.

At any juvenile hearings, youth must be represented by counsel, often a public defender. If the child is detained, a hearing on the facts of the case may not occur for several months, during which time the young person must be detained in a "juvie prison" until the hearing. At the adjudication hearing on the youth's fate, the state's attorney presents witnesses and any evidence to show the youth committed the alleged crime. As in adult court, the public defender or other attorney has an opportunity to present witnesses and cross-examine the state's witnesses. All misdemeanor juvenile hearings in Maryland are closed to the public to conceal the identity of the minor.

If a court determines the juvenile is delinquent, a disposition hearing is held. Multiple options are available. Like adults, the child can be placed on probation with specific terms, such as restitution, counseling, or treatment. In Maryland, delinquent youths are placed under the supervision of the Maryland Department of Juvenile Services. Even if they are not originally detained pending a hearing, they eventually can be placed in a juvenile detention facility for a specific term that cannot exceed their twenty-first birthday. Although Black youth make up only 15 percent of all US youth, they represent 41 percent of all youths in juvenile detention.[15]

Youth enter the juvenile justice system mostly through a police arrest, a school law enforcement referral, or an arrest on school grounds. On rare occasions, parent intervention involves them in the juvenile justice system. For example, I encountered Margaret (not her real name), a witness for a client in an unrelated case, after she'd already filed a complaint with juvenile authorities for an assault against her by her then fifteen-year-old son. Margaret, a former police officer, confronted him when he lost the keys to the house. She was upset because he had lost house keys in the past, which meant that a locksmith had to replace the locks on their house. As she stressed that he should be more responsible, her son became frustrated and agitated by her tone of voice. He grabbed and shoved his mother into a corner of the kitchen, punching and pounding Margaret's small body with blows to her lower body and then fleeing the house. Margaret went to the nearest emergency room, where X-rays revealed multiple bruises but no broken bones. Several days later, Margaret contacted juvenile authorities. In this case, prosecutors did not charge Margaret's son, a Black teen, with a crime. Instead, he entered into an informal intake agreement with the Maryland Department of Juvenile Services that required counseling sessions for ninety days without the involvement of the prosecutor's office unless he failed to comply. Both parents signed the agreement to support their son with compliance. No lawyers were involved. No further action was warranted or taken. Margaret's son was one of the lucky ones.

In another example of parent intervention involving the juvenile justice system, an African American Baltimore mother became involved in an argument with her fourteen-year-old daughter after she came home late from shopping. As with Margaret's son, the argument became physical when the daughter shoved her mother, and the mother called the police. When the police arrived, they charged the daughter with second-degree assault, a misdemeanor. With that decision, her daughter went from being a teen coming home late from shopping for a prom dress to a juvenile delinquent. The prosecutor charged the daughter in juvenile court, and the court placed her on probation, which required that she abide by the terms of her probation or be subject to a return to a juvenile detention facility for any violations. Over the next two years, her daughter ended up in a juvenile detention facility twelve times due to minor infractions of her probation, such as coming home after her curfew or leaving home without permission. A mother's desperate cry for help one evening went awry and resulted in her daughter's involvement in the juvenile prosecutorial process for several years and multiple detentions. An investigative report by the *Baltimore Sun* found that in Maryland, Black girls are five times more likely to be referred to Maryland's juvenile justice system than white girls, which is far greater than the national average.[16]

BLACK YOUTH DISPARITY

Like adults, many youths are detained while awaiting trial because of a prosecutor's recommendation. The Sentencing Project, a research and advocacy organization, analyzed detention rates and found that in 2021 Black youth were four times more likely to be detained than their white peers nationwide.[17] In Louisiana, which has a large Black population, the detention rate for Black youth is six times the rate for white youth, but in places with a small Black population, like Scott County, Iowa, the numbers are even worse, with Black youth 8.7 times more likely than white youth to be incarcerated.[18] This means that in Scott County, Iowa, 1 out of every 22 Black kids is detained versus 1 out of every 457 white kids. In New Jersey, Wisconsin, Connecticut, and the District of Columbia, the same study found that Black youth are at least ten times more likely than white youth to be held.[19] According to the Equal Justice Initiative, on average, Black youth are five times more likely than white youth to be incarcerated.[20] These racial disparities have not changed since the 1980s and 1990s, when Black youth were more likely to be sent to a juvenile facility, and white youth were more likely to be sent to a psychiatric hospital to receive treatment or evaluation.

In Baltimore, where I prosecuted, public defenders represent most of the youth in court on any given day. An eleven-year-old child does not have money to hire a lawyer, and their parents typically lack funds to hire private counsel. One Baltimore juvenile public defender estimated that the population her office represented was 95 percent to 99 percent Black youth, who faced charges for crimes such as possession and distribution of drugs, robberies, thefts, many low-level misdemeanors, and school fights, including fights where their clients were the victim but fought back and ended up in jail. Youth crimes include a range of actions from trespassing by playing in a vacant house all the way up to committing rapes and murders.[21] Her clients are taken to the Baltimore City Juvenile Justice Center, nicknamed "baby jail," "juvie jail," or "juvie prison," where they (some as young as eight years old) are placed in a cell, handcuffed, and shackled, while they cry and scream and tears flow.

Each juvenile public defender is assigned hundreds of active juvenile cases, and standing across the aisle of the courtroom is a prosecutor who has the discretion to make decisions about young people, usually Black children or teens, that may impact their lives for many years to come. The prosecutor bears responsibility for what happens to youth who enter the juvenile or adult system, particularly the thousands who do not belong there.

In many states, youth are shackled in chains when brought to juvenile court. It is heartbreaking to see small children shackled together. And it is inhumane. As a prosecutor and later as private counsel, I saw young children who were wearing handcuffs, leg irons, and belly chains and accompanied by jail guards who had brought them to courtrooms in Maryland and Washington, DC, with these restraints, regardless of whether they were accused of a nonviolent misdemeanor or violent felony. It didn't matter. Children as young as seven years old have appeared in shackles. Imagine a white male prosecutor on the opposite side of counsel table in prosecution of a ten-year-old Black girl in shackles.

Although thirty-two states prohibit the use of unnecessary shackles, subject to a determination by a judge, this does not mean they have abolished shackles. It is an abhorrently bad practice, but it is still legal in many states. Using shackles on children treats them as subhuman, not as children. As a

Black woman, every time I saw Black youth in shackles—some who had not been convicted or adjudicated as delinquent—I couldn't help but think of my enslaved ancestors.

The use of shackles for youth came about after the late 1990s amid high nationwide crime rates and the demonization of Black youth. In 1995, John J. Dilulio Jr. coined the term *superpredator* to refer to teens, mostly Black teens who were deemed remorseless about the impulsive and violent crimes they committed.[22] The term served to dehumanize Black youth and further weaponized the criminal justice system against them.

In many states, the age of a young child does not matter when someone is making an arrest. In Florida, there is no minimum age for charging a child. In 2019, an Orlando, Florida, police officer arrested a six-year-old Black child, Kaia Rolle, for having a temper tantrum in school, during which she allegedly kicked three school employees. Kaia's grandmother told school officials that her granddaughter suffers from sleep apnea and that the incident was a side effect of her medical condition.[23] Nevertheless, Kaia was restrained with zip locks around her small wrists, placed in a police car, and taken to the Orange County Juvenile Assessment Center, where she was fingerprinted, photographed, and charged with battery. The charges were dropped against Kaia, but the damage was done. On the same day as Kaia's arrest, the same officer arrested an eight-year-old Black child. These incidents are not an aberration.[24]

Children as young as Kaia are sometimes arrested, but prosecutors usually decide to drop charges. In 2020, in Maryland, prosecutors dropped charges against over a thousand children under the age of thirteen who had been arrested.[25] During the school year 2018–2019, school police arrested seventy Maryland elementary school children,[26] and 56 percent of all Maryland school arrests were Black youth, who represented only 34 percent of the Maryland public school population. Until recently, Maryland, like Florida, had no minimum age to prosecute a child. But in June 2022, Maryland enacted a law that raised the minimum age to thirteen for juvenile court prosecution, except for children ages ten to twelve alleged to have committed the most serious violent crimes. This law will preclude prosecution of any youth under the age of thirteen except for serious crimes that are mandated for adult court.

School arrests result in a high number of Black children entering the juvenile justice system, where they face prosecution at an unusually young age. US law enforcement officers arrest Black boys in school to face prosecution at a rate that is three times higher than the rate for white boys.[27] These racial disparities exist in forty-three states and the District of Columbia. Just as police arrest Black adults for often bogus or questionable disorderly conduct offenses, the same thing happens with Black youth, particularly in schools. Before a school disciplinary problem reaches a prosecutor, a principal may start the process to approve the arrest, after which it goes to the law enforcement officer or security resource officer stationed at the school. (A federal grant for school security that began after the 1999 Columbine High School mass shooting allowed many Maryland schools to assign police officers to high schools in 2002.) After the officer arrests the student, the prosecutor decides whether to charge or release a child. By then, the trauma to the child or teen has already been done—regardless of the outcome. Due to racial bias, Black students have suffered far more than white students from arrests made by the school security officers and police officers stationed at schools.[28]

JUVENILE LIFERS

The most egregious types of juvenile incarceration involve people who committed a crime as a teenager and remain in prison decades later with only a slim chance of release. Children as young as thirteen can be sentenced to life without the possibility of parole.[29] They are called juvenile lifers. In 2004, Brett Jones had just turned fifteen. He lived in Shannan, Mississippi, with his grandparents, Bertis and Madge Jones. One year earlier, he had moved from Florida to Mississippi to live with his grandparents to escape an abusive stepfather after his mother remarried. His father was in prison.[30] On the morning of August 9, 2004, Brett's grandfather, Bertis, discovered that Brett was watching television with a girl, Michelle Austin, in a bedroom.

The grandfather asked Michelle to leave the house, and Brett and his grandfather argued about the incident. That afternoon, Brett was in the kitchen making a sandwich when he and his grandfather resumed the argument with shouting, shoving, and punching. He stabbed his grandfather with the knife he was using to make the sandwich, and when the knife broke, he used another knife to continue stabbing his grandfather for a total of eight times. He was arrested, tried, convicted, and sentenced to mandatory life in prison without the possibility of parole. A jury took just four hours to convict him and sentence him to life in prison at age fifteen.[31]

In 2012, the US Supreme Court decided *Miller v. Alabama*, which declared that mandatory life in prison without parole sentences for youth offenders under eighteen was unconstitutional but that discretionary life without parole was allowed.[32] This meant that a court could not automatically sentence someone under eighteen to life without parole but could use its discretion and impose that sentence or a lesser punishment after considering mitigating qualities such as age. After two Mississippi courts still found that a sentence of life without parole was appropriate for Brett Jones, he appealed to the US Supreme Court. In *Jones v. Mississippi*, Jones argued he was not permanently irredeemable and should therefore be eligible for parole at some point in his life because he was just fifteen when the murder occurred. In 2021, Justice Kavanaugh wrote the opinion for the court and struck down Jones's arguments. Brett Jones remains in a prison with a life sentence without the possibility of parole.[33]

The Sentencing Project has reported 62 percent of all youth sentenced to life without parole were Black children and teens at the time the crime was committed.[34] Twenty-five states, including Maryland, have abolished life without parole sentences for youth offenders under the age of eighteen.[35] No adult is the same person they were at fifteen. Our brains do not fully develop until we are twenty-five years old.[36] For the justice system to punish someone forever for a crime committed at age fifteen is an injustice.

Like Brett Jones, Joe Ligon was a fifteen-year-old teenager when a judge sentenced him to life in prison without the possibility of parole on two counts of first-degree murder, to which Ligon had pleaded guilty in 1953.[37] In 2016, the US Supreme Court made retroactive its 2012 decision that juvenile lifers serving without parole were eligible to be resentenced. A Pennsylvania judge resentenced Ligon to a sentence of thirty-five years in 2017, which meant Ligon was immediately eligible for a parole hearing. Against his attorney's advice, Ligon appealed his resentencing so that he could be free without parole. After being held in prison for decades, parole meant that he would remain under the penal system's rules while on parole for years to come, and any minor infraction of his parole terms and conditions could send him right back to prison. In 2020, a federal appeals court sided with Ligon, and at age eighty-three and after serving sixty-eight years in six different prisons, he was free.[38] Ligon is the longest-serving person to have received a "juvenile lifer" sentence.

MISPERCEPTIONS OF BLACK TEENS AND MURDER CASES

Despite the media-induced and racially motivated fears of Black teens as superpredators in the 1990s, very few Black adolescents face prosecution for murder or other serious violent crimes.[39] I had the misfortune to prosecute a murder case that involved three Black teenage students, all under eighteen and one barely fifteen years old. They were charged with the murder of another teenager, a high school classmate. In Maryland, adult courts have automatic jurisdiction over cases where youth between the ages of fourteen to eighteen years old are accused of serious crimes like murder. In this murder case, like many others, the defense lawyer requested a reverse waiver to send the case to juvenile court. I opposed the motion. Ordinarily, I would have remained quiet, but in this case, I spoke up at the urging of the victim's mother and sister, who strenuously opposed a juvenile transfer and hoped that the defendants would face a more severe punishment in adult court. Although it was rare for the prosecutor to have ongoing communication with a murder victim's family, in this case, the victim's family stayed in close contact with me throughout. The family was especially distraught that the three defendants and victim had been friends. In opposing the motion for transfer to juvenile court, I felt that I was fighting for the family to obtain justice and accountability, but I also felt pulled in two directions.

Although the judge denied the defense request to transfer the case to juvenile court, the jury in adult court found all three young defendants not guilty. The victim's mother and older sister cried uncontrollably at the verdict, and I expressed my remorse to them. Underneath, however, I was conflicted, feeling sadness for the victim's family but also relief because I knew that had the three defendants been found guilty, they would have faced upward of thirty years in prison. The victim did not deserve to die at the hands of his three friends. But at the same time, these defendants did not deserve to spend decades in prison, lose constitutional rights, and live with the burden of a felony conviction. I knew the ramifications of a murder or manslaughter conviction for Black teenagers meant that their lives would never be the same—just as my cousin Edward's life was never the same.

DENIAL OF RIGHTS BEFORE VOTING AGE

Once young people charged as adults leave prison, their conviction has a lasting impact, not just on them and their families but on America's ability to build a just society. For instance, most teens convicted of a felony can never serve on a jury, and that matters much more than you might think. Jury selection is one of the most important phases of a trial. Studies show that racially diverse juries make fewer errors and can result in fairer trials.[40] The public often associates felonies with heinous crimes like murder, rape, or other crimes of serious violence. But felonies have a wide range of severity, and their definitions differ from state to state. In Maryland, a theft of $1,500 is classified as a felony with a maximum punishment of five years in prison.

People have a right to be tried by a jury of their peers. That does not mean that a jury must be made up exclusively of the defendant's race, but race is certainly a factor. In a city that has a majority Black population, one would assume juries would be composed of mostly Black jurors. But in many jury trials, I had fewer Black prospective jurors from the jury pool to choose from, partly because, nationwide, one-third of Black men have felony convictions. So even before I could strike anyone from a jury pool, the law had already excluded many Black people from service. As Justice Thurgood Marshall once said, the exclusion of a segment of the community "deprives the jury of a perspective on human events that may have unsuspected importance in any case that may be presented."[41]

In many states, including Maryland, people do not need a felony conviction to lose their civil rights. They just need to commit a certain class of misdemeanor punishable by one year or more and receive one year or more in jail.[42] Texas bars people who committed misdemeanor theft. The District of Columbia even excludes people who are facing misdemeanor charges but have not yet been convicted of a crime. In total, studies show that 36 percent of 19 million people excluded from jury service due to exclusionary felony conviction laws were African Americans, who comprise 13 percent of the US population. That amounts to almost seven million Black Americans prohibited from jury service. Only Colorado, Illinois, Iowa, and Maine have no automatic felony exclusion laws that prevent an individual's service on juries.

If prosecutors would carefully consider transferring a youth's case to juvenile court or allowing it to remain in juvenile court, they would allow the youth to keep the right to serve on a jury. In Maryland juvenile court, there is no conviction—only adjudication of delinquency. When a state law prohibits a large segment of the population who are mostly Black people from jury service, it further dehumanizes Black youth and penalizes them for a prosecutor's acts. In the case of *Batson v. Kentucky* (1986), the US Supreme Court ruled that a prosecutor cannot exclude or challenge a juror from jury service based on the race of the juror.[43] State jury exclusion laws, along with the help of prosecutors, already do most of the work to ban Black Americans from jury service for acts committed before their brains fully formed as adults. Black Americans are racially disproportionately overly represented in the juvenile and criminal court system as defendants and racially disproportionately excluded from jury service on cases that affect the lives of African Americans—long after their juvenile case ended.

States differ on the process of removing a juvenile to adult criminal court, but generally, juvenile court jurisdiction runs up to age eighteen. Nevertheless, in most states, a person under age eighteen, the highest legal age people can be tried as a juvenile, can be tried and convicted as an adult for serious crimes such as murder and sent to prison for life. Most states do not allow individuals to drink legally until age twenty-one. Teens cannot vote until age eighteen. Most states require teens reach age sixteen to drive. However, in the criminal justice system, a teen can be sentenced in adult court before reaching eighteen.

Before my young clients and other children's brains are fully developed to maturity, they can spend years in prison with adult prisoners. Justice Sonia Sotomayor, in quoting retired Justice Anthony Kennedy in *Miller v. Alabama* (2012), said that "even if the 'juvenile's crime reflects unfortunate yet transient immaturity,' he can be sentenced to die in prison."[44]

We should work to give youth an opportunity to reform within the juvenile system instead of subjecting them to the horrors of adult prisons. In some states, this would require prosecutors, activists, and lawmakers to align and change the current laws. Wherever possible, we need our individual prosecutors to intervene, protect our children, seek fairness, and deliver justice.

We recognize as a society that children are often too young to think responsibly. Yet we decide that some children—mostly Black children—are so nonhuman in their behavior that we must ban them from society for the rest of their lives. Adult prisons leave an indelible mark on teen psyches. Prisons are violent places, and these youth are held with adults who are often repeat offenders who have committed multiple crimes. This practice sets youth on the path to becoming repeat offenders themselves and appearing before prosecutors on multiple occasions. It does nothing to keep the public safe. And a never-ending cycle of prosecution is created and perpetuated, continuing to overwhelmingly target Black youth.

5 PROBATION: WASH, RINSE, AND REPEAT

The very serious foundation of racism is distraction.
—Toni Morrison, novelist

In January 2007, nineteen-year-old Robert Rihmeek Williams was arrested in Philadelphia for illegal possession of a gun, possession of drugs, and misdemeanor assault charges. In 2008, Williams was convicted of the charges, served five months in prison in 2009, and was released and placed on seven years of court-supervised probation. Almost thirteen years later, Williams was thirty-two, still on probation for those charges, and famous for his music, which he performed under the name Meek Mill.[1]

The terms of his probation required Meek Mill to obtain permission to travel out of state, regularly report to a probation officer, pass drug tests, and receive no subsequent arrests or convictions. These terms, while customary, are restrictive for the average person and even more so for a successful touring artist. In 2014, Mill went on a multistate concert tour without approval from his sentencing judge. That decision landed him in jail for five months, and the judge added five more years of probation.[2] In December 2015, Mill found himself in court again for failure to obey travel restrictions and missing meetings with his probation officer. In January 2016, the judge sentenced him to ninety days of house arrest and community service.[3]

In August 2017, Mill was arrested for "recklessly driving a dirt bike" while filming a music video. Even though the prosecutor dropped the charges, Judge Genece Brinkley ruled that the arrest violated the terms of

Mill's probation. In November 2017, she sentenced him to two to four years in prison for riding a dirt bike.[4] By this point, a number of high-profile celebrities—rapper Jay-Z, comedian Kevin Hart, NFL executives and players, civil rights activists including Reverend Al Sharpton, and representatives of national racial justice organizations—had spoken in defense of Mill. After Judge Brinkley's ruling, Mill filed an appeal. With support from national groups keeping his case in the public eye, Mill's attorneys argued before the Pennsylvania Supreme Court that Mill should be released pending his appeal on the grounds that his 2008 trial was flawed and for other legal reasons. That release request was granted in April 2018.

In July 2019, Mill was successful. A Pennsylvania appeals court overturned his original 2008 conviction and granted him a new trial with a new judge.[5] Shortly after this, in August 2019, Philadelphia reformist district attorney Larry Krasner declined to further prosecute because the only witness to the original arrest was a now-disgraced police officer.[6] In exchange for the nonprosecution agreement, Krasner's office offered Mill a deal to plead guilty to a misdemeanor firearm charge. Mill received no further probation. Krasner stated that Mill's case was one of police corruption, excessive parole/probation court supervision, and an unfair process inherent in the criminal justice system.[7] With that, Mill's court saga finally ended.[8]

In this case, one arrest and conviction resulted in almost thirteen years of a repeat cycle of probation, and each time Mill was rearrested or violated the terms of his probation, it was for technical violations or a minor arrest but no new conviction. Yet he still almost ended up in prison for four years. Mill spent millions of dollars on his high-powered legal defense to secure his freedom.[9] It paid off for him, but the average Black person on probation does not have access to such well-financed representation or celebrity advocates.

HOW PROBATION WORKS

Probation adds an additional pipeline of people for prosecutors to send off to jail. In 2022, the United States had 4.6 million people on probation, which is more than the 2.1 million people on parole or in prison or jail.[10] Probation is often dismissed as a slap on the wrist or a walk in the park, but it involves some fairly burdensome requirements that can easily land people in jail or prison. People under supervised probation (as Meek Mill was) need to make regular, compulsory visits with their probation agent; pay mandatory monthly probationary fees, court costs, fines, and any court-ordered restitution; and pay for drug or alcohol testing (if ordered) and home detention monitoring equipment (if ordered). Probation officers will accuse defendants of noncompliance and file a petition for a violation of probation for any number of small missteps called technical violations. These include not paying the above fees, missing a meeting, showing up late, failing to complete drug/alcohol counseling, failing to complete anger management classes, testing positive for an illegal substance, or being unemployed. Defendants with jobs must manage to show up for work as well as complete community service hours in a timely fashion, do drug or alcohol testing (often weekly or twice weekly), and make weekly visits to the probation officer. I have seen judges impose probation requirements such as getting a job for those who are unemployed, earning a high school equivalency degree, writing apology letters, reading books, and a myriad of other conditions. Missing in the equation is providing any help that the person may need to remain compliant. Prosecutors who offer probation deals do not offer assistance in finding a job, becoming drug or alcohol free, or finding transportation to attend meetings and substance abuse tests.

A single individual can be subject to ten or more probation requirements—any of which could trigger a violation of probation hearing. Some of these requirements can also include not contacting victims or witnesses on a no-contact or do-not-call list, not changing an address without notifying a probation officer, not making child support payments (if ordered), or providing copies of job applications on a weekly basis and any specific terms of an individual case. The sky's the limit on the types and number of technical probation requirements a person can be subject to, and they all depend on the prosecutor making the recommendation at sentencing. As many Black people quickly discover, a probation plea is not a get-out-of-jail-free card. It's like walking on a tightrope with no safety net underneath.

When I prosecuted in Baltimore, even a technical violation like the ones that confronted Meek Mill resulted in the imposition of an entire suspended sentence. Fortunately, in 2017, the Maryland law was changed, and it now limits the amount of jail time that a person can receive for technical violations to fifteen days in jail for a first offense, thirty days in jail for a second offense, and forty-five days in jail for a third offense. After a third offense, however, the individual is subject to the full suspended time. At least thirty-four other states have laws to limit the amount of time a person may serve on a technical violation.[11] The same law does not apply to new arrests or convictions, which can result in the entire imposition of an imposed suspended sentence.

When individuals are placed on unsupervised probation, they do not have to report to a probation officer. In those cases, the likelihood of a revocation is significantly lower. The most likely way to violate unsupervised probation is to be arrested for another crime. Unfortunately, Black people are three and a half times more likely than white people to be mandated to supervised probation.[12] Of the 4.6 million people on probation, one-third of them are Black, and they often cannot afford the financial costs associated with probation, including the transportation costs to visit a probation agent once or twice a week.[13] African Americans make up 30 percent of those on community probation supervision but just 13 percent of the US adult population.[14] Plea bargains drive the racial disparity in Black people placed on supervised probation and fuel overall mass probation.

RACE DISPARITY AND PROBATION

In 2014, the *Virginia Daily Press* studied 110,000 probation records from across the Commonwealth of Virginia on a case-by-case basis. The study found that when defendants appear before Virginia judges for a violation of probation, more white defendants than Black defendants are treated leniently. In Virginia, 19.2 percent of white people's probation charges are dismissed versus only 13.7 percent of Black people's cases. Of those cases that resulted in a violation of probation, 45 percent of white people received no jail or prison time versus only 31.4 percent of Black people. A 2014 study published by the Urban Institute that analyzed four locations that included New York City, Multnomah, Oregon, Dallas County, Texas, and Iowa's Sixth

Judicial District found that Black probationers had their probation revoked at significantly higher rates than white and Hispanic probationers in all four study sites.[15] Revocation rates for white probationers were between 18 percent and 39 percent lower than for Black people on probation.[16] For example, in Dallas County, the study revealed that Black probationers' revocation rates were 55 percent higher than the rates of white probationers.[17] Iowa's Sixth Judicial District and Multnomah County, which are predominately white, had the greatest racial disparity during the time studied, as Black people experienced probation revocation at twice the rate of white people. Overall, nationwide, Black people remain on supervised probation for longer periods than white people.[18] These results suggest that probation supervision contributes to the racial disparities in the criminal justice system, both by initially placing more white defendants on unsupervised probation and by revoking Black probationers at greater rates.

As discussed in chapter 3, the targeting of Black people by overpolicing in largely Black communities is well documented and leads to more arrests for Black people. If an individual is already on probation, a new arrest alone will result in a petition for violation of probation. For Black people who live in Black neighborhoods targeted and harassed by police for nuisance crimes and noncrimes, it is difficult to avoid an arrest while on probation. Once an arrest occurs, even if the person is found not guilty, an individual can be detained in jail for months until the case and probation revocation hearing are resolved. The racial disparity in marijuana arrests alone shows the fragility of Black people on probation. A 2020 ACLU research report covering arrests between 2010 and 2018 found that Black people are over three and a half times more likely to be arrested for marijuana offenses than white people, despite equal rates of marijuana use by both races.[19] These results occur in every state and the District of Columbia and even in locations where simple marijuana possession is legal.[20] Even "driving while Black" becomes a challenge, as police officers continue to stop Black motorists at higher rates than white drivers.[21] If any stops lead to a misdemeanor traffic violation, it's off to jail for a probation revocation.

Meek Mill's case underscores the profound power of the prosecutor as, once again, the most influential actor in the criminal justice system. As a prosecutor, I handled a docket of violation of probation cases for felony and misdemeanor cases. The misdemeanor unit might be the bread and butter of the prosecutor's office, but a probation plea offer is often the knife used to cut the bread and spread the butter. One key element of a violation of probation hearing is that criminal rules do not apply. A violation of probation is not a criminal proceeding. It is a civil case. Yes, a prosecutor handles the violation of probation docket, and a person can be sentenced to a jail or prison term, but that person is not protected by norms like a right to a jury trial or the right to confront witnesses. This is one of those legal quirks that are hard to understand. The proceedings are fairly informal except for the person facing a revocation of probation and possible incarceration. A stand-in agent or substitute probation officer who probably has never seen the defendant can testify for the defendant's probation officer, if unavailable, and read the violation report to the presiding judge. Hearsay evidence is acceptable, which means witnesses who support a violation are not required to testify in person because the probation agent can testify from notes. Most important, the state's burden of proof is not beyond a reasonable doubt as in a criminal case but is the much lower standard of preponderance of the evidence. For instance, it is the same burden of proof used in a car accident case.

An assistant state's attorney proves the probation case with very little evidence, including identifying the defendant in the courtroom, advising the judge that the defendant was lawfully placed on probation by the court, stating that the conditions or rules of probation were explained to the defendant at the time of sentencing and were acknowledged as understood by the defendant, providing the basis of the violation through the agent's testimony, and stating that there is no legal justification or excuse for the violations. A defendant has the right to a defense to explain or rebut the allegations, but unless a defense attorney has an acceptable legal justification for the violation, the hearing is over.

And prosecutors and judges are not consistent in how they view violation defenses. For some, if there is documented proof that a defendant is indigent and unable to pay court-ordered costs and restitution, the defense may be considered acceptable. A subsequent arrest and a charge that gets thrown out of court may not be considered a valid defense to prevent a violation—as Meek Mill discovered when he was sentenced to two to four years for a probation violation. In the blink of an eye, the defendant faces sentencing. A probation agent normally makes the recommendation, and often I would concur unless I had overriding reasons to differ. If the probation agent preferred to continue to work with the defendant, I would not stand in the way of continuing probation. Even in cases where a defendant escapes the revocation of his probation and the imposition of a prison or jail sentence, the length of the probation could be extended up to five years, additional stricter terms imposed with the nightmare of future violations hanging over the individual's head. As a prosecutor, the days when I handled a violation of probation docket were always my least busy. An entire probation docket could be completed in less than one hour.

Whenever a serious conviction served as the basis of the violation, it was customary for the prosecutor to request that the probation be terminated and a sentence of incarceration be imposed. In the case of an arrest only, I had the flexibility to recommend we await the outcome of the new charge before a decision on the violation. In that case, the individual is usually held in jail pending the outcome of the new charge and probation revocation hearing. As always, any prolonged detention in jail can easily result in the loss of a job, a place in school, a house or an apartment, a car, and any other possessions, even if the defendant is allowed to remain on probation.

For people who await trial while in jail, a prosecutor's offer of probation seems like a life jacket. Most defendants I encountered, even those who maintained their innocence, jumped at a probation plea deal offer. In misdemeanor court, I offered far more probation pleas than jail sentences. A probation plea meant that a jail or prison sentence is suspended and left dangling unless and until the person is found guilty of a violation of probation. Even for defendants who post bail, probation offers them a chance to avoid the possibility of prison—or so they think. Often, as was the case with Meek Mill, probation disrupts people's lives and keeps them in the criminal justice system under the crosshairs of a prosecutor, sometimes for much longer than the original suspended sentence time period as a judge can continue the length of the probation.

I recall one defendant early in my career who declined what I thought was a reasonable probation offer. The case was regarding illegal possession of a firearm, and I discovered later that it had deep flaws. The ballistics report revealed that the gun was inoperable and incapable of being fired. Technically speaking, this meant it was not a firearm and therefore was not illegal. Due to the lack of comprehensive trial training by my office, I did not know that a gun needed to be operable and capable of being fired to be illegal, so I pushed for a probation plea deal. (I did not make the decision to prosecute alone. Several prosecutors had reviewed the case and decided to proceed. A prosecutor reviewed the case for legal deficiencies before the defendant's arraignment and then offered a plea bargain at arraignment.)

The defendant refused. The defense attorney was convinced his client was not guilty. It perplexed me that a defendant would decline probation and risk jail time. We went to a trial before a judge without a jury. The police officer testified, and I submitted the gun ballistics report into evidence. The judge read the report and quickly found the defendant not guilty. That defendant escaped the probation system and avoided a hanging suspended sentence over his head and possible incarceration down the road. He was one of the lucky few.

CASE STUDY OF ALLEN BULLOCK

Allen Bullock was not so lucky. In April 2015, when Bullock was eighteen, his friend Freddie Gray's neck was broken while Gray was in Baltimore police custody during transport in a police van. Gray died one week later from his injuries, and Bullock joined in the public protests following Gray's death. An iconic photograph published on the front page of the *Baltimore Sun* captured Bullock and an unidentified Black man as they stood on top of a police car. The photo became the face of the Baltimore protests against the police mistreatment of Freddie Gray. Other photos and TV videos showed Bullock holding the traffic cone that he used to smash the police vehicle's side window and windshield during the protests. At the time of the April protests, the state's attorney for Baltimore City had not yet charged the four police officers with the murder of Freddie Gray. Seeing Bullock's photo on

TV in the news and knowing that an arrest would be imminent, Bullock's mother and stepfather told their son to turn himself in to the police. Bullock did the right thing and turned himself in to the authorities, presuming that he would be charged with misdemeanor malicious destruction charges for damage to the police vehicle. He was wrong.

Allen Bullock was right to turn himself in to the police. Whenever I have clients with an outstanding arrest warrant, I counsel them to turn themselves into the authorities. I recommend voluntary surrender as opposed to police arrest on the basis that when they appear before the judge for a bail hearing, their compliance should indicate their trustworthiness to appear for future court appearances, which factors into the judge's consideration of bail. Bullock was wrong, however, to think that prosecutors would charge him only for the crime that occurred—malicious destruction of property. Instead, he was charged with malicious destruction of property and with eight counts of rioting. Malicious destruction of property with a value over $1,000 carries a maximum penalty of three years and a fine to not exceed $2,500. When the value of the property is less than $1,000, the maximum penalty is sixty days in jail. When I prosecuted, malicious destruction of property would have been the appropriate charge. But the state's attorney increased the charges to include eight rioting counts, which theoretically carried life in prison. Bullock committed no violent crime. No crime against any person occurred at all—only damage to a vehicle. A prosecutor recommended that Bullock's bail be set at $500,000, much higher than the bail of the four police officers who were eventually charged with Freddie Gray's murder.[22]

At age eighteen, it was Allen Bullock's first case in adult court. High bail is usually subject to the criteria of flight risk, risk to public safety, and lack of ties to the area. Bullock was a Baltimore resident who had turned himself in and committed no crime against a person. His attorney called the bail amount "ransom."[23] Bullock had a juvenile record for fighting and theft, but there were no serious charges in his juvenile file, according to his mother in an interview given to the media. He took three types of medications for his attention-deficit/hyperactivity disorder.[24] Bullock remained in jail for ten days until crowdfunding and assistance through an anonymous person or organization posted the necessary $50,000 to secure his bail of $500,000.[25]

At Bullock's initial court appearance, assistant state's attorney Mark Jaskulski, under Marilyn Mosby's leadership, recommended eleven years of incarceration as the state's plea offer—for broken car windows. Clearly, with the high bail and overzealous prosecutorial charges, Jaskulski intended to make an example of Bullock. And Judge Peters agreed, stating, "I guess what's happened here is the state wants to make an example of him. Is that what it is? . . . Trust me, I see a lot of cases coming in through here, and this is basically, unfortunately, malicious destruction. It happened to be a police car, it happened to be very well publicized, but I see malicious destruction impacting private citizens all the time coming in here. I don't get anywhere near that kind of [prosecutorial] response."[26] In response to the state's recommendation of lengthy incarceration, Bullock's attorney asked for a fifteen-year suspended sentence and five years' probation—still much higher than the circumstances warranted. Bullock entered a guilty plea with the hope that he would receive a suspended sentence. In 2016, the judge sentenced Bullock to twelve years with all but six months suspended, five years' probation, and conditions that included performing four hundred hours of community service, obtaining his GED, and writing a letter of apology to the Baltimore Police Department.

In June 2017, Bullock's probation agent filed a violation of probation petition on the grounds that Bullock had missed court appearances in Frederick County, fifty miles outside of Baltimore City, had two missed meetings with his agent, and had failed to notify the probation agent of a change in address. At the hearing in July, Bullock addressed the reasons for his absences. He stated: "I ain't really have no transportation, no family, no way to call or nothing."[27] Bullock's mother had put him out of the house after a dispute. At the hearing, Bullock's public defender told the judge and prosecutor that Bullock had been working at a car wash and was planning to enroll at a Baltimore Learning Center and nonprofit adult literacy organization to earn his GED. Despite this, at the conclusion of the hearing, Jaskulski asked the court to sentence Bullock to the entire eleven and a half years for what amounted to minor violations. Judge Peters imposed a sentence of eleven years and six months and suspended seven years to be followed with five years of probation. In essence, he received four years in prison but was credited for time spent in jail before the violation sentencing as well as time off for good behavior in prison—and then an additional five years' probation after his release.

In October of that same year, three months after Bullock was sentenced, the new Maryland law limiting jail or prison time for technical violations went into effect. Under the new law, Bullock would have been sentenced to fifteen days in jail.

In November 2020, Bullock's probation agent filed another violation of probation petition. This time, the reason was due to a felony conviction for second-degree rape, which was a nontechnical violation, so the new law limiting sentencing did not apply. This time, Bullock received a prison sentence of seven and a half years on the probation violation—the remaining time left on his original suspended sentence of eleven and a half years—to be served consecutively at the end of the felony rape sentence of twelve and a half years. This time, the prosecutor got what he had wanted since the day Bullock stood on top of that cop car back in 2015. Bullock was sentenced to twenty years in prison.

Bullock's case reveals how everything in the criminal justice system—charges, bail amount, probation plea offers, probation terms, and probation revocation—is subject to the whim of an individual prosecutor. Bullock's long suspended probationary sentence that began at age eighteen and continued until he was fully sentenced under his original sentence at age twenty-three cannot be viewed in a vacuum. Bullock represents how a prosecutor unfairly works to ensnare young Black adults through the probation system, with staggering end results. Bullock entered the Maryland prison population, of which 70 percent are African Americans in a state with 31 percent Black population,[28] higher than any other state. Bullock is considered an emerging adult (age eighteen to twenty-four) serving a long sentence, and in Maryland, eight out of ten emerging adults who are serving a sentence of ten years or more, like Bullock, are young Black adults.[29] Of those in Bullock's age category serving ten or more years, 41 percent are Black men.[30] As discussed in chapter 4, the brain does not fully develop until at least the mid-twenties. Studies show that before age twenty-five, individuals tend to have heightened impulse reactions, increased sensitivity to peer pressure, and immature decision making, when compared to adults over age twenty-five. All of these tendencies can become risk factors in dealing with criminal behavior, risk factors that are exacerbated by histories of trauma[31] (and the death of a friend and a prison sentence would certainly qualify as trauma).

Regardless of the felony committed with the subsequent conviction, Bullock should never have received a suspended sentence of eleven and a half years for standing on top of a patrol car and breaking car windows. And the prosecutor should never have recommended an excessive twelve-year prison sentence for what amounted to vandalism. The prosecutor should never have ignored Bullock's age, maturity, and socioeconomic issues when faced with a probation revocation for nontechnical terms. Unfortunately, most prosecutors just wash, rinse, and repeat the probation cycle without considering a person's specific circumstances.

A prosecutor's duty is to seek justice, not convictions. Where was the justice for Allen Bullock? Whenever I had a case of vandalism, which is the crime of malicious destruction with a first-time offender, I offered probation before judgment (to avoid a conviction and criminal record), restitution, and usually unsupervised probation. Bullock, barely past the legal age to remain in juvenile court and still on juvenile probation, needed help in the form of mental and physical health counseling to address his ADHD and anger management, a GED, and job counseling. The malicious and excessively long suspended sentence ultimately landed Bullock in prison for an extra twelve years. Sadly, prosecutors have the discretion to offer high sentences at trial and probation violations, even when they are totally unjustified.

THE OTHER RACE SIDE OF PROBATION

When I think about Meek Mill, Allen Bullock, and the countless Black defendants I offered probation pleas to, I also think about cases that merited incarceration but received probation. In 2014, Justin Craven, a twenty-five-year-old white South Carolina police officer, shot and killed Ernest Satterwhite, a sixty-eight-year-old Black man in the back. As an unarmed Satterwhite sat parked in his driveway, Craven fired multiple shots at him.[32] Family video and police dashboard camera video showed that Satterwhite was unarmed and that Craven killed him. Craven had attempted to stop Satterwhite on a traffic violation, but Satterwhite continued driving until he safely reached his driveway and then stopped with Craven in pursuit. The prosecutor presented the case to the grand jury to obtain a manslaughter indictment. The grand jury declined to indict on manslaughter and indicted on a felony gun charge, which carried a maximum of ten years in jail. A prosecutor offered a plea deal to Craven to plead guilty to a lesser misdemeanor charge. Craven received three years of unsupervised probation and community service hours[33] for killing a man for no reason. Contrast that with the sentence that Bullock received for breaking car windows. As Jack Swerling, Craven's attorney, stated after the sentencing, "He's pretty much free to go live his life."[34]

Peter Liang, a Chinese American and former New York City police officer, was indicted in 2014 on manslaughter charges in the killing of Akai Gurley, an unarmed African American man. Liang shot and killed Gurley as he walked down steps in a housing project. Liang was convicted of manslaughter, and a prosecutor recommended that he serve house arrest for six months and then complete five hundred hours of community service.[35] A judge reduced the manslaughter charge to criminally negligent homicide and sentenced Liang to five years of probation and eight hundred hours of community service—and no jail time.[36] Would that sentence ever be given to a Black defendant convicted of manslaughter? I doubt it.

PROBATION AND BLACK LIVES

Over 45 percent of Black men ages twenty-four to thirty-two without a high school diploma have been on probation at some point in their lives.[37] Studies show that probation supervision is heavily concentrated among economically disadvantaged Black people, with estimates of one out of every twenty-one Black adults (one out of every twelve Black men) on probation supervision versus one out of every sixty-five white adults (one out of every forty-one white men).[38]

Even when an individual has reoffended while on probation with a new arrest and a conviction, a prosecutor's recommendation should consider all of the circumstances. Every case should not be handled with the same heavy hand. I encountered several judges who had a "no excuse" policy for supervised probation violations. These judges sentenced people to the entirety of their original suspended sentence for even a minor nonviolent subsequent offense and conviction and did not accept any excuses for the offense.

A few years ago, I sat in a Charles County courtroom in LaPlata, Maryland, while I waited for my client's case to be called. La Plata is a small town in southern Maryland whose population is just under 30 percent Black residents.[39] A middle-aged Black man appeared before the court on a violation of probation. He had almost completed his probation without any prior issues when he was convicted of stealing some building materials left outside a building. It was a misdemeanor, but it was a conviction, and the prosecutor sought jail time for the balance of the man's suspended sentence. I was drawn to the man's case because I thought he had a compelling reason as to why he should not face jail time or at least not immediately. He was the sole caretaker for his wife, who had terminal cancer and likely had less than twelve months to live. He requested that the court either forgo a jail sentence and impose additional time to his probationary period or, if his probation was revoked, allow him sufficient time to arrange for his wife's care. The prosecutor and probation agent opposed both requests. At the conclusion of the hearing, the judge sentenced him to a prison term of over one year to commence immediately. He left the courtroom in handcuffs while his wife stoically looked on.

Every day in every state, countless defendants leave courtrooms with a suspended sentence and terms of probation. The key word is *suspended*. If people successfully complete all of the terms during the probationary period, the probationary period ends, but this is not what usually happens. Instead, people follow a winding road of more court dates for technical and non-technical violations. Individuals who are locked up because they are unable to make bail before trial jump at the chance to return home on the same day as their trial. They don't pay much attention to the finer details of their probation and rarely realize that probation is fraught with booby traps and that, as studies show, those traps are more numerous and more dangerous for

Black defendants. For many Black defendants, probation is far from being their way out of the criminal justice system.

As a prosecutor, I often offered probation as a plea bargain in misdemeanor cases where a defendant was not already on probation and had little involvement with the criminal justice system. I thought I was doing a good deed. After all, the person received no jail time. But surveys of adults who have been entangled in the probation system show that they often prefer a shorter prison term over a longer period of probation.[40] A Texas probation director himself admitted that if faced with prison or probation, he would pick prison.[41] How's that for transparency on probation? Probation is still a punitive sentence. The devil is in the details.

Most probationary terms and conditions fail to address drug or alcohol substance abuse, mental health issues, unstable family and living arrangements, or other socioeconomic issues that relate to crime. This systemic prosecutorial failure to offer assistance and support to people who desperately need it results in a revolving door of thirteen million misdemeanor cases annually, and this door continues to swing open to bring in repeat people for prosecutors on probation violations.

Probation positions people with one foot in the prison door and waits for them to trip and fall the rest of the way in.

III   PROSECUTORIAL REFORM IN ACTION

6 POWER OF THE PROSECUTOR

Where you see wrong or inequality or injustice, speak out, because this is your country. This is your democracy.
—Thurgood Marshall, US Supreme Court Justice

On May 1, 2015, I sat in a Montgomery County, Maryland, courtroom for a hearing with my client. When the hearing ended, I walked out to the hallway to check my phone and found an extraordinary number of missed calls and messages. I listened to one voicemail left by a friend, a former Baltimore prosecutor. It said, "Wow, I didn't see that one coming. Where are you? Call me."

I called her back. "What's going on? I'm in court."

"Marilyn Mosby filed murder charges against the police officers in the Freddie Gray case. It's all over the news."

Two weeks earlier, on April 12, 2015, Freddie Gray had been taken for what many Black residents call a "rough ride" in a police van that ended with severe spinal injuries. He died one week later on April 19. Many young Black people took to the streets in protest to express years of pent-up anger and frustration over Baltimore police officers' brutality, misconduct, unlawful acts, and excessive force against mostly young Black men like Freddie Gray. After the medical examiner's report ruled Gray's death a homicide, the state's attorney for Baltimore, Marilyn Mosby, made her announcement on the steps of Baltimore's War Memorial Plaza, adjacent to City Hall, symbolizing the change she wanted to bring to Baltimore's political and prosecutorial landscape.

But can any prosecutor change the prosecutorial blueprint of a city built on the overpolicing and overprosecution of its Black residents?

THE START OF PROGRESSIVE PROSECUTORS

Marilyn Mosby, a Black woman, was elected as state's attorney for Baltimore City in 2014 and sworn into office in January 2015, less than four months before she announced charges in the Freddie Gray case. At thirty-four years old, she was the youngest state's attorney or district attorney of any major US city. Mosby worked five years as a Baltimore assistant state's attorney for almost the same number of years that I did. Elected just three months after a police officer shot and killed unarmed Michael Brown with his hands raised up in Ferguson, Missouri, on August 9, 2014, Mosby became one of the first round of elected prosecutors who dubbed themselves "progressive prosecutors"—a term used to describe prosecutors who work to reform prosecutorial policies toward overall fairness and racial equity in the prosecutor's office. (As of 2022, less than 3 percent of the 2,400 elected state prosecutors referred to themselves as progressive or reform minded.) These prosecutors' policies, while not uniform in nature, often seek to reduce cash bail, decline prosecution for various low-level misdemeanors, increase pretrial diversion and restorative justice practices, and establish conviction integrity review units and sentencing review units in an effort to reduce racial disparity caused by the prosecutor's office. Since 2014, voters elected reform-minded prosecutors in large urban cities like Baltimore, St. Louis, Philadelphia, and Los Angeles and in smaller areas such as Durham, North Carolina, Portsmouth, Virginia, and Chatham County, Georgia. Buoyed by support of the Black Lives Matter movement and protests in cases such as Michael Brown (stopped and killed while jaywalking), Eric Garner (choked to death), Stephon Clark (killed in his grandmother's backyard), and others, it took a new generation of Black elected prosecutors—like Wesley Bell (who defeated Bob McCullough), Marilyn Mosby (who defeated Gregg L. Bernstein), Kimberly Gardner, Kim Foxx, and Minnesota Attorney General Keith Ellison—who were joined by white, Hispanic, and Asian American reform prosecutors across the country to begin the sea change toward prosecutorial reform.

Marilyn Mosby's decision to prosecute police officers quickly catapulted her onto the national stage and into the discussion of reforms that a prosecutor could make. In Baltimore, in the forty years from 1987 to 2023, nearly every elected state's attorney was a Black person. For one four-year term from 2011 to 2015, a white man, Gregg L. Bernstein, held the position. Marilyn Mosby defeated Bernstein in 2015. Despite Black prosecutorial leadership, the Office of the State's Attorney for Baltimore City did not change from traditional prosecution until the election of Marilyn Mosby. All others were traditional prosecutors.

Ultimately, the six police officers charged in Freddie Gray's homicide ended up with acquittals, a hung jury, and dismissals. In other words, they got off scot-free. One officer, Alicia White, was even promoted to captain.[1] And police retaliation soon began against the reform-minded Mosby. Five of the six police officers filed a lawsuit against Mosby in federal court for malicious prosecution and other charges for what amounted to doing her job.[2] One officer's attorney audaciously stated the officers were "humiliated at the criminal charges,"[3] which is horrifyingly laughable in the face of what happened to Freddie Gray while in custody at the hands of these same police officers.

As a former prosecutor, I know that prosecutors have absolute immunity under the law in their discretion to pursue a case, regardless of the case's outcome against a defendant. I have had to explain to many of my private clients that there was no legal recourse against a prosecutor who filed charges against them when the trial ended with an acquittal, dismissal, or hung jury. The US Court of Appeals for the Fourth Circuit ultimately dismissed the police officers' malicious prosecution, defamation, and invasion of privacy lawsuit against Mosby, and in 2018, the US Supreme Court declined to hear their appeal.[4] The police officers would have known this would be the result but brought the lawsuit anyway as payback. This lawsuit shows how far police unions will push back against a prosecutor's progressive efforts aimed at police accountability. And reform-minded prosecutors must be prepared for tough fights against reform efforts and refrain from any compromises.

While a few reform-minded prosecutors will prosecute law enforcement officers for crimes committed on duty, the vast majority of on-duty police killings go unpunished. The *Washington Post* database of fatal police shoot-ings, kept since 2015, shows that, on average, a thousand fatal shootings by police occur yearly with 30 percent being Black victims even though African Americans represent only 13 percent of the US population.[5] In 2022, police killed more people than any other year, with 1,176 lives lost.[6] Most fatal police shootings get swept under the rug without charges. Many prosecutors prefer to avoid charging police officers for crimes committed rather than face retaliation that could cost them their working relationship with the police department, their reelection success, a recall, an impeachment, or a lawsuit. This reluctance is understandable but is not a reason for compromising or refraining from charging police officers for crimes committed while on or off duty. Quite the opposite: prosecutors must treat police officers as they treat anyone who breaks the law. As the often repeated saying goes, "No one is above the law." The law is supposed to be applied equally to all people and citizens, but this expectation is sadly more aspirational than reality-based. Prosecutors must be bold and charge police officers regardless of any poten-tial backlash.

Despite prosecuting the six police officers, the Baltimore state's attorney also aggressively prosecuted the Freddie Gray protesters and recommended excessive bails and prison terms. For instance, Allen Bullock, Gray's friend, who had harmed no one but damaged a police car's windshield, faced a line prosecutor's plea bargain offer of over nine years in prison for what amounted to damage to a police vehicle.[7] Reformist prosecutors cannot talk out of both sides of their mouths to appease police officers.

Just slightly more than a hundred miles north from the State's Attor-ney's Office for Baltimore City is the Philadelphia District Attorney's Office. Philadelphia's district attorney, Larry Krasner, sued the police department seventy-five times as a private civil rights attorney before he took office.[8] Philadelphia, nicknamed the City of Brotherly Love, is known more for decades of unrest, police killings, and police bombing of an entire Black neighborhood without accountability than for brotherly love when it comes to police, prosecutors, and their treatment of Black people.[9] In 2022, Kras-ner's office won a manslaughter conviction against a white police officer charged with murder for the killing of an unarmed Black man—believed to be the first Philadelphia jury conviction for an on-duty killing by a police officer in at least forty years.[10] Krasner's office charged another police officer in 2022 in the unarmed shooting of a twelve-year-old kid.[11] Krasner's actions have been criticized by those who desire to maintain the status quo of failing to charge police officers. In 2021, in his first reelection campaign, the Philadelphia police union opponents of his reforms ran Carlos Vega, a law-and-order candidate, against him. Krasner overwhelmingly won reelection.[12]

José Garza, the district attorney for Travis County, Texas, who was elected in November 2020, told me that he is excited and hopeful about recent prosecutorial reforms.[13] By the end of Garza's first two years in office, he had already implemented major changes in charging police officers for crimes. His office handles all felonies in Travis County, which includes Austin, Texas. Garza told me that he secured indictments of thirty police officers in just his first twenty months of office through a newly formed civil rights unit.[14]

PROSECUTOR POWER TO MAKE PROGRESSIVE CHANGE

I recommend the creation of a unit that is outside of the local state district attorney's office that can independently investigate police cases, particularly when an elected DA refuses. The Minneapolis attorney general, Keith Ellison, removed the cases of Derek Chauvin and his fellow police officers from the local district attorney and successfully prosecuted them. An objective investigation from a state agency or independent prosecutor's office without ties to local police will allow for a more just outcome. In October 2021, Maryland passed a law that established a new division in the Maryland Attorney General's Office that partners with the Maryland State Police to investigate all killings by police officers. In 2019, Maryland had thirty-one police-involved deaths.[15] Local state's attorneys and district attorneys work closely with police officers every day, but when it comes to police officer accountability, an unbiased prosecutorial lens is crucial.

While efforts to prosecute police officers will help address police misconduct going forward, they will do nothing to redress the egregious damage already done by police officers. To right past wrongs, I recommend the formation of integrity units in all prosecutor offices to review convictions and throw out any that were obtained through police misconduct or unlawful acts—including ones obtained with guilty pleas by many Black defendants or even after a person has served a sentence. In conviction integrity units, prosecutors also conduct reviews of convictions to investigate allegations of actual innocence. As a result of the process, prosecutors should implement policies to ensure that past practices that caused the wrongful conviction do not continue in the future.

To exonerate people who have been falsely accused or convicted, progressive prosecutors, including former Baltimore state's attorney Marilyn Mosby and Manhattan DA Alvin Bragg, have created such units around the country.[16] In her first year in office, Mosby created the Conviction Integrity Unit to review and investigate claims of actual innocence. In another instance, her office vacated nearly 800 convictions of mostly Black people, including previous guilty pleas, that were due to police misconduct. A federal investigation into a Baltimore Police Department specialty unit known as the Gun Trace Task Force resulted in federal charges against the unit. Mosby's office threw out the convictions for arrests made by the unit due to officers' criminal conduct of planting guns and drugs on people and then arresting them.[17] Many people had already served time in prison as a result of the officers' crimes. In 2022, the Manhattan District Attorney's Office under Alvin Bragg reviewed cases through its Post-Conviction Justice Unit. The Manhattan DA prosecuted eight police officers, who were convicted of on-duty crimes and sentenced to as much as fifteen and a half years in prison, and vacated 188 convictions that resulted from the testimony of these officers. The Manhattan DA's office identified more than 1,100 cases for further review after twenty-two former police officers were convicted of on-duty crimes. Justice requires that prosecutors perform ongoing reviews to identify corrupt officers whose tainted testimony or illegal acts violated rights and resulted in unjust convictions.[18]

As a just society, we cannot allow prosecutors to convict people and lock them away, potentially forever. Justice requires a second look, but that second look frequently does not happen because we do not see race as the driving force behind these prosecutions. Jamila Hodge, executive director of Equal

Justice USA, told me in an interview that "the only reason that we can just completely throw someone away is because we don't see them as a human person deserving dignity, respect, anyway. And that's rooted in race. Because we do treat those who are accused differently when they're not Black."[19]

For most prosecutors, justice ends with a guilty plea or a judge's or jury's guilty verdict. During my term as a prosecutor, I don't recall that my office ever affirmatively reviewed any cases of individuals who were serving time. We encountered inmates who won their appeals and returned to court for a new trial, for resentencing, or for a post-trial hearing. Even then, we were instructed to argue in support of a person's incarceration—almost never for release. In 2020, the Baltimore state's attorney's office created a sentencing review unit to examine lengthy and excessive sentences imposed disproportionately on Black people, sentences of individuals who no longer threatened public safety, and sentences that might have other just reasons for review. The creation of prosecutorial sentencing review units could go even further by reevaluating sentences of individuals who have spent more than twenty years on a life sentence for a crime committed as an adolescent, individuals who were punitively sentenced under habitual offender and mandatory sentencing enhancements, and individuals who due to age or health reasons no longer present a threat to public safety. In other instances, a review would allow a prosecutor to review sentences of twenty-five years or more, review convictions that are no longer a crime, and review other cases whenever justice merits a review regardless of the amount of time served. The pursuit of justice should not end with a conviction in a system that is rigged against Black people. Other reform-minded prosecutor offices—in Seattle, Philadelphia, Brooklyn, Los Angeles, New Orleans, Prince George's County, Maryland, and other jurisdictions—have started similar sentence review work. California, Washington, Illinois, Oregon, and Louisiana have passed laws that allow a prosecutor to initiate a resentencing. Five other states—Maryland, Minnesota, New York, Massachusetts, and Georgia—had similar bills come before the legislature without a vote in 2022. Even when a new prosecutor is elected, the law ensures that the resentencing review work will continue.[20] A prosecutor's sentencing review unit should receive petitions for review from public defender offices, defense attorneys, individuals, government officials, and other offices. Increased staff of paralegals and investigators would allow for ease of review and swifter justice.

A sentencing review unit would be ideal for cases like that of Michael Thompson, a Black man who was convicted in 1996, sentenced to forty-two to sixty years for gun possession charges and up to fifteen years on marijuana charges, and sent to a Michigan state prison.[21] His charges arose from a 1994 encounter of selling three pounds of marijuana to an undercover cop. After the undercover purchase of marijuana, police obtained a search and seizure warrant to search Thompson's house, where they retrieved multiple guns from a locked safe, some of which were antique. Because Thompson had prior felony convictions, he was sentenced as a habitual felon. He would have been eligible for parole in 2038—the year he would turn 87.[22] Due to public outcry, including from Michigan's attorney general, Governor Gretchen Whitmore commuted Thompson's sentence, and he was paroled in 2021. At the time of his commutation, Thompson had served twenty-six years.[23] His case, like similar cases of thousands of prisoners, merited a much earlier review. Thompson remains under the supervision of the criminal justice system, as any violation of his parole conditions will land him back in prison.[24]

To help us move past mass incarceration, prosecutors' sentencing reviews must examine both violent and low-level nonviolent cases. In New Orleans, the resentencing unit of the office of the Orleans Parish District has obtained the early release of 168 people. As of 2022, the DA, Jason Williams, estimated his office saved the state $10 million per year with those early releases due to the high cost of incarceration. Williams has another 1,500 cases under possible consideration, which represents half the prison population from New Orleans.[25]

DECLINE PROSECUTION IN FAVOR OF JUSTICE

Reforms should also include declining prosecution of most misdemeanors and some felonies and moving toward diversion or restorative justice. So often the prosecutor's office leans toward a conviction even when justice would demand that the case be dismissed at the initial review stage—before a defendant ever has to walk inside a courtroom. A decline to prosecute a host of misdemeanor categories could significantly lower the number of cases, reduce racial disparities, and eliminate the upheaval of people's lives when they are faced with the threat of prolonged probation.

In March 2020, at the beginning of the Covid-19 pandemic, the Baltimore state's attorney's office declined to prosecute drug possession and prostitution cases. A Johns Hopkins research study released on October 19, 2021, found that no increase in crime, citizen complaints, or threats to public safety occurred over a fourteen-month period.[26] The Baltimore police chief, Michael S. Harrison, concurred, and admitted that crime did not rise after the prosecutor declined to prosecute certain charges. The Johns Hopkins researchers found that the state's attorney's refusal to prosecute 741 drug possession and prostitution cases also did not increase crime and that less than 1 percent were rearrested. And 78 percent of the arrests averted due to this policy were Black residents.[27] Other prosecutors—including the Brooklyn district attorney, Eric Gonzalez; the Cook County state's attorney, Kim Foxx; the Los Angeles DA, George Gascón; and the former Suffolk County, Massachusetts, DA, Rachael Rollins—took similar actions.[28] Former Suffolk County DA Rollins enacted policies to decriminalize at least fourteen misdemeanors. Like Marilyn Mosby, Rollins partnered with researchers to study her results. Rutgers University professors found that diverting low-level crimes actually reduces future crime and thereby makes the public safer.[29]

While I applaud these prosecutors' efforts during the pandemic and give them an A for effort, those efforts did not go far enough. On a national level that averages thirteen million state misdemeanor cases annually, prosecutors must expand the list of misdemeanors and nonviolent felonies that they will decline to prosecute if they don't risk public safety. Many nuisance and survival crimes that I encountered daily as a prosecutor should never have been charged in the first place.

Prosecutors must also rigorously review and screen misdemeanor and other cases after an arrest or summons to appear in court to determine whether those cases should be dismissed or diverted at the pretrial stage, preferably before or at arraignment.

DIVERSION AND RESTORATIVE JUSTICE

Diversion takes different forms. The DA for Travis County, Texas, José Garza, spoke to me about a pilot pretrial diversion program he started shortly after taking office. Because of this program, one individual went from arrest and charges of cocaine possession to a diversion program with the Carpenter's Union that allowed him to successfully complete the program and become a carpenter's apprentice earning $22 an hour instead of receiving a criminal conviction. Garza's office intends to build on the pilot program. We need more programs like this that will help people and fewer prosecutors who will convict or incarcerate on a police officer's whim. These diversion efforts will help increase public safety and decrease mass incarceration.[30]

In the interest of public safety, prosecutors should favor a restorative justice approach that works to rehabilitate offenders and helps offenders reconcile with victims and the community. Restorative justice is not new to America's court system. Thirty-five states use some form of restorative justice.[31] The concepts differ but center on a victim-focused approach and accountability for the offender. The key to a transformed justice system is to use restorative justice for a greater number of cases without involving the criminal court.

Common Justice is the first restorative justice program for ages sixteen to twenty-six that focuses on violent felonies, excluding sex offenses, shooting cases, and attempted murders.[32] It works as an alternative to incarceration. Danielle Sered, founder and director of Common Justice, recognizes that "we will not end mass incarceration without taking on the question of violence."[33] Common Justice is based in New York, and the Brooklyn or Bronx DA's office refers cases to it with the consent of all involved parties. Trained facilitators work with the parties to determine an approach of rectifying wrongs and obtaining healing for the victim. An agreement is reached between the parties, and the offender might be required to, for example, pay restitution, perform community service, attend school, or find a job. Offenders must also complete an intensive violence intervention program for twelve to fifteen months. In his description of the program, DA Eric Gonzalez stated, "We involve the victims rather than simply incarcerating people. We have been doing that increasingly with violent cases as well. We do it in cases where you might typically think a DA would seek incarceration, but the decision is made by the victims and their families. We take our cues from them. In a lot of cases, it doesn't serve the victims to send someone to jail."[34]

Victims overwhelmingly prefer restorative justice programs over traditional prosecution, and 80 percent to 90 percent are satisfied with the process and results.[35] Restorative justice allows victims to have a say in what happens in a case affecting them. Many prosecutors, however, treat victims as though they are pawns in a chess game, and these weakest pieces are used only as a means to an end—conviction. Many prosecutors do not ask victims for their recommendation on a case. Instead, they tell victims about the proposed plea bargain. A victim may not want incarceration for the defendant, but if the prosecutor believes that prison or jail is appropriate, prosecutors will ignore the wishes of the victim. When a victim fails to come to court, prosecutors use victim shaming or an arrest warrant for failure to abide by a subpoena. When victims have appeared in court on multiple occasions without resolution of a case, the most common question asked is, "Do I have to come to court—again?" I always told them yes, and at the conclusion of a victim's case, I called the victim's name and said, "You're free to leave." Many victims have no understanding of what happened in court. Many crime victims have indicated that they would prefer that offenders be held accountable with rehabilitation rather than with incarceration.[36] There are so many more cases that would benefit from restorative justice that satisfies the victim's concerns and provides accountability for the offender—if prosecutors would use the tool. In my almost five years as a prosecutor, there were many times when I wished that restorative justice practices had been available. I encountered serious felony cases where both the victim and defendant did not want imprisonment but still wanted accountability. Time and again, I have seen how the prosecutorial system does not allow for the victims' desires for leniency, particularly in felony cases.

In 2016, Karl Racine, the District of Columbia attorney general, implemented a comprehensive restorative juvenile justice program based on fairness to reduce the number of adolescents and young adults who pass through the formal court system. This in-house restorative justice program focuses on crimes committed by adolescents and emerging young adults between the ages of eighteen and twenty-four. The Office of the Attorney General for the District of Columbia does not accept homicides, sex crimes, gun offenses, or domestic violence in the restorative justice program.[37] Racine states that "it's the only restorative justice program housed in a prosecutor's office in the United States of America."[38]

The DC program accepts individuals when a prosecutor is planning to bring charges. It operates with trained counselors instead of prosecutors. Racine says that restorative justice places the keys of justice directly in the hands of the victim. At any time, the victim has the right to stop a prosecution. If the offender and victim both agree to participate, a written agreement is signed that establishes how the offender can repair the harm caused. The offender also receives services and cognitive behavior therapy to prevent future harm. Based on the data collected after completion of the program, Racine's office found that the youth recidivism rate was significantly lower and thereby increased public safety.[39] If offenders satisfactorily complete the program, the charges against them are dismissed.

Neighborhood Courts is a restorative justice model that launched in San Francisco in 2012. The office of the District Attorney of the City and County of San Francisco diverts nonviolent misdemeanor cases precharge to one of ten neighborhood courts that are facilitated by trained community-based volunteer adjudicators who facilitate hearings where individuals who caused harm accept responsibility for and discuss the impact of their actions.[40] Adjudicators then create directives based on the facts of each case and needs of each party, such as cognitive therapy, letters of apology, or community service. Neighborhood court costs the taxpayer up to 82 percent less than traditional prosecution.[41]

One restorative justice program conducted by the Longmont Colorado Community Justice Partnership (LCJP) works completely outside the criminal justice system and yields excellent recidivism rates. Police refer arrested people directly to LCJP, and all cases are accepted except for sexual assault, domestic violence, motor vehicle offenses, and crimes that involve a mandatory minimum sentence. Once offenders successfully complete the program, their records will not show the arrest. While a restorative justice program's success varies, LCJP's restorative justice measures have decreased reoffending rates to as low as 10 percent in a year. Traditional recidivism rates are as high as 80 percent.[42]

Funding sources for restorative justice programs vary, with some programs sourced with philanthropic funds, community partnerships, and government funds. A report by the Beyond Big Cities initiative at John Jay College's Institute for Innovation in Prosecution states that in Alameda County, California, "The one-time cost for restorative justice was $4,500 per accused person, versus $23,000 per year on average for a young person on probation."[43] In another example, if Maryland freed up just a fraction of the $300 million that taxpayers spend to incarcerate residents of Baltimore City annually, it would be able to allocate substantial funds to effectuate public safety, add restorative justice measures, and achieve justice simultaneously.[44]

REFORMS INCREASE FAIRNESS, NOT CRIME

Many who oppose reform-minded prosecutors claim that their views about fairness are soft on crime and lead to an increase in crime. This argument is not backed by research. A study conducted by the University of Toronto with research teams from Rutgers University, Temple University, Loyola University in Chicago, and the University of Missouri in St. Louis found no evidence to suggest that violent crimes increased in areas where progressive prosecutors took office. The study researched sixty-five cities from 2015 to 2019 and twenty-three cities from roughly 2018 to 2021. The study compared cities both before and after the election of progressive prosecutors. It found no increase in violent crime or homicide in Chicago, Philadelphia, and Los Angeles after progressive prosecutors took office.[45] So why don't reform-minded prosecutors do more to reduce the mass incarceration of Black people?

Jails are overcrowded with people who cannot afford to pay bail. In the United States, every day almost half a million legally innocent people remain in jail for low-level crimes because they are unable to make cash bail[46] and purchase their freedom. Eighty percent of people in jail are awaiting trial because they either are unable to pay a bail bond or have a no-bail status.[47] Although the US Constitution presumes innocence until proven guilty, many people stay confined in jail before trial. A cash bail system allows people with financial means—even those charged with violent crimes, including murder—to purchase a get-out-of-jail-free card. Cash bail penalizes poor people, including those charged with minor crimes. An inability to post bail puts the accused at risk for losing jobs, children through social services, family and community ties, health, and even life. Elimination of cash bail is an equitable way to deal with overcrowded jails. Many reform prosecutors campaigned and won on the promise to eliminate cash bail. In jurisdictions where reformist prosecutors have implemented bail reform and allowed people to await trial at home, studies confirm no increased harm to public safety occurs.[48]

Most people remain in jail pretrial as a result of an inability to pay a bail bond, which amounts to 10 percent of the amount of bail—not as a result of a concern that they will commit more crimes. The United States and the Philippines are the only two countries with a for-profit bail bond system.[49] Whenever a person is placed on bail, continued release before trial is conditioned on various criteria, such as drug testing, alcohol testing, weekly visits with pretrial release personnel, orders to stay away from victims, making all court appearance, no new arrests, and other criteria related to a specific case and as ordered by a judge. Failure to abide by any of the required conditions may result in revocation of bail and forfeiture of release to await in jail pending trial.

In places where cash bail reform has occurred—including New York, New Jersey, Washington, DC, and Santa Clara County, California—at least 99 percent of people completed pretrial without an arrest for a serious crime.[50] Cook County, Illinois,[51] Harris County, Texas,[52] Kentucky, and Philadelphia maintained the same rearrest statistics before and after the new cash bail reforms were implemented.[53] And New Mexico and Yakima County, Washington, surprisingly showed that a larger percentage of people completed their pretrial period without a new arrest than before reforms were enacted.[54] These results show the need to overhaul the states' cash bail system. Some people may need to remain in jail pending trial due to either being a flight risk or risk to public safety, but this description does not apply to the half million people held every day in jail on low-level crimes.

INCARCERATION FAILS TO TREAT MENTAL HEALTH

Incarceration has a minimal impact on public safety. Drug possession and prostitution cases are just two types of low-level misdemeanors that make up 80 percent of state court dockets and result in thirteen million cases in the United States each year.[55] The vast majority of prosecutorial time and energy goes to handling misdemeanor cases and a few theft and other felonies that should be classified as misdemeanors, most of which do not need a conviction or punishment but rather alternative noncarceral programs to address treatment options and necessary social services. Instead of helping adolescents and young Black men, prosecutors often prefer to remove them from society through incarceration or endless probation, which ultimately leads to incarceration. Prosecutors see themselves as a hammer and Black people as the nails that secure their conviction rates. The entire criminal justice system revolves around punishment and cancel culture—removing the individual from society—rather than rehabilitation. This leads to tremendous waste and causes irreparable, needless harm. Society and prosecutors ignore the prior trauma faced by many Black people whose cases land on a prosecutor's docket. When we see crime in the news, we often fail to consider that many Black youth and young adults face trauma at home, in school, and in their neighborhood.

Fifty-six percent of state prisoners and 64 percent of people in jail have mental health issues, and these issues often contribute to the actions that lead them to a prosecutor.[56] For example, a Black male client of mine in his early twenties suffered from Asperger's syndrome, impulse control disorder, and several other mental disorders. Due to his Asperger's, he struggled to understand interpersonal relationships, and after a romantic breakup, he was charged with misdemeanor harassment and stalking. At his bail review hearing, I argued before the judge that nothing in his background indicated that he was a violent threat to society and that he therefore should be eligible for pretrial release with regular mental health treatment with a psychologist or psychiatrist. I provided the judge and prosecutor with a psychologist report and mental health examination that stated my client presented no risk of harm to himself or others and that showed the psychologist's recommended course of treatment and therapy. Unfortunately, the white male prosecutor in the case disagreed, and so did the white male judge: he set bail at $100,000, which my client and his family could not afford to pay. My client remained in jail, where he received no mental health treatment and no assistance in understanding the harms he committed on the victim, and there was no way for the victim to become involved in a mutually agreeable outcome. Instead of giving my client the help he needed and the tools to better understand appropriate behavior in relationships, the prosecutor and the judge opted for punishment. On his trial date months later, my client accepted a plea bargain with a suspended sentence with five years' probation and no additional jail time. My client was one of the luckier defendants with mental health issues.

Reginald Cornelius "Neli" Latson, an eighteen-year-old Black youth, was diagnosed with Asperger's syndrome in the eighth grade and often spent his free time at his neighborhood public library in Stafford County, Virginia. In Stafford County, 69 percent of the population identified as "Caucasian."[57] On the morning of May 24, 2010, he was waiting for the library to open when an unknown person called 911 to report that a suspicious male was sitting outside the library and "possibly" had a gun. Latson had no gun and had committed no crime. When the sheriff approached and attempted to restrain Latson, a fight ensued. Many people who suffer with Asperger's are hypersensitive to touch and unwanted touch often invokes a fight or flight response. Latson did not understand why the officer was restraining him, and he panicked and assaulted the officer. The officer sustained injuries, and Latson was charged with assault and maiming a law enforcement officer. Latson's attorneys argued that he suffered from a disability and recommended an alternative to incarceration—mental health services. The prosecutor disagreed, and a judge sentenced Latson to ten years in prison. After spending five years in prison, including nine months in solitary confinement, he received a conditional pardon from Virginia Governor Terry McAuliffe. After he was released from prison, he remained under probation supervision. In 2021, Reginald Cornelius "Neli" Latson received a second conditional pardon, this time from Virginia Governor Ralph Northam, which ended his probation. It took a total of eleven years, including five years in prison with solitary confinement stays and pardons by two governors, to finally free him.[58] Mental illness is not a crime, and a person with psychological challenges is not going to get better in prison.

The lack of alternative options to punishment also affects those who are dealing with substance abuse. When I was a prosecutor, I saw countless individuals charged with misdemeanors who had proof of acceptance into an in-house drug or substance abuse program. Yet the state's attorney and presiding judge often opted to keep them in jail and out of treatment. Even today, when drug courts are prevalent and judges and prosecutors can refer defendants to treatment, enough program openings often are not available. Perhaps the most heartbreaking situation is the overwhelming number of juveniles who enter into the criminal court system due to issues from their own abuse and trauma, parental neglect, and socioeconomic challenges. These children need support services and counseling instead of a jail cell.

PROSECUTORIAL RACIAL BIAS AND ANIMUS

While most of these reforms will work toward eliminating systemic racial disparities, reducing mass incarceration, and reducing mass probation, prosecutors must address the individual implicit racial bias in DA offices, including line prosecutors, investigators, and other employees. Every office has its workplace dynamics, quirks, or peculiarities, but the office of the DA or state's attorney can legally destroy lives, dismantle rights, and seek death for people—all in a day's work. Combating implicit racial bias will require a complete overhaul of the prosecutor's office. The district attorney for Travis County, Texas, José Garza, told me his office seeks and recruits diverse prosecutors and employees who are driven to do the work of reforms. Less than two years in office, Garza stated his office became 40 percent more diversified in staff.[59]

How prosecutors see Black people reflects how they prosecute Black people. Diversity appointments of senior DAs is an important factor. Black people and people of color should have a say in the policy making of the offices responsible for disproportionately charging and convicting Black people. To change how prosecutors prosecute, we must change the culture of the office, which includes both the individual implicit bias and structural racial bias inherent in the prosecution of Black people.

In most of the country, inexperienced prosecutors receive very little substantive trial and legal training. Racial bias training is even rarer. In prosecutor's offices, where the majority of attorneys and their elected bosses are white, racial bias training is paramount so they can first be made aware of their own biases and then continually assess both the explicit and subtle implicit biases that are informing their decisions, which in some cases, are literally a matter of life and death. The American Bar Association recently adopted racial bias training for law students. A robust training program with an eye toward justice instead of conviction rates and a goal to uphold racial justice will produce more informed and upstanding prosecutors. I highly recommend that ongoing racial bias training be provided. Ongoing educational trainings, workshops, and webinars on skills, racial bias, juvenile justice, and implementation of policy reforms should be regularly conducted among prosecutors.

Kristin Henning, a Georgetown University law professor and nationally recognized educator and author on race and juvenile justice, told me that she has led countywide trainings of police officers, judges, and prosecutors. In her trainings, she provided prosecutors with a playbook and worksheet they could use to check their racial bias in adolescent and adult cases.[60] Her trainings for state prosecutors on racial bias showed prosecutors "how to interpret bias in the legal system when you see it on a day-to-day level, at the individual in a court hearing, or when somebody says something that reflects bias or is racially discriminatory or would serve to have a traumatic impact on somebody in the court system."[61]

After I left the prosecutor's office and entered private practice, I took courses and attended webinars and conferences in my practice areas to learn the best ways to represent my clients. Prosecutors who represent the public should require that line prosecutors and other essential employees attend regular trainings on skills, racial bias, and juvenile justice issues to increase their skills and practices for fair and just prosecution.

PROSECUTORIAL COMMUNITY OUTREACH

Along with ongoing office trainings, all line prosecutors and supervisors should be required to be directly involved in the communities they serve. Sometimes the only interaction that a prosecutor may have with the community served is in a courtroom. Every day in most courts, prosecutors require that some defendants obtain community service hours to obtain diversion of their case or a dismissal. The reasoning is that if defendants are involved in the community, they will be less likely to cause harm to the people who live there. The same theory applies to prosecutors. Prosecutors need exposure to the group of people they represent. Every time I called a case on my docket, I said the words, "Your Honor, Deborah K. Hines on behalf of the state." If the state of Maryland or Baltimore City was my client, shouldn't I become acquainted with my client? The community needs to see prosecutors engaged in their community, not just in a courtroom where they are ready to convict a family member or other loved one. Some community residents see prosecutors in the community only when they are campaigning for reelection. Prosecutor community service activities could include a day spent cleaning a community playground, playing a basketball game with youth, starting a softball league, or tutoring and reading to school children. The possibilities are endless—as they are for my clients who are ordered to perform community service hours. A certain number of community service hours should be required every year for line prosecutors. The prosecutors who prosecute Black children and young adults should not lack knowledge of the community that the office serves. I want prosecutors to see firsthand the traumas faced by many Black people in the community. As prosecutors visit jails, prisons, and juvenile detention centers, they will better understand the community harm caused by their carceral policies.

PROSECUTORIAL OVERSIGHT

A prosecutor's office usually undergoes no oversight—either from within or outside the office. For justice to be achieved, a state's attorney or DA must be willing to give up power. An oversight unit within the state attorney general's office or a special prosecutor's office would be an option for investigating serious claims of civil rights violations within a prosecutor's office. A former Philadelphia district attorney, R. Seth Williams, who was the predecessor of Larry Krasner, accepted lavish gifts (such as vacations, sixteen airline tickets, and a car) when he served as district attorney and, in exchange for the gifts, provided lenient sentences. After a grand jury indicted Williams on twenty-three counts of corruption, he was tried for bribery and sentenced to five years in prison.[62]

Young inexperienced prosecutors, despite honorable intentions, overwhelmingly feel they have no voice in the office. They might notice corruption—such as obviously falsified evidence from police officers, intentionally missing documentation from police, or all sorts of abuses by their leaders—but they keep silent. Mainly, this is because most prosecutor's offices lack any sort of mechanism for an employee to openly or anonymously report wrongdoing without fear of reprisal. Line prosecutors know that if they report misdeeds, they will face repercussions. Additionally, since prosecutors, especially those in specialized units, rely on police officers, they hesitate to report or punish police misconduct. For these reasons, prosecutors need to set up an ethical unit inside or outside of the confines of the prosecutor's office that allows anyone in the office to anonymously report prosecutorial or police wrongdoing and address ways to correct it.

DAs must instruct line prosecutors to seek and review all pertinent discoverable information from a police officer's administrative disciplinary files and then to provide it to defense attorneys, where permissible under state law. Prosecutors may know by word of mouth that an officer has committed wrongdoing in the course of his duties. The police personnel management system files contain information of prior misconduct, investigations, use of force complaints, theft of objects or an arrestee's money, racial slurs used, or other examples of racial bias that may have a bearing on a present case. Vida Johnson, criminal defense attorney and associate professor of law at Georgetown University Law Center, states, "It's like 12 or 13 states where this is accessible to them (prosecutors)."[63] In fact, police records are available to the public in twelve states.[64]

A POLICE DO-NOT-CALL LIST

DAs must provide prosecutors with a "do not call" list of unreliable, untrustworthy, or corrupt cops. In 2022, the Office of the State's Attorney for Baltimore City released a do-not-call list of over three hundred police officers. The office had concerns about using the officers' testimony due to integrity issues such as perjury, corruption, theft, and other reasons that deem an officer's testimony as unreliable.[65] Prince George's County, Maryland, St. Louis, Missouri, Philadelphia, Houston, Seattle, and other DA offices are developing and maintaining do-not-call lists. St. Louis DA Kim Gardner dropped a hundred cases where untrustworthy officers were witnesses.[66]

EXONERATION AND UNDOING HARMS

Line prosecutors commit egregious and illegal acts that go unreported because others lack a clear means to report them. In 1997, for example, a jury convicted Louis Charriez of stabbing a man based on the testimony of five state's witnesses. Charriez asserted self-defense, but the jury believed the government's witnesses. In 2021, the truth finally came to light: the key witness provided testimony to convict Charriez in exchange for money from Brooklyn DA prosecutors and for leniency in her sentence. Brooklyn prosecutors paid one witness $35,000 for an apartment, rent, food, hotel rooms, and other items. A total of $56,000 was paid to five prosecution witnesses to convict Charriez. A judge threw out Charriez's conviction, but by then he had already served twenty-five years in prison. Charriez's attorneys discovered the new exonerating information through multiple searches and utilization of the Freedom of Information Act.

Whenever a person's case is dismissed or a conviction overturned, as in the case of Louis Charriez, the records of the police department, courts, and probation department remain in files without an expungement or sealing filed by the person. A person's criminal records are maintained in multiple databases. My clients often think that a prior conviction or arrest without a conviction automatically drops off their record after a certain time period. While that may occur with credit records, a criminal arrest or criminal case information often remains forever. All prosecutors should provide the necessary expungement forms whenever they enter a nolle prosequi (dismiss the case) or a jury or judge acquits an individual. It should go without saying that a prosecutor should not oppose an expungement, yet I have had a prosecutor oppose an expungement request in a District of Columbia case for a client. The judge agreed with the prosecutor, and my client, though he was not convicted, could not get his case records sealed.

Prosecutors serve the public and owe a duty to protect the public—and not to protect corrupt police officers. It cannot be overstated that prosecutors owe a duty to "seek justice within the bounds of the law, not merely to convict."[67] Prosecutors' policies, the rules they play by, serve as a destructive force in the lives of so many Black families. Reform prosecutors must massively overhaul the prosecutorial system and bend it toward racial justice.

Prosecutors, progressive or otherwise, must define success differently. Prosecutors must move away from defining success as convictions. Many prosecutor offices give promotions for high conviction rates and successful jury trial outcomes. Instead, what if prosecutor offices could offer raises or other incentives for high compliance with an office's protocols on justice and fairness? For example, why not offer incentives for the most community service hours performed, for satisfactory restorative justice or pretrial diversion outcomes, and for largest amount of decreased juvenile cases processed through the court and referred to outside agencies? Let's upend the thinking around incentives for line prosecutors. Let's look toward justice instead of convictions.

7 POWER OF THE PEOPLE

The power of the people is much stronger than the people in power.
—Wael Ghonim, "Inside the Egyptian Revolution," TED Talk,
March 2011

On May 19, 2018, seventeen-year-old Charles Battle II was a high school senior in Denver, Colorado, with less than two weeks to graduation. At the end of the summer, he planned to enroll in college and eventually earn a business degree. Late that evening, as he was walking home, four police cars approached, stopping him in his tracks. Battle kept his hands up at all times and did what the officers instructed him to do, remaining calm even as three guns were pointed at him. As a young Black teenager terrified at the sight of police officers wielding guns, Battle thought the obvious: he was going to die that night at the hands of police.

Once Battle was handcuffed and seated in the back of a police car, another officer brought a Hispanic woman to the scene. Earlier that evening, the woman had called police to report that two Black men who wore grey sweatpants and grey hoodies had attempted to steal her husband's truck and then chased and threatened her with a knife. The officers drove her to where Battle was then standing near a patrol car, dressed in black jeans, a black coat, and a grey hood and wearing handcuffs, and one officer asked her if Battle was one of the men involved in the crime. Seated in the back seat of the car, she gave a positive identification, and police placed Battle under arrest, charging him with attempted aggravated robbery—a crime that carries a penalty of six years imprisonment.

In the flash of an eye, Battle, a teenager with no prior involvement with the law, became a criminal defendant. Meanwhile, as the hours passed with no word and no ability to reach him by phone, his parents, Sharon and Charles Battle, worried that the worst might have happened to him—that he had been murdered. It was somewhat of a relief to receive a call from authorities in the early morning hours informing them that their son was alive and in police custody. Police released Battle to his parents' custody the next day.

He denied the charges. Later at court, he refused any diversion programs and plea bargains offered by the prosecutor. What happened next is an example of one mother's unwavering advocacy for her son and organized activists' efforts to change the law that led to his arrest.[1] Battle questioned the fairness of a law that allows a police officer to show a suspect to a victim while the suspect is in custody and held in handcuffs.

A MOTHER'S FIGHT FOR JUSTICE

Sharon Battle is a mother, a pastor, and a volunteer activist and board member of Together Colorado, a faith-based community organization of 220 diverse congregations with mostly white members. She urged the group to become involved in her son's case, and members packed the courtrooms during his hearings and wrote letters to the Denver district attorney. Six months after Charles's arrest, the prosecutor dismissed his case without prejudice—which meant it could be reopened.

After her son's case ended, Sharon Battle's efforts as an activist went into high gear. She had no legal, political, or research experience. Armed only with an unrelenting passion to change a law that impacted thousands of defendants, mostly Black men like her son, she embarked on a journey.

As a prosecutor, I reviewed and prosecuted multiple cases where the identity of the crime's perpetrator is unknown to the victim and the victim later identifies the accused. Several techniques are used to obtain an eyewitness identification. The most common one, which many people are familiar with, is the lineup. When the victim can describe the suspect, the police show the victim four or more people who are similar in facial description, hair, height, and weight to the victim's description of the perpetrator and stand them in a straight line at a police station for the victim to view and identify. Another commonly used technique is a photo array. The police show the victim photographs of people who look like the victim's description of the perpetrator and ask the victim to make a positive identification. The most unreliable technique for obtaining an eyewitness identification is what happened to Charles Battle II and is known as a "showup." With this technique, the victim is brought near the scene of the crime and asked to identify one person who has already been detained by police and is held in handcuffs. According to the National Registry of Exonerations database, 28 percent of all exonerations were due to wrongful or mistaken eyewitness identifications, and according to the Innocence Project's database of 375 DNA-based exonerations, 69 percent were due to eyewitness misidentification. Exonerations occur after a person has been convicted.[2] If misidentification had not occurred in the first place, there would be no need for an exoneration. Mistaken identification is more prevalent in cross-racial eyewitness identity as in the case of Charles Battle II, a Black man, and his accuser, a Hispanic woman. The Innocence Project's research reveals that 42 percent of exoneration cases based on eyewitness identification result from cross-race identification.[3]

Sharon Battle and members of Together Colorado educated themselves on relevant topics, held community forums and virtual statewide church presentations, talked to eighty lawmakers, including the Denver attorney general, and asked everyone they met to talk to other lawmakers and support a call to action. Together Colorado engaged a lobbyist to draft a bill on showups[4] and obtained support and cosponsorship for its Eyewitness Identification Showup Regulations bill from State Senator Julie Gonzales and State Representative Jennifer Bacon. The bill did not gain enough legislative support to outlaw showups but was written to eliminate suggestiveness in the way showups are handled, like showing Charles Battle II while handcuffed standing next to a police car. The bill passed in January 2022 and creates practices that all Colorado law enforcement officers must follow. For example, police can no longer show a suspect to a victim in handcuffs or in poor lighting. If the officers are noncompliant, the law could affect the prosecutor's ability to use an eyewitness showup as admissible evidence in Colorado cases. What started as a mother's advocacy for her son was channeled into activism that helped to pass a new law.

The new showup eyewitness identification law passed almost four years after Charles Battle II's arrest. His trauma still remains. The emotional and psychological scars of his arrest and prosecution affected him and resulted in his decision to defer his dreams of pursuing a college education, earning a degree in business, and building his own business—for now. He hopes to get his life back on track.[5]

REFORMERS WILL CHANGE THE GAME

Prosecutors hold the most power over the justice system, and they are public servants. The 2,400 district attorneys and state's attorneys elected in the United States have a responsibility to the public, and the public has a responsibility to hold prosecutors accountable to the ideals of justice. To do that, we need a grassroots movement centered on increasing education, advocacy, lobbying, and protests and voting reform prosecutors into office and keeping them there.

We need advocates for prosecutorial reforms who will lobby representatives at their offices, lobby at local and state lawmaker sessions, and testify before committees and hearings. Many significant prosecutorial reforms will occur by changing existing laws.

Therefore, supporters of reform must be ready to support bills that advance the restructuring of criminal justice and oppose those that erode reforms. Such support means that we must be vigilant in our efforts to educate both ourselves and others on proposed legislation when the state or city legislature is in session and to follow closely the policies, laws, and budget of the prosecutor's office.

In 2016, the District of Columbia Criminal Code Reform Commission (CCRC), an independent District of Columbia agency, was tasked with revising the District's criminal code of offenses and penalties. The criminal codes define and clarify criminal laws, the laws' intent, and penalties for sentencing and resentencing. In essence, they are the bible that prosecutors swear on. According to attorney, professor, and criminal justice reform advocate Patrice Sulton, a Black woman who served as an adviser to the CCRC and who was the founder and executive director of the DC Justice Lab, few Black people have the opportunity to become involved in revisions of state and local criminal law codes. Some people have ranked DC's criminal code as one of the worst in the country,[6] perhaps because the District of Columbia has made few updates to its criminal code since 1901.[7] Many of the laws on the books are unconstitutional, outdated, or incomplete.[8]

Whenever there is a well-written revision of a town or state's criminal statutes, the laws' intent is more clearly defined, and they pare down the authority of prosecutors to overcharge in opposition to the law's original intent. Most prosecutors do not look at a law's intent when they are drafting charges against a defendant. They just want to see what they can use. For example, prosecutors often use the crime of kidnapping to charge a person whenever victims are moved or pushed to another location against their will. This sounds logical. But when I prosecuted, kidnapping was interpreted as using any slight movement of a victim to another location—including to another room in the same house, which is certainly not the intent of the law. In many jurisdictions, kidnapping charges carry a thirty-year penalty, and prosecutors often overcharge to obtain a plea. Revisions of criminal laws allow the actual intent to become clear and consistent.

In 2021, the Criminal Code Reform Commission submitted its recommendations to the Council of the District of Columbia, and the council (the District's legislative body) started public hearings on the proposed changes. Before proposed changes to criminal laws are accepted in final form or voted on by a legislative body, public hearings allow concerned citizens to appear and voice opinions. Advocates should partner with criminal justice reform organizations or advocacy groups that work toward prosecutorial reforms.

Those who are most impacted by criminal laws, whether victims or former defendants, should become involved and have a say in the reform process. In Sulton's work with the DC Justice Lab, the people most impacted by the criminal law statutes voiced opinions and provided helpful insights about the proposed changes to expand the District of Columbia's expungement law, to allow additional people arrested for or convicted of a crime to have their records sealed or if the crime is later decriminalized.

In 2023, the District of Columbia's proposed changes were overruled by the US Congress. Because DC is not a state and is unable to self-govern like a state, the proposed crime bill needed approval from Congress, and it failed to receive such approval. So the process will begin all over.[9]

US Supreme Court Justice Ruth Bader Ginsburg once famously said, "Fight for the things that you care about, but do it in a way that will lead others to join you."[10] The goal of a successful reform effort must include education for the purpose of bringing people from all walks of life into the movement, and one of the best ways to learn is through firsthand experiences. Many nonsecular organizations have prison services groups that meet with individuals serving time behind prison walls. Other organizations engage in services to assist those citizens returning from prison. These types of direct experiences with people directly affected by the criminal justice system help to reveal the carceral whims of prosecutors.

WATCH AND REPORT

Advocates can also become watchdogs to observe and learn firsthand how prosecutors work and to hold them accountable. When I prosecuted, a group of citizens that we called our "court watchers" showed up to watch felony trials and talk to the prosecutors and defense attorneys before, during, and after the jury returned a verdict to ask questions and discuss the facts, the evidence, the law, and the strengths and deficiencies of the case to gain a better understanding of how the system works.

The public generally can attend any court hearings, proceedings, or court trials. One exception is juvenile court, where the identity of the juvenile and proceedings are kept secret to protect the youth. Other exceptions include grand jury proceedings and other matters that may require privacy, such as protecting the identity of a child or an informant. Court watchers have existed for years in many courtrooms across the country.[11] Court watchers started in the Chicago and Cook County, Illinois, area in the 1970s; in New Orleans after Hurricane Katrina; and later in other places such as Massachusetts and New York City.[12]

The purpose of a court watcher activist is to become familiar with how courts run, monitor the actions of prosecutors to see if elected prosecutors' promises made are being kept, and report findings or take other actions. As many court watchers soon discover, their perception from TV or other media of how prosecutors work is vastly different from reality. The focus of court watchers can be on bail hearings, sentencings, other criminal pretrial hearings, and trials, and some court watcher groups also align themselves with other organizations such as bail or civil rights organizations. Court Watch NOLA (New Orleans, Louisiana) has collected data and published reports on prosecutors' use of arrests to compel victims and witnesses to testify by sometimes using fake subpoenas.[13] CourtWatch MA discovered that many of the crimes listed on a "Do not prosecute" list circulated by Rachael Rollins, the former progressive Suffolk County, Massachusetts, district attorney, were still being prosecuted.[14]

During my tenure as a prosecutor, court watchers had no formal training that I was aware of, but today, many organizations run training sessions for court watchers. The American Bar Association (ABA) recognizes and encourages court watchers as an effort to promote accountability, recognizing the importance of the public's access to the courts as mandated in the US Constitution.[15] The ABA offers training materials and manuals on how to start a court watch program and will soon offer trainings.[16]

Court Watch PG is based in Prince George's County, Maryland, a part of the Washington, DC, metropolitan area, and is run and founded by two formerly incarcerated Black women, Qiana Johnson and Carmen Johnson.[17] Court Watch PG observes bail hearings in Prince George's County District Court to collect data, educate the public, and hold the county state's attorney's office accountable to the will of the people. State's Attorney Aisha Braveboy campaigned and won on her promise to end cash bail.

After graduating from high school and before starting Court Watch PG, Qiana Johnson, a mother, worked for ten years for the federal government, content to have a good government job and start building a pension.[18] In 2012, however, Quiana became involved in a real estate scheme with Shamika Staggs to fraudulently sell a vacant house that did not belong to her and split the proceeds. They drafted a bogus real estate deed; forged the signatures of an attorney, a notary, and the property owner; and filed the deed in the Prince George's County land records office. Staggs sold the property to an investment company for $238,000 and split the net proceeds of almost $200,000 with Johnson. In 2014, a grand jury indicted Johnson on a ten-count indictment that included theft of over $100,000, filing a false document, and forging a deed. She pleaded not guilty and requested a jury trial, and in 2015, a Prince George's County circuit court jury convicted her on two charges. A judge sentenced her to ten years' incarceration but suspended five years and gave her five years of probation after her release. She was released in August 2017 (early due to good time served)[19] and began to volunteer with Progressive Maryland, an organization that works to elect progressive lawmakers.[20] That work led her to start Life After Release and Court Watch PG.

Court Watch PG cofounder Carmen Johnson, also a formerly incarcerated individual, heavily invests her time in Prince George's County court watch work. After her conviction in federal court on mortgage loan schemes and a sentence of fifty-seven months in 2015, she served her time.[21] Now she has trained over seventy court watchers and observed over 2,400 bail hearings in Prince George's County. She also works with law students from the DC area in her capacity as director of Court Watch PG.[22]

Before the Covid-19 pandemic closed or partially closed courts, Carmen Johnson was one of only a handful of in-person court watchers in Prince George's County. During the pandemic, hundreds of court watchers, from high school students to retirees, began watching Prince George's County bail proceedings on their computers or phones, and other court watcher organizations across the country began similar virtual practices.[23] After courts reopened fully due to decreased outbreaks of Covid-19, Maryland courts began to move toward shutting down virtual access to bail hearings, which would have required that court watchers attend hearings in person.

In 2022, in response to the threat that Maryland courts would return to decreased accessibility, Court Watch PG, with assistance from Georgetown University law students, drafted a proposed bill to continue the virtual platform permanently. They were joined by other interested parties—including civil rights organizations, state public defender's offices, celebrities Jamie

Lee Curtis and Fiona Apple, grassroots organizations, high school and college students—in advocating to keep the court's virtual system open to the public. A University of Virginia student who started watching bail hearings on Court Watch PG in high school joined other volunteers to write 250 accountability letters to prosecutors and other court officials.[24] Fiona Apple used her 2021 Grammy Awards platform to ask her Instagram followers to sign and support the petition to keep Prince George's County and other Maryland courts open virtually.[25] The 2022 legislative bill to keep Maryland courts open on a virtual basis did not reach a vote. For now, the decision to keep available virtual access to Maryland court hearings remains with the decision of individual judges, and Court Watch PG advocates will continue to fight for accessible accountability with future bills.[26]

EDUCATION IS KEY

Activist and author DeRay McKesson told me that over the course of the decade he has spent working as an activist, he has learned that "few people sort of know what the prosecutor does anyway . . . and we just need to educate people on the basics."[27] The work of activists will require educating other people about the work, power, and limits of the prosecutor, including cash bail, mandatory sentences, diversion programs, juvenile justice issues, the death penalty (where still legal), simple drug possession laws, mental health issues, and misdemeanor nonviolent crimes that cause no threat to public safety but disproportionately harm the lives of Black people.

Other educational opportunities include hosting community events to engage friends, colleagues, and family to work for reform; starting a group or event on specific criminal justice issues through faith-based organizations and secular groups; hosting a book club that reads criminal justice and mass incarceration literature and holds deep discussions about it; joining and partnering with racial justice organizations for support and guidance; subscribing to a criminal justice newsletter; and donating time, talent, and money to local, state, and national organizations for the purpose of expanding the movement. Opportunities abound for ways to hold prosecutors accountable and advocate for reforms.

One simple way to become educated about the prosecutorial process is through jury service. A court summons for jury duty is often viewed with dread. In fact, whenever I have engaged in the jury selection process known as voir dire, I find that many young people of all races balk at jury duty. Prospective jurors that I would love to have sit on a jury trial often have multiple excuses to avoid jury duty—and backup excuses in case one doesn't work. On the other hand, I have found that middle-aged to older more conservative Black and white people usually express a willingness to serve on a jury. This dynamic causes an imbalance of power that reflects who serves on a jury and votes on the fate of a person, often a Black person, who is charged with a crime. Jury service is one way that activists see firsthand how prosecutors handle trials. Activists who fight for reforms must be willing to serve on a jury when called for jury service. One person and one trial will not make a major difference, but collectively, diverse juries do matter. Juries decide the lives of Black people—those most disproportionately impacted by prosecutors. Courts across the country show a lack of diversity in juries for a variety of reasons.[28]

Statistics since the George Floyd protests in 2020 show a sea change in the willingness of more people to become engaged in the legal process, including sitting as jurors.[29] I hope that this trend continues. Jurors serve in one of two ways—either as a trial juror to hear evidence in an individual civil or criminal case to reach a verdict or as a grand juror to decide whether criminal charges should be brought and which charges to bring in an indictment against one or more defendants. Most jurisdictions require trial jurors to serve on one trial or for one day without a trial. Grand jury service is much longer, and grand jurors may review multiple cases for indictments on many charges presented by the prosecutor. After jurors have served, most jurisdictions will not call them again for jury service for several years.

PROTESTS AND MARCHES RAISE AWARENESS AND BRING CHANGE

Protest marches harness great power to raise the general public's awareness of prosecutorial and police accountability issues. On August 1, 2014, eighteen-year-old Michael Brown graduated from Normandy High School in St. Louis, Missouri, intending to enter a trade school,[30] something only about 30 percent of Normandy High School students go on to do.[31] Eight days later, Brown's life was ended at the hands of white police officer Darren Wilson, who shot the unarmed teen six times. Wilson was in his police vehicle in Ferguson, Missouri, when he stopped Brown and a friend, Dorian Johnson, who were walking in the middle of the street. A physical and verbal confrontation ensued, which led Wilson to exit his vehicle. He did not call for backup.

In his grand jury testimony, Wilson said that Michael Brown appeared like "Hulk Hogan" (a former professional wrestler), an angry grunting "demon" who made Wilson "feel like a 5-year-old." Both Wilson and Brown were six feet, four inches in height.[32] Wilson used racially motivated and biased words derived from the 1990s Black superpredator rhetoric to describe Brown, a Black teenager, to the grand jurors. Wilson testified that he feared for his life multiple times and that Brown was nonhuman and possessed superhuman strength. An officer's statement that he was in fear for his life has become synonymous with a refusal to file criminal charges for taking the life of an unarmed person—usually a Black person. It is hard to imagine that Wilson, a police officer armed with a gun, actually feared an unarmed teenager due to his professed belief in Brown's "power to overcome" him. Wilson stated: "The only way I can describe it, it looks like a demon, that's how angry he looked."[33]

The grand jury believed Wilson's racially charged words and his portrayal of himself as a helpless cop with a gun overpowered by an unarmed citizen and declined to indict Wilson on murder or any other charges. In one week, Michael Brown went from a high school graduate with his full adult life ahead of him to another unarmed young Black man in America killed at the hands of a white police officer.

The incident proved intolerable for Ferguson's residents. After years of unfair treatment by a prosecutorial and police system that failed to protect Black residents, the dam finally broke, and people poured into the streets to protest. Ferguson's protests continued for a year and spread to other parts of the country as they drew attention to police brutality, a broken prosecutorial system, and the failure of white St. Louis prosecutor Robert McCullough to protect the rights and lives of Black people by appointing a special prosecutor to oversee Wilson's investigation and indict Wilson. The young protestors chanted "Hands up, don't shoot" and fired up a movement.

The Ferguson protests were among the first to use social media in real time. The protestors' use of Twitter and their ability to connect with others as the uprising unfolded was unprecedented. Years earlier, on March 7, 1965, TV and print journalists covered civil rights demonstrators near Selma, Alabama, who were beaten as they crossed the Edmund Pettus Bridge on their way to Montgomery. The continuous real-time worldwide observance of a protest would have been unimaginable in that time.

The United States has a long history of marching protests. The United States was founded on protest. It is in our country's DNA from the 1773 Boston Tea Party and the American Revolution of 1776 to Martin Luther King Jr.'s 1963 March on Washington and the George Floyd marches in 2020.[34] In between those touchstone moments, countless protests have led to significant change. For example, in 1913, people who supported women's suffrage marched in Washington, DC, and that march led to the passage of the nineteenth amendment to the US Constitution, which guaranteed women the right to vote on August 18, 1920.[35] On March 7, 1965, approximately 600 activists attempted to march across the Edmund Pettus Bridge in Selma, Alabama, to protest the unlawful denial of Black people's right to vote in the South, and their efforts led to the passage of the Voting Rights Act of 1965.[36] Their success set the standard for a long line of celebrated protests. The 1963 March on Washington, where Dr. King delivered his "I Have a Dream" speech, brought needed attention to the economic inequalities facing Black Americans and led to the passage of the Civil Rights Act of 1965. An alliance of civil rights organizations, clergy, and labor unions drew approximately 250,000 people to Washington to demand a national program to provide jobs and livable wages, a prohibition against the discrimination of Black people in hiring, decent housing, integrated public schools, voting rights, protection against police brutality, and self-government rule for the District of Columbia, a majority Black-populated city. Over sixty years later, the United States still has not addressed the impact of the trauma of racism on its economic and criminal justice systems, including the prosecutorial system. King's March on Washington helped to end Jim Crow laws in the South, but the US government did little to address systemic racism embedded in US systems, including the prosecutor's office.

In the 1960s and 1970s, protests against the Vietnam War galvanized hundreds of thousands of demonstrators. In November 1969, in the Moratorium March, one of the largest antiwar marches, over a half million people rallied to end the war.[37] In 1981, President Ronald Regan fired twelve thousand air traffic controllers across the country for speaking out against their work conditions, after which the Solidarity March in support of labor unions and the air traffic employees drew over 250,000 protestors.[38] In 1995, the Million Man March attracted hundreds of thousands of Black men, who converged on Washington, DC, to support the solidarity of Black families. In January 2017, on the day after the inauguration of Donald Trump as US president, 4.2 million people in six hundred cities participated in the Women's March to protest Trump's policies that threatened the rights of women. It was the largest one-day march in American history.[39]

Many of these marches sent powerful messages to the world, but unlike their earlier predecessors, few brought about tangible change. While the 1969 antiwar Moratorium March drew over a half million people, the 1981 pro-union Solidarity March over 250,000, the 1995 pro-Black family Million Man March nearly a million, and the 2017 pro-women's rights Women's March over four million, each one fell short of achieving its goals. These marches made important statements but offered little action beyond the march itself.

In contrast, the marches that protested the murder of Michael Brown by police galvanized a Black Lives Matter movement and concrete political action. On August 8, 2018, almost four years to the day that Michael Brown was killed by Darren Wilson, Wesley Bell, a criminal justice activist, defense attorney, and city council member, was elected prosecuting attorney for St. Louis County, Missouri. Bell was supported by grassroots organizations and activists who canvassed door to door, texted and called voters, educated voters on prosecutorial issues, and registered voters as young as high school seniors. He beat Robert McCullough, who had held the position for twenty-eight years, with 56 percent of the vote.[40] Like McCullough, Bell is the son of a police officer,[41] but the similarity ends there. When McCullough was first elected, Bell was fifteen years old, younger than Michael Brown was at his death. Bell ran on promises to end cash bail for nonviolent cases, oppose mandatory minimum sentences, use diversionary practices, and appoint a special prosecutor to oversee police killings. After four years of collective social and political action, a new prosecutor had replaced McCullough.

THE SAGA OF KEITH DAVIS JR.

Protests also have been used as a tool against progressive prosecutors. For example, in 2015, Baltimore prosecutors charged Keith Davis Jr. with the murder of a Baltimore security guard, Kevin Jones. In 2017, Davis's first murder trial ended with a hung jury. A 2017 retrial resulted in a guilty verdict. The conviction was overturned due to the prosecutor's failure to disclose evidence that consisted of the jail house informant-witness's criminal record. In 2018, a third trial resulted in another hung jury. Finally, in 2019, a fourth trial ended with a conviction for second-degree murder and a sentence of fifty years in prison. While on appeal, the fourth trial's sentence was vacated, and the court granted Davis a new trial on the basis of unfair jury selection.[42] The Office of the State's Attorney for Baltimore City under Marilyn Mosby sought to bring a fifth trial against Keith Davis. If tried again, Keith Davis would have been only the second person tried five times for the same incident in US history.[43] The other person, Curtis Flowers, endured six trials before being released after spending decades in jail.[44] In my almost five years as a prosecutor, I can't recall a single instance where prosecutors retried someone for the same charges more than twice.

Throughout all of these prosecutions, Davis's supporters maintained that police planted a gun on Davis. They recognized that the only way to end this cycle and ensure Davis's freedom was for the prosecutor to drop the charges. So activists applied pressure with marches, rallies, mobile billboards, and other campaigns. Kelly Davis, Keith's wife, who was his girlfriend at the time of the alleged incident, fought tirelessly for his freedom.[45] Although

Kelly had no training in the law or involvement with activism, she began a seven-year real-life course in activism to free Davis. Kelly told me that she took a crash course on the justice system to learn how to be an advocate for someone. She attended town hall meetings, asked questions, started a social media campaign, organized an advocacy campaign recruiting other individuals, attended court trials to hear evidence, and printed and distributed flyers in neighborhoods to inform voters.[46] In January 2023, Baltimore State's Attorney Ivan Bates, who had defeated Marilyn Mosby, dropped all charges against Keith Davis Jr.

The marches in the wake of the deaths of Michael Brown, Eric Garner, and Breonna Taylor—which focused on police brutality and killings of Black people—also highlighted the failure of prosecutors to take action against these injustices. And those protests have made a sizable impact on the criminal justice system. In 2014, after delaying his decision for almost four months, the prosecuting attorney for St. Louis County, Missouri, Robert McCullough, ultimately declined to bring charges against the officer who killed Michael Brown. In contrast, in 2020, the attorney for Hennepin County, Minnesota, Mike Freeman, took just four days to charge Derek Chauvin for the murder of George Floyd, making him the first white police officer to be charged in the killing of a Black person in Minnesota's history.[47]

We need marches and protests to bring about change in our legal system and society, but they are not enough on their own. Long-term approaches are necessary, such as building broad bases of support among allies and working with a plan to target the levers of power. What comes after the march may be more important than the march itself.

While the above-mentioned measures are critically important, voting is one of the best ways to raise one's voice. Voting supports the belief that the people have the power to change a broken system. Voter registration proved to be an extremely useful tool in the 2020 election and will continue to be so in 2024 and beyond. That work should continue into the future and at all times, not just during presidential election years. Unfortunately, America's voting population tends to pay attention only to national politics—voting only in presidential election years—and frequently skips midterm and other interim elections. Most prosecutorial elections take place during these less popular elections on the state or local level.

The work should emphasize local elections, where most impactful decisions are made, particularly the elections of prosecutors, who typically run for office every four years in almost all fifty states. Some prosecutors run for decades without opposition or term limits. Voting also helps to elect other state and local lawmakers who will support and sponsor progressive legislative bills to reign in the carceral power of the prosecutor's office and to make prosecution more just and equitable—even if a reform-minded prosecutor fails to be elected or stay elected.

While I recommend voting as one method to enact reforms, I am also mindful of the voting restrictions that disproportionately disenfranchise Black people. For example, when people are charged with and convicted of a felony, many states prohibit them from voting. Felony crimes have a wide range of severity, and their definitions differ from state to state. What felony convictions all have in common, however, in almost every state, are felony disenfranchisement laws. Only two states, Maine and Vermont, have no felony disenfranchisement laws, including while a person is serving a prison sentence.[48] Felony disenfranchisement laws offer another opportunity for reform activists to become involved.

Fourteen states take away the right to vote while a person is serving time. Thirty-four states either disenfranchise people who are convicted of a felony for an extended time after leaving prison or indefinitely take away the right to vote after committing certain felonies.[49] In 2020, Iowa became the last state to remove the permanent lifetime ban on a person's right to vote due to a felony conviction. However, it left intact a provision that requires people to complete their entire parole or probation before restoring their right to vote. This process could take years.[50]

Alabama, Arizona, Arkansas, Florida, and Tennessee require the payment of all fines before restoring the right to vote.[51] While the amount of fees and costs may vary by state, estimates average at $10,000 and may reach $500,000 in fines.[52] I have handled cases as prosecutor and private counsel where individuals have no means to pay the high fines and costs they have incurred. Reform activists should lobby for reforms in this area.

State laws regarding disenfranchisement hit African Americans the hardest. One in ten eligible African Americans of voting age could not vote in eleven states due to voter disenfranchisement laws.[53]

Given US history, it should come as no surprise that felony disenfranchisement of African Americans is highest in southern states, including Alabama, Florida, Kentucky, Mississippi, Tennessee, and Virginia. In those states, one in seven eligible voting age African Americans are disenfranchised.[54]

In 2006, the United Nations Human Rights Committee charged the United States with violating international law due to its discriminatory felony voter disenfranchisement laws. If the United States had followed the United Nations' recommendation, then the laws of over thirty states would have been repealed, and millions of formerly incarcerated people would have had their right to vote restored.[55] Activists will need to work and lobby in conjunction with organizations for removal of the ability to vote caused by prosecutorial felony convictions.

ELECT, SUPPORT, AND AGITATE REFORM PROSECUTORS

State prosecutors, which include all municipal jurisdictions except federal, are mostly elected positions. There are over 2,400 elected state and local prosecutors across the United States, of which 95 percent are white[56] and only 1 percent are women of color.[57] Given that America's criminal justice system disproportionately incarcerates African Americans, we need to elect progressive prosecutors with a clear criminal justice reform platform.

The protest marches in the wake of Michael Brown's murder in Ferguson, Missouri, in 2014 helped spark a nationwide movement to replace conservative or traditional prosecutors with reformers.[58] Since those protests, more progressive prosecutors have won offices (although still far too few), including Kimberly Foxx (the Chicago area), José Garza (Travis County, Texas), George Gascón (Los Angeles), Larry Krasner (Philadelphia), Karen McDonald (Oakland County, Michigan), Marilyn Mosby (Baltimore), and Monique Worrell (the Orlando area). Protest marches bring awareness, and reform legislation and fair prosecutorial policy initiatives bring about change. We need to engage all available avenues.

An elected prosecutor is first and foremost a politician. Most politicians desire to remain in office once elected, particularly if no term limits exist for the office. The job of the people is to use and exert power to push politicians and prosecutors to make systemic changes in a prosecutorial system that was built and designed to harness power against African Americans. The election of progressive politicians and prosecutors is key but is only part of the answer to injustice. Activists must continue to agitate the prosecutorial system, including applying pressure against reform prosecutors when necessary. Despite their good intentions to advance transformational reforms, politicians want to win future elections, and reform-minded prosecutors may make compromises—like failing to indict police officers to appease police unions—to win reelection. Prosecutors need to feel the breath of activists down their necks. Progressive prosecutors sometimes need to confront police, who can detrimentally sway criminal case outcomes that might affect public safety. Conservative lawmakers hold power over elected prosecutors' office budgets and in other ways. Powerful police unions, like the Fraternal Order of Police, often oppose police reforms and accountability. Citizens who support public safety sometimes favor a "lock them all up" approach. Conservative district attorney associations sometimes oppose and call for the ouster of reform-minded prosecutors. As the movement grows, it faces pushback.

These hostile groups often advocate for punitive policies to increase the carceral power of the prosecutor or try to thwart the efforts of reform prosecutors.[59] Activists must be keenly on the lookout for reform prosecutors who are tempted to remain in office by making compromises that thwart progressive reforms. This is a push and pull situation. Progressive prosecutors need activists to shield and support them when attacked, or else reforms will be either stalled or reversed in the next election or recall election or with threats of impeachment. This occurred with Chesa Boudin, who was recalled before his first term was completed in San Francisco; George Gascón, who survived failed recall efforts in Los Angeles; Larry Krasner, who remained in office after impeachment efforts failed in Philadelphia; and Marilyn Mosby, who lost reelection after two terms in Baltimore. Activists who are in favor of reforms must keep up their mobilization efforts for reform prosecutors because attacks inevitably will occur. Efforts must continue to elect, reelect, protect, and support progressive prosecutors.

There is no one right way for activists to fight for prosecutorial changes. The point is to start where you are and do what you can. Many activists become impassioned about a particular issue due to a family member's experiences or personal experiences with the justice system. Activists will learn by experience of what works, what fails, and what might succeed. Education on prosecutorial issues is a key factor. To bring others into the fold of reform activism, protests and advocacy require that activists become knowledgeable about their issues. The battle requires sacrifices of time and effort.

Activists and advocates possess more experience in some areas than others. Some people are new to activism, but no experience is necessary to get the job done. No titles are needed. Whether you call yourself a reform advocate, a protestor, an activist, an ally, an accomplice, or something else, the goal is the same—transformational prosecutorial reform for a more just society.

The current prosecutorial system was not built overnight. It will take sustained efforts to build a new, equitable justice system that serves all Americans with equality, fairness, and integrity. The key is to make a lifetime commitment. Acts of individuals mobilized collectively through groups play a critical role in pushing elected prosecutors toward transformational reforms. As advocates and activists for prosecutorial reform, we must do what author and social activist bell hooks once said: "To be truly visionary we have to root our imagination in our concrete reality while simultaneously imagining possibilities beyond that reality."[60]

8 POWER OF WHITE ALLIES

It is impossible to struggle for civil rights, equal rights for Blacks, without including whites. Because equal rights, fair play, justice, are like the air: we all have it or none of us has it. That is the truth of it.
—Maya Angelou, "America's Renaissance Woman," Academy of Achievement interview, January 22, 1997

In April 2021, Kimberly Potter, at the time a forty-six-year-old Minneapolis police officer, shot and killed Daunte Wright, a twenty-year-old unarmed Black man. During her trial for first- and second-degree manslaughter, Potter testified that she had stopped Wright for a traffic citation, an expired registration, and an air freshener hanging from his rearview mirror and claimed that she accidentally shot him when she drew her revolver instead of her taser. On the stand, Potter dressed like a middle-aged white soccer mom, wearing a high-necked floral blouse, a semisheer shawl, and a bright yellow neck lanyard. She repeatedly cried. Her freedom hinged on a twelve-person jury that included only one Black juror.

The jury deliberated for over twenty hours and found Potter guilty on both counts. After the verdict, Black Americans breathed a collective sigh of relief—although it was hard not to feel disappointed and resentful at the judge's sentence of only two years in prison.

Several weeks earlier, I had watched a Georgia jury of eleven white jurors and one Black juror find three white men—Gregory McMichael, his son Travis McMichael, and their neighbor William Bryan—guilty of murdering Ahmaud Arbery, another young unarmed Black man as he jogged less than two miles from his home.[1] A prosecutor recommended and a judge sentenced all three men to life in prison.

Just a few years earlier, these verdicts and prosecutor sentencing recommendation would have been unimaginable. White men and women who had killed unarmed Black men were rarely found guilty. But in these cases, the white jurors saw the humanity of Daunte Wright and Ahmaud Arbery as equal to that of the white defendants. Courts do not allow cameras in the jury room, but I believe that the white jurors must have listened attentively to the lone Black juror in each case to reach these verdicts.

This shift in verdict outcomes comes, in part, from a new degree of racial consciousness inspired by the protests following George Floyd's murder in Minneapolis in 2020. Those racial justice protests, some of the largest since the days of Martin Luther King Jr., included tens of thousands of white people. In fact, at several of them, white faces made up the majority. Research data from June 6–7, 2020, showed that white people accounted for 65 percent of protestors in Washington, DC, 61 percent in New York City, and 53 percent in Los Angeles.[2] In contrast, protests dating back to Michael Brown in 2014 in Ferguson, Missouri, were populated mostly with Black people.

ROLE FOR WHITE ALLIES

Thus far, the fight against police brutality and for prosecutorial reform has been carried out mostly by Black people, and it is encouraging to see some marches populated primarily by white Americans. Conversations within the Black community have questioned whether white Americans would ever step forward to take a pivotal role in dismantling a system that was created and maintained for more than four hundred years by and explicitly in favor of white Americans. The United States is still a country dominated by white people, and true change cannot occur if white Americans do not work to undo these prosecutorial harms. Yet this outpouring of white support also inspired some skepticism in Black communities. White Americans have built and maintained a system that explicitly benefited them for centuries. How many of those who joined the marches truly wanted to work to dismantle that system? How many of them showed up just to play the white savior role?

White allies are necessary in the fight for prosecutorial reforms. But some of these prosecutorial reforms are more difficult to see. The convictions of the McMichaels and their neighbor for the murder of Ahmaud Arbery, for instance, are easily seen as justice. But white people must learn to accept the full humanity of Black people even when it does not involve a Black person's heinous murder at the hands of a white person. They need to recognize the intricacies involved in Black recidivism, plea bargaining, sentencing, and all of the other many inequities discussed in this book, and this requires being able to see the racist soup they're swimming in.

White people who want to be allies in the struggle for prosecutorial and racial justice reform often struggle with understanding the most effective way to do so for fear that their unacknowledged prejudices will interfere with good intentions. The intergenerational racism they carry is so ingrained that they cannot always recognize it in themselves. In Portland, Oregon, on July 18, 2020, Beverly Barnum started a group of mostly white women to protest George Floyd's murder by linking arms, wearing yellow T-shirts, carrying yellow roses and sunflowers, and using their bodies as a physical barricade between federal law enforcement officers and Black Lives Matter protesters.[3] News media carried photos and videos showing the Wall of Moms protecting Black protesters. Whether consciously or inadvertently, the premise of Barnum's organizational structure suggested that white people needed to rescue and save Black people. In addition, using the Wall of Moms as a human shield between the police and Black protesters rather than standing in protests interspersed among Black protestors amplified the myth that Black people need to be saved by white people. Ten days after it was formed, Barnum's group imploded very publicly amid accusations that Barnum coopted the cause for her personal gain and abandoned the original Black Lives Matter message.[4]

America's inherited social structures flow from one generation to the next and carry risk factors that cannot be ignored. This inheritance moves from one individual to the next and is passed down from one generation to the next. We have genetic traits and predispositions to diseases, but we also have predetermined positions in a race system that was designed to keep everyone in their places. The good news is that our structural DNA not only reveals risk factors but also can inform a diagnosis and treatment plan for the underlying disease of racism. We need to be aware of America's DNA in order to manage risks and prescribe a treatment plan for its diseases to correct past wrongs and effectively work for change.

The Portland Wall of Moms demonstrated ineffective white ally participation through a failure to recognize that the white savior mentality is not only abhorrent to African Americans but also ineffective. Consciously or unconsciously, Barnum's group of mothers, with their yellow shirts, yellow roses, sunflowers, and linked arms, sought to bring attention to themselves rather than to the cause of police brutality, prosecutorial inaction when police kill unarmed Black Americans, and George Floyd's life. Hundreds of white women in a sea of thousands of Black protesters already stand out— without the bright yellow clothing. Their white skin color was sufficient to grab media attention. Barnum's actions suggested that she wanted to make a statement about her white privilege rather than a statement with her white privilege in support of a laudable cause. Since long before Black Lives Matter protests, "support" from groups like Barnum's has caused Black leaders to question the motives of white allies: Is the support exploitative, or is it true allyship?

PLEASE, NO WHITE SAVIORS

The role of the white savior has a long history in American history. It is so embedded in our culture that its practices permeate works by white people for white audiences. For example, the Hollywood movie *The Help*, based on the novel by Kathryn Stockett, a white author, explores the life of a Southern white woman who writes about the work experiences of Black maids in an effort to help them but fails to understand the real-life racial issues of life in the Jim Crow South. The author centers this story of Black women around a white woman, as if Black people have no story unless white people are present and at the center of it.

Another example of the white savior story is *The Blind Side*, first a book written by a white author, Michael Lewis, and later a Hollywood movie that portrays the story of Michael Oher, who as a teenager became homeless, was adopted by a white family, and eventually played in the National Football League. In the movie, the white mother, played by Sandra Bullock, shows Oher how to throw a football, and the rest is history. The real-life person, Michael Oher, told the press that it was hurtful to see the film portray him as a Black teen who needed help from a white woman to learn how to play football and that his success in the NFL was due to his white adopted mother rather than his hard work, discipline, skill, and determination.[5]

Hollywood has consistently remade the world in its image. Frederick Douglass had himself photographed wearing beautiful suits and a confident expression because the only images of Black people at that time were degrading and humiliating and led the world to believe that the "Negro" had nothing of value to offer. Unfortunately, Hollywood has spent decades undoing Douglass's intentions.

The white savior mentality is borne partly of a paternalistic attitude pervasive among white Americans that compels them to view the issues of Black Americans through their own lens. Such a skewed perspective does not require input or dialogue with Black leaders in order to advocate on their behalf. Such a viewpoint sees Black Americans only in relation to whiteness—as if Black people do not exist outside of whiteness and cannot exist without white people.

In his article "On Being White and Other Lies," James Baldwin says that the Black condition created white people.[6] In other words, white people would not exist if Black people did not exist. For example, before coming to America, white people were known by their nationality, such as Polish, Italian, Greek, Spanish, and British. The white community in the United States is a creation of social conditions born of a need to subjugate Black people. Baldwin continues, "No community can be based on such a principle, or, in other words, no community can be established on so genocidal a lie."[7] He calls this choice one of moral erosion, which makes it impossible for anyone who identifies as white to have the moral authority to lead. And Black people, Baldwin goes on to say, "have paid for the crisis of leadership in the white community for a very long time and have resoundingly, even when we face the worst about ourselves, survived and triumphed over it. If we had not survived, and triumphed, there would not be a Black American alive."[8]

White allies are not, have never been, and were never meant to be the "savior" of Black people. The role of a white ally in the fight for prosecutorial reform must always be one of a supporting actor.

EARLY WHITE ALLIES

Early white abolitionist allies publicly voiced their opposition to slavery, wrote newspaper and magazine editorials, assisted with monetary investments, and supported the Underground Railroad, an abolitionist network composed of Black and white people that was organized to help enslaved Black people escape to freedom in northern states and Canada. Few white allies were as outspoken as the early abolitionist William Lloyd Garrison, who in 1831 started *The Liberator*, the first abolitionist newspaper, and who argued for emancipation and legal equality for enslaved Black people.[9] While some white abolitionists, like Garrison, sought freedom and full equality for Black Americans, they proved to be outliers in the fight for full equality. The work of white abolitionist allies abruptly ended with the issuing of the Emancipation Proclamation (1863) and passage of the thirteenth amendment to the US Constitution (1865). Even though white allies saw their goals as being fully achieved with the end of slavery, their cause was only half achieved because political and social equality for Black people lagged behind that of whites. Black abolitionist Robert Hamilton saw a tremendous loss and argued that if Black people did not receive full equality with their freedom, it would take another hundred years before they achieved it.[10] (He underestimated.)

White allies missed an opportunity to continue the fight for justice and equality for Black Americans after their emancipation. And forty-four years passed after the thirteenth amendment was enacted before white allies joined forces to fight again for the equality of African Americans. In 1909, sixty people founded the National Association for the Advancement of Colored People (NAACP) to address systemic criminal injustices. Only seven of the original members were Black, including the scholar W. E. B. Du Bois, journalist Ida B. Wells-Barnett, and activist educator Mary Church Terrell. Du Bois became the only Black American among the group's first executives.[11]

Eleven years later, in 1920, James Weldon Johnson became the first Black American to serve as executive secretary, and that appointment marked the beginning of Black leadership of the NAACP.[12]

In 1942, another ally organization, the Congress of Racial Equality (CORE), began with a group of white middle-class students from Chicago who, along with Black students, initiated efforts to integrate Chicago businesses, public facilities, and restaurants.[13] By the 1950s, when the organization became involved with Dr. Martin Luther King Jr. in the Montgomery, Alabama, bus boycotts and later in the 1960s Freedom Rides in the South, it had become a predominately Black organization.

In the 1950s and 1960s, a burgeoning civil rights movement was structured around Black leadership and made impassioned calls for white ally participation. Dated April 16, 1963, King's famous "Letter from Birmingham Jail" was published eight years after the start of the civil rights movement, and in it, Dr. King expressed his concerns about a failed effort to connect and make a clearer case for more white allies to join the civil rights movement. Among his thoughts about police brutality, racial injustice, and the unfair treatment of Black Americans at the hands of prosecutors in the courts, he also expressed his expectation that more white allies, particularly white clergy members, would become the strongest supporters of the movement. He articulated his disappointment as a Black clergy member that white clergy did not join in the civil rights movement and, with few notable exceptions, remained silent and uninvolved.[14]

King also wrote that while he was disappointed with the small number of white allies, what was small in quantity was big in quality. Those who supported the civil rights movement participated in Freedom Rides, marched in protest marches, sat at segregated lunch counters that prohibited Black and white people to eat together, suffered police abuse and brutality, and sat in jail after arrests.

Even so, he argued that few members of a race that has oppressed another race could fully understand or appreciate the feelings of the oppressed. He was mindful that fewer still would take persistent and strong action. In his letter, King named allies who used their voices—such as author James Dabbs, activist Harry Golden, journalist Ralph McGill, and writer Lillian

Smith—to write about the Black struggle. McGill, a Pulitzer Prize–winning journalist, consistently for decades used his editorial voice to write about racial disparities.[15]

Dr. King recognized the need for the support of white allies with "strong, persistent, and determined action."[16] Before the March on Washington in August 1963, statistics reveal that most white people felt disconnected from the civil rights movement and believed it was a Southern problem—not an American problem. Very few white people actively supported the movement.[17] The six Black leaders of the March on Washington—including King, John Lewis, and representatives from CORE and the National Urban League—planned a march that would include white allies to support the idea that injustice against Black people was an American problem caused by white people.

They invited four white allies to join them as coleaders—a rabbi, a Catholic leader, a Protestant minister, and a labor leader. The strategy worked perfectly. But the inclusion of the labor leader led to the biggest payoff. Tens of thousands of white people, mostly union members, joined as allies in support of workers' rights and poor people's rights, sending shock waves through the nation as white people interspersed in a massive sea of Black American marchers.[18]

Eight years passed from the start of the civil rights movement with the Montgomery bus boycott in 1955 to the August 1963 March on Washington before white allyship took root. In April 1968, less than five years after the civil rights movement built stronger white allyship after the March on Washington, King was assassinated, and the civil rights movement and white ally support stalled again. In their place, law and order prosecutors—who fueled mass incarceration, mass probation, and unprosecuted police killings of unarmed Black people—eventually took root.

ECHOES OF PAST WHITE ALLIES

Like a perfectly coded DNA sequence in our nation, it was eight years between the Montgomery bus boycott and the March on Washington, and it was eight years between Trayvon Martin's death, which launched the

Black Lives Matter movement, and the rallying of masses of white allies in response to the George Floyd murder. Even more striking, there were forty-four years of dormancy between the passage of the thirteenth amendment and the founding of the NAACP, and there were forty-four years of dormancy between the assassination of Martin Luther King Jr. and the murder of Trayvon Martin, which ignited the Black Lives Matter movement. If we don't get it right this time, will the support of white allies become dormant for another eight years—or worse, another forty-four years?

Black Lives Matter began as a Twitter hashtag and then became a movement. In 2012, a self-appointed neighborhood watcher, George Zimmerman, a white man of Hispanic descent, shot and killed Trayvon Martin, an unarmed seventeen-year-old Black American. The jury acquitted Zimmerman, and white allies remained silent. King's 1963 Birmingham letter on white allies and Black injustices could have been written at that moment. The nation erupted and violence rippled across its cities as Black people's long-unheard voices rose to demand justice and accountability.

Black people will need effective ally support to dismantle a harsh prosecutorial system established over four hundred years ago. It will take hard work on the part of white allies. In the words of Dr. King, it will take "strong, persistent and determined action."

AMPLIFICATION OF EFFECTIVE WHITE ALLIES

Effective white allies will use their voices to amplify racial disparities in prosecution within the criminal justice system. But in order to do so, they must first examine the personal lived experiences passed down through America's history. Assessing their own implicit racial bias by active and constant self-interrogation is a good place to begin. Such assessments will reveal how white Americans have viewed Black lives through a distorted white lens. As racial justice advocate Dr. Judy Lubin, a sociologist policy analyst and founder and president of the Center for Urban and Racial Equality, states, "If you're a white person in this space, you need to develop your racial equity lens." According to Dr. Lubin, white people need to understand how to talk about race and build a comfort level in doing so. This work includes joining with white colleagues and friends, groups of white allies, or white accountability groups to discuss these issues among themselves as they work with their colleagues of color. She encourages white allies to examine how they have internalized ideas around white superiority and the ways racism shows up in themselves.[19]

White people must make a choice to become antiracist, and that choice must be made daily and not just when a Black person is killed at the hands of police. Whiteness comes with advantages, and confronting the consequences of whiteness requires a continual presence of mind. Just as Black people are aware and reminded daily of what it means to be a Black person in the United States, white people can become effective allies only if they recognize what author George Lipsitz calls the possessive investment in whiteness. They must recognize that they are already part of the problem.[20] The possessive investment in whiteness results from the original lie about Black people that dates back to 1619—that Black people are inferior to white people. It shows up when white people, faced with the reality that unarmed Black people are disproportionately killed by police and massively incarcerated and prosecuted in the United States, argue that something besides racism must be the cause. This belief system defies the Human Genome Project, whose work confirms that all humans are 99.9 percent the same. Racial superiority is based on a biological lie.[21] As Lipsitz states, the United States and by extension its prosecutorial system cannot get well if white people remain deeply attached to the things that are making us all sick.[22]

Well-meaning white Americans seem to equal the blindfolded symbol of justice with their own level of color blindness. "I don't see color," is their frequent response in racial discourse. However, insisting on the idea of a colorblind society, while well-intentioned, leaves people without the language to discuss race at any level, especially to examine their own biases. Color blindness relies on the concept that race-based differences don't matter and ignores the realities of systemic racism in our carceral prosecutorial system.

African Americans learn how to navigate a white world through immersion. White allies must now similarly begin to immerse themselves in Black lives and Black culture by reading books, listening to lectures, participating in workshops on antiracism and racial bias, volunteering at racial justice organizations, visiting African American art institutions, investing in African American literature, and having open and honest dialogues with Black people, including those most impacted by the prosecutorial system. Dismantling a broken prosecutorial system will require knowledge, sacrifice, and action.

Often, as a prosecutor, my white colleagues asked me to explain or interpret what a Black witness said, as if I were a translator for people who spoke another language. It is equally overburdening to expect Black people to teach white America about what it means to be Black in America as it is to require Black Americans to learn how to live in a white world. This expectation is simply the other side of a privilege coin. White America's privilege says, "If you don't teach me, how will I learn?" Black Americans had no access to such privilege. They learned how to effectively navigate white life at the expense of their lives—literally. Similarly, it is white America's responsibility to learn about the country's history and a movement that requires the affirmation of the value of the lives of an entire group of people: "Black lives matter" needed to be said in response to the prosecutorial practices that suggest that they do not.

PITFALLS OF DNA AND WHITE ALLIES

The dogged persistence of America's DNA has transferred the inherent values, myths, and lies that ripple throughout our society in history books, advertisements, entertainment, and the prosecutor's office. White allies need to study and debunk the mythological lies that have been circulated about Black people for centuries.

These long-standing lies say that Black people commit more crime, Black people who are in jail or prison belong there, white police officers shoot and kill unarmed Black people because they must have committed a criminal act or did something wrong to cause the shooting, only a few police officers are bad, Black people are more prone to violence and more dangerous than white people, most Black people are in jail due to drugs, and perhaps most insidious of all, slavery is in the past and bears no relationship to today. African Americans need white allies to talk to other white people about systemic racism in America and bring more allies into the process in the fight for prosecutorial reform.

In order to support African Americans, white allies must remain open to receiving and accepting concrete criticism, leadership, and advice from African Americans. It is the responsibility of white America to critique its role in the establishment of carceral systems and ideals that have relegated people of color to the outskirts of society and many to prisons and jails at the hands of prosecutors.

Ideally, relationships with incarcerated or formerly incarcerated Black individuals will allow white allies to gain firsthand knowledge and understanding of the prosecutorial process and its effect on Black people. These relationships can be forged through prison support groups and organizations. For white allies, it will take daily constant awareness—an effort Black people have been forced to put in for centuries.

Brazilian education philosopher Paulo Freire argued in his famous book *Pedagogy of the Oppressed* that only the oppressed can liberate themselves and their oppressors.[23] The process begins when individual people become aware of their own social context, political context, economic context, gender, social class, and race and the ways these play important roles in the shaping of their reality. That awareness can then lead the oppressed and the oppressors to understand their own power. Each one has power. The power of the oppressed is to be aware of their agency to choose and create their own reality. The power of the oppressor is to be fully aware of their privilege and to position that privilege in support of the work of the oppressed. It's like a relay race in which each of four runners has a role to play. The lead runner sets the stage, and the last runner (the anchor and fastest one) pulls off the win. The middle runners are the support team. No runner drops the baton. White Americans who want to be allies in this race for prosecutorial reform can stand firmly in the middle, working cooperatively with African Americans in the struggle to undo centuries of prosecutorial injustice. Otherwise, the firmly entrenched system of racism and privilege will corrupt the process.

When white allies take control and attempt to lead, it reinforces the paternalistic nature of white superiority. It never works. Quite the opposite, it is counterproductive. As Paulo Freire notes, only the power of the oppressed is sufficiently strong to free both the oppressed and the oppressor. Effective allyship requires that white allies work in solidarity as a team to eradicate prosecutorial injustices. When I worked as a Baltimore prosecutor, the felony unit was organized in four-person teams. Each team had a designated team captain. On occasion, a team captain and another assistant state's attorney, a team member, would prosecute a high-profile murder case together. The team captain was designated at trial as first chair. The other prosecutor served as second chair. The role of second chair was not inferior or subservient to the first chair. Both served as co-counsel on the same trial team with the same goal. However, the first chair had more trial experience and more knowledge of criminal law. Whenever I served as second chair, I never felt less responsible than the first chair for the outcome of the case. Like a first chair in a criminal trial, African Americans bear the burden of having lived firsthand experiences of racial disparities in the criminal justice system and therefore must be the ones to lead. As Dr. King wrote from that Birmingham jail, "Freedom is never voluntarily given by the oppressor, it must be demanded by the oppressed."[24] African Americans must lead the reform of a broken prosecutorial system with white allies who contribute and serve in important roles.

Effective allies must hold intimate and intricate conversations with those they support. And like all good conversations, there will sometimes be missteps. Those who seek to be allies often fear that they will do something wrong in the learning process, that they will accidentally offend Black people and cause further harm. It is a legitimate concern. No one wants to make matters worse.

But it is important to remember that perfection isn't necessary or even required. Persistence—not perfection—is key. As with any new learning process, it will take time. The key is to remain committed for the long haul, stay open to learning and receiving criticism as opportunities to grow. In any education process, there will be mishaps, mistakes, and missteps.

Consider this experience as analogous to your first days on a new job with little experience. A new, inexperienced member of a team often learns the job by sinking or swimming. My own first days as a prosecutor had many sink days. Mistakes, mishaps, and missteps will be made by white allies. The important thing is what you do next—to learn from those mistakes and grow in knowledge. The key is to apologize (if appropriate), accept responsibility for the mistake, and move forward in the education process. The reward is mutual respect.

RECOGNITION OF ONE'S WHITE PRIVILEGE

An important point of learning is the recognition of white privilege and the ways it works in everyday practices. The progress in this area is encouraging. In June 2020, 57 percent of white Americans recognized that white privilege exists, up fourteen points since 2016 and up twelve points since 2019.[25]

The word *privilege* does not mean that a white person has had an easy life. It means that in the United States, the color of some people's skin affords them opportunities and advantages often denied to Black people. Nowhere is privilege more apparent than in the criminal justice system at the prosecutor's door. Rory Fleming, an attorney and a writer, said he began to recognize his own privilege as he saw how the criminal justice system treats people of color and his white relatives in similar situations: "it made me acutely aware of the privilege I was born with."[26] When white people see the daily rewards afforded them and systemic advantages due to their whiteness and the ways power works, they are better able to become effective allies in prosecutorial reforms.

Black intellectual W. E. B. Du Bois introduced the concept of white privilege in the 1930s when he explained that even if white people are poor, they still benefit from the color of their skin. Peggy McIntosh, in her 1989 essay "White Privilege: Unpacking the Invisible Knapsack," brought the term to prominence when she compared white privilege to an invisible package of unearned assets that a white person cashes in every day but that is denied to African Americans.[27] White privilege is a powerful tool allies can use to advocate for radical reform to the systemic injustices in our nation's DNA—and it does not look like the Portland Wall of Moms.

Here's what it can look like. In April 2018, two young Black men, Donte Robinson and Rashon Nelson, were waiting inside a Philadelphia Starbucks café in Rittenhouse Square, an affluent, majority white neighborhood, to meet with their white business associate, Andrew Yaffe. They asked to use the restroom but were told it was for paying customers. A white cashier called the police after Nelson and Robinson refused to leave. Police arrived and asked the two men to leave, ultimately handcuffing, arresting, and perp walking them out of the Starbucks and placing them in a police vehicle. A white customer, Melissa DePino, who saw that the men had done nothing wrong, filmed the police encounter and tweeted the video. DePino further addressed the incident in an essay posted on CNN's website.[28] She noted that although incidents like the one in the Philadelphia Starbucks happen every day to Black people, most white people either don't see them or believe them.[29]

Unlike Bev Barnum and her Wall of Moms, DePino diverted any attention from herself and directed it to the two young Black men. Her video was retweeted over ten million times.[30] Many white people were surprised to learn that while they may sit in a Starbucks for hours without a purchase and without an arrest and potential prosecution, the same rules do not always apply for young Black males. Because of DePino's actions, Starbucks went into damage control by closing all of its US stores for one afternoon to hold diversity training for all 175,000 employees.[31] The charges against Robinson and Nelson were dropped, and their criminal cases were expunged, unlike many Black men who are wrongfully arrested, charged, processed, and convicted at the hands of prosecutors.[32] Starbucks entered into a settlement of an undisclosed sum with an agreement to pay college tuition for Robinson and Nelson.

The difference between what a white savior would have done and what Melissa DePino did is subtle but comes with radically different outcomes. DePino used the white privilege of her voice to amplify what unjustly occurred in the racially motivated encounter at Starbucks, and she directed the attention of the world to the two young men who had been negatively affected. The story was not about her. She was merely a conduit for the story to reach the world. Sometimes being an effective ally is as simple as speaking up when injustices occur.

In America, the defects of racism and criminal injustices through prosecutorial malfeasance against African Americans cannot be ignored. Those defects run freely and deeply throughout its people and may prove harmful to the next generation. The American disease of racism tightens a prosecutor's grip on the freedom, minds, and bodies of Black people. Yet although it has proven fatal for generations, it is treatable. And as is often the case with a complex illness, the treatment plan will require a joint venture led by the most experienced members of the team.

WHITE ALLIES AND VOTING POWER

One powerful tool of white allies is the power of the vote—and not just in general elections but in focused, community-specific elected offices, including elections for prosecutors. The work of allies requires persistence as they campaign for reform prosecutors, vote them into office, and vote to maintain them in office once elected. The often-used phrase "Every vote matters" is most important in prosecutor elections where slim margins or slim voter turnout means the difference between success or failure, particularly in white majority populations.

Former public defender Chesa Boudin was elected San Francisco district attorney in 2019 and took office in January 2020. He campaigned on his support for reforms for the prosecutor's office and won with 35 percent of the first-place votes in an election with only 42 percent turnout. After taking office, Boudin delivered on his reform promises to review and overturn wrongful convictions, end the prosecution of children in adult courts, and eliminate cash bail. Public safety was reduced to the lowest rate in almost four decades.[33] Then calls for his recall began to be made.

At the same time that Boudin was elected, a massive sea change was occurring in San Francisco—gentrification. Wealthy tech workers could afford expensive apartments and houses, which inflated prices. Many people lost their homes as evictions multiplied. Because of the displacement of many minorities, who sometimes ended up camping on public streets, Boudin declined to prosecute for low-level crimes. The new gentrifiers became a vocal minority with money and blamed Boudin for the homelessness and resultant poverty that affected their quality of life.[34] Without help from the legislature, however, a prosecutor has no authority to invest in community resources to alleviate poverty and homelessness.

A recall election allows voters to decide whether to oust an elected official before the elected term expires. Under California law, to commence a recall election, 12 percent of the voters from the last election must sign a petition and publicize an intent to recall, along with other criteria.[35] In Boudin's case, at least 51,325 signatures were needed to start the process.[36] The necessary signatures exceeded the required number, so in January 2022, two years after Boudin took office, the San Francisco Department of Elections set a recall election date of July 2022.

In July 2022, 60 percent of voters voted for Boudin's recall, with a 25.8 percent voter turnout.[37] An army of recall supporters, mostly from wealthy real estate and tech groups, raised an astounding $7.2 million to remove Boudin from office.[38] Reform prosecutors always walk a fine line between reforms and public safety concerns. That balancing act, coupled with the failure of reform supporters to vote in significant numbers, sealed the coffin for Boudin.

Chesa Boudin's recall is a cautionary tale for white allies, shining a light on the need for their continued support. San Francisco is the seventeenth largest city in the United States and has just under 6 percent Black population, according to census data.[39] In contrast, similar complaints about Philadelphia's reformist district attorney, Larry Krasner, had to reckon with the city's 43 percent African American population.[40] With that broad support, Krasner easily won reelection with almost 70 percent of the vote.[41] But in San Francisco and other cities with a low Black population, when white people become disenchanted and move beyond reform prosecution, Black Americans lose. The stark realities of racial disparities in prosecution still oppress Black Americans. This is where white allies needed to step up their game in support of Black people by communicating with their white counterparts to support prosecutors like Chesa Boudin.

A 2017 study on racial disparities in the prosecution system in San Francisco points to substantial racial disparities—despite the city's small Black population.[42] Charges added after an arrest of a Black person are more likely to be added as felonies, as opposed to misdemeanors when compared to similar white cases. And when Black defendants are convicted either through a guilty plea or trial by judge or a jury, sentences for Black defendants are 40 percent longer than sentences for their white counterparts. A Black defendant booked into a San Francisco jail will receive on average a sentence of roughly 6.1 months, which is 3.4 months longer than a comparable white defendant will receive. White defendants' cases are resolved in a shorter period of time than Black defendants. The additional eleven days spent in a San Francisco jail by Black defendants over white defendants may seem small or trivial, but they are statistically substantial and have a real-life impact, including loss of jobs or child custody.

Chesa Boudin's recall is a cautionary tale of what happens when white allies drop the baton handed to them by Black Americans—and fail to engage other white people in the cause of prosecutorial reforms. Before Boudin completed his first term, many white voters became disillusioned, viewing his reforms through their own lens and not that of Black San Franciscans.

America's prosecutorial reform team must be led by Black citizens who are assisted by white allies. With this joint task force, we can treat the disease of systemic racism and racial bias in the prosecutorial system. The support of allies must continue to grow, as they educate and bring others in the fold to work toward change and equality. It is a lifelong journey to become an effective ally and an antiracist. It will be a challenge. But it is the only way to free us all.

9 POWER OF ALLIANCES

Our struggle is not the struggle of a day, a week, a month, or a year, it is the struggle of a lifetime. Never, ever be afraid to make some noise and get in good trouble, necessary trouble.
—John Lewis, congressman, June 2018

In October 2020, State Senator Joseph D. Morrissey introduced a bill in the Senate of Virginia that would allow a defendant to choose between a judge or a jury for sentencing. Since 1796, Virginia law had required juries, not judges, to sentence defendants after a jury trial. The only other state where this happens is Kentucky.[1] In all other states, a jury decides an individual's fate after a jury trial only in a death penalty case. Some might wonder what is wrong with having a jury sentence an individual in a case where the jury rendered a verdict. It almost seems to make sense. But the 2018 annual report of the Virginia Criminal Sentencing Commission revealed that, on average, Virginia juries sentenced people to terms that lasted four years longer than sentences imposed by judges in nonjury trials,[2] and the rate was even higher for African American defendants, even though Black defendants' sentences were already 17 percent longer than white defendants when sentenced by a judge using a risk-assessment tool.[3] Virginia's law and the harshness of jury sentences led most defendants to plead guilty or to take a trial by judge to avoid being sentenced by a jury. While the vast majority of defendants in all states will choose a plea bargain over a jury trial due to the prosecutor's trial penalty, Virginia's law further ensured the prosecutor's preferred outcome of plea bargains over a jury trial.

In a felony sentencing in other states, after a jury reaches a verdict, a judge sets a sentencing date, usually four to six weeks after the verdict. The judge orders a presentencing investigation report, which is compiled by probation services. The probation officer conducts an investigation, looking at criminal background, family history (including the convicted person's immediate family), financial history, job history, education, history of substance abuse, a victim statement, and the circumstances surrounding the crime for which the person was convicted. The individual convicted is able to meet with the probation officer to increase chances for leniency by providing positive information such as character letters from friends, family, employers, and neighbors and any other pertinent information, such as enrollment in counseling or treatment programs. Both the defense attorney and prosecutor offer information for the presentence report, which in a felony case establishes a range of recommended sentencing from minimum to highest based on the criteria in the report. Members of a Virginia jury lack the presentencing information provided to the judge. They are given the statutory penalties but not the recommended guidelines or report.

The 2018 annual report of the Virginia Criminal Sentencing Commission found that juries exceeded the recommended sentencing guidelines in half the cases.[4] More important, judges may sentence below the recommended guidelines if they deem it appropriate to do so. For example, a judge might issue a noncarceral sentence such as probation or community service. A jury does not have that option. Juries also cannot recommend substance abuse treatment, mental health treatment, or other services as part of probation.

Virginia is a conservative jurisdiction. Virginia's incarceration rate of 749 per 100,000 people is among the highest in the world.[5] Opponents of the bill argued that it would increase jury trials and thereby cost taxpayers more money. Jury sentencing made it easier for prosecutors to get plea deals and therefore convictions, so most prosecutors vehemently opposed the bill. Despite their opposition, a broad coalition came together—including eleven Virginia progressive district attorneys, the Public Defender's Office of Arlington County, the Virginia NAACP, progressive advocacy groups, attorneys, lawmakers, and citizen groups—and advocated for change.[6] In July 2021, the bill became law[7] and allowed Virginia defendants to choose whether a judge or jury will provide sentencing after a jury trial.

ALL HANDS ON DECK

Meaningful reform is possible. But transformational changes that go beyond the purview of individual prosecutors require a coalition. It's time for all hands to be on deck.

The members of the Virginia Progressive Prosecutors for Justice, calculated by cities and county jurisdictions, represent 40 percent of the state's population. They aligned with lawmakers and other coalitions, such as Justice Forward Virginia, a nonpartisan advocacy group, to pass reform laws like expungement reforms that allow formerly incarcerated individuals to be reintegrated back into society. They ended three-strikes laws under certain circumstances.[8] They also abolished the death penalty. In 2021, Virginia became the first formerly Confederate state to abolish the death penalty. Until that point, Virginia had executed more people than any other state in US history. Of the 376 people that the state executed for murder in the twentieth century, 296 were Black people.[9] When the death penalty was outlawed, the remaining 2 people on Virginia's death row had their sentences converted to life without parole. We must eliminate the death penalty in all remaining states through similar alliances. In 2020, 42 percent of death row inmates nationwide were Black people.[10] The death penalty remains legal in twenty-four states and suspended in three other states.[11]

During the 2022 legislative session, Justice Forward Virginia worked to eliminate all mandatory minimums in Virginia except aggravated murder of a law enforcement officer and to consider the feasibility of resentencing individuals already sentenced under mandatory minimums.[12] Although the bill failed in 2022, the work continues.

The Maryland Alliance for Justice Reform, another nonpartisan group, works to support meaningful criminal justice legislation and address inequities, such as repealing Maryland's mandatory law that automatically places youth charged with certain crimes in adult court, as well as reforming and broadening expungement of cases.[13] They also advocated for the passage of a bill that would eliminate Maryland's felony murder rule.[14] The felony murder rule allows a person to be found guilty of first-degree murder if a victim dies during the committing of a felony, regardless of whether the person killed the victim. A person can be sentenced to life in prison in Maryland under felony murder even if the party did not participate or was not present during the killing but served legally as an accomplice. The classic description is the getaway driver in a robbery that ends with someone dying or being killed. It is still considered felony murder where a victim dies of a heart attack during a felony.

In 1973, Marie Scott, a nineteen-year-old Black teenager, was convicted of felony murder for acting as a lookout in a gas station robbery. Marie was under the influence of pills supplied by her codefendant, which impaired her judgment, and while she was standing outside, her codefendant killed a station attendant. Marie did not know or expect that her codefendant would kill anyone. Marie was sentenced to life without parole in a Philadelphia County court. Marie's codefendant received the same sentence. In 2022, Marie Scott, age sixty-seven, was a writer, editor of a newsletter for children, legal aid assistant, and advocate for children with incarcerated parents—but she was still incarcerated.[15] Her codefendant, a juvenile at the time of the murder, was released on parole after the 2016 Supreme Court decision in *Miller v. Alabama* allowed retroactive reconsideration of juveniles' sentences of life without parole. In Pennsylvania, 70 percent of the people serving time for a felony murder conviction are African American.[16]

Beauford White, a Black man, also stood as lookout outside while two other men went into a house looking for drugs and killed six people. White was convicted of felony murder and sentenced to the death penalty. He was executed in 1987, and the two shooters were later executed, as well.[17]

In the United States, the doctrine of felony murder began in Maryland in 1776,[18] but it has since been abolished in most other countries, including England and Wales (1957) and Ireland (1964), and countries whose origins of the felony murder rule also date back to the 1700s.[19] The Sentencing Project and Fair and Just Prosecution have called for an end to the felony murder rule, which remains legal in forty-eight states and the District of Columbia.

The only excluded states are Hawaii and Kentucky.[20] In fifteen states, a felony murder conviction results in a sentence of life without parole.[21]

RESHAPING REFORM PROSECUTORS WITH ALLIANCES

The Vera Institute of Justice, a national research and policy organization, has formed Reshaping Prosecution initiative, which works with local prosecutor offices around the country for at least one year and often up to eighteen months. Reshaping Prosecution initiative works with local prosecutor offices to adopt reforms through a racial equity lens focused on systemic disparities based on data.[22] The reforms include, declining or diverting cases, building evidence for alternative approaches to address systemic racial disparities with a focus on a safer community.[23] Reshaping Prosecution helps to change racially disparate policies and practices by exploring the worst racial disparities, developing alternatives, and weighing the benefits of policies against their drawbacks [24] Members of Vera's Reshaping Prosecution staff worked with Ramsey County, Minnesota, Attorney John Choi after the Philando Castile police shooting case.[25]

On July 6, 2016, Castile was shot and killed in St. Anthony, a Minneapolis suburb, by a police officer who stopped him for a broken taillight.[26] Castile's girlfriend and her four-year-old daughter were passengers in the car. As Jeronimo Yanez approached the vehicle, Philando told the officer that he possessed a firearm and a legal permit to carry it. Yanez told Castile, "OK, don't reach for it then. Don't pull it out." Castile replied, "I'm not pulling it out." The officer repeated his command, "Don't pull it out," and within seconds, pulled his gun out of his holster and fired seven shots in close range at Castile as his girlfriend and her young daughter watched in horror. Castile's last words were, "I wasn't reaching for it."[27] He later died at the hospital. Castile was a thirty-two-year-old Black cafeteria manager who was beloved by the community at a Montessori school in St. Paul, Minnesota, and exhibited no actions to cause the officer to shoot and kill him.[28]

Within five months of his killing, Ramsey County Attorney John Choi filed criminal charges against Jeronimo Yanez for second-degree manslaughter and dangerous discharge of a firearm.[29] Choi filed charges without waiting for a grand jury to indict because he believed that Yanez killed without justification. Choi also became the first county attorney in Minnesota history to file charges against an on-duty police officer for killing someone.[30] Jeronimo Yanez's jury trial took place in 2017, and the jury found him not guilty—like so many other police officers who were tried for killing unarmed Black people.

A few years after the verdict, in 2019, Choi's office partnered with the Reshaping Prosecution initiative for eighteen months to work to end pretextual police traffic stops such as the one that cost Philando Castile his life. Pretextual stops are minor traffic infractions that don't affect public safety—such as a broken taillight (Walter Scott shot and killed in 2015), an air freshener hanging from the rear-view mirror (Daunte Wright shot and killed in 2021), a missing front license plate (Samuel Dubose shot and killed in 2015), mismatched license plates (Patrick Lyoya shot in the back of the head and killed in 2021), failure to use a turn signal (Sandra Bland died in a jail cell three days after her arrest), a missing car inspection or registration sticker, illegally dark tinted windows, and expired license plates. All of these people who were stopped for minor traffic violations and killed by police officers—Philando Castile, Walter Scott, Daunte Wright, Samuel Dubose, Patrick Lyoya, and Sandra Bland—were Black victims.

Traffic stops that affect public safety—such as driving recklessly, using excessive speed, or a suspicion of driving while intoxicated—are non-pretextual. A valid safety reason exists for the stop. In pretextual stops, police officers often stop a vehicle for a minor traffic violation as a pretext for searching for contraband or illegal substances. Over the course of thirteen years, police stopped Philando Castile over forty-nine times for minor traffic stops such as failure to wear a seatbelt, no proof of insurance, missing taillight— and the last stop ended his life.

In 2020, the population of St. Paul, Minnesota (the largest city in Ramsey County) was 16 percent Black residents, and 43 percent of motorists stopped were Black drivers. A report published in 2020 found that on a nationwide level, Black drivers were 20 percent more likely to be stopped than white drivers and twice as likely to be searched.[31] And those stops could be deadly for Black motorists. Despite the disproportionate police searches of Black drivers, the study found that out of almost 100 million motorist stops nationwide, Black people were less likely than white people to possess guns, drugs, or illegal contraband.[32] The Ramsey County Attorney's Office and the Reshaping Prosecution initiative found that less than 2 percent of all pretextual stops resulted in the discovery of illegal contraband. In 2021, Ramsey County Attorney Choi announced that his office would no longer prosecute felony cases that arose out of minor traffic stops.[33] Based on the research and evidence that was compiled by his office and Reshaping Prosecution, Choi concluded that it was both safer and more just for the community if these stops did not occur.

This is but one example of how Reshaping Prosecution has helped prosecutors to change their thinking on racial disparities and community safety.[34] As of November 2022, according to Akhi Johnson, director of the Reshaping Prosecution initiative at the Vera Institute of Justice, at least sixteen local prosecutor offices from around the country have enrolled in the program since its launch in 2017.[35]

In 2019, the Vera Institute for Justice expanded its prosecutorial initiatives and alliances by joining forces with John Jay College's Institute for Innovation in Prosecution.[36] This partnership brought together experts from around the country (including scholars, practitioners, advocates, and other system-impacted people) to develop concrete ideas that prosecutors can use to tackle racial disparities. Their efforts resulted in the Motion for Justice initiative, which works to transform the prosecutor's role by implementing racial equity strategies in partnership with community organizations. We won't end mass incarceration without looking through a racial equity lens, and this must be done in collaboration with the community. As the saying goes, "Those closest to the problem are closest to the solution." The former director of the Reshaping Prosecution initiative, Jamila Hodge, stated, "If we were trying to address these hard problems, we had to hear from community members. . . . Then we needed prosecutors to hear from them, and that any policy changes be deeply informed by the real-life experiences of those who are impacted by these decisions and policies."[37]

CHANGE THROUGH COMMUNITY PARTNERSHIPS

Growing up in Baltimore, I saw the work of community organizations in partnership with local elected officials through the lens of my mother. My mother and other members of community organizations regularly met with elected officials to address the socioeconomic issues that my community faced. I often heard her tell stories about the necessity for elected officials to partner with the community to hear its perspectives on ways to improve life.

The Vera Institute for Justice's Motion for Justice initiative provides financial resources to community-based organizations to establish such programs and provides training, educational materials, support, and data analysis. It focuses on safety by centering racial equity. It also provides prosecutor offices with policy expertise to guide them to a better understanding of racial injustices and fairer and more equitable processes. Motion for Justice has partnered with community programs and district attorney offices in Georgia, Hawaii, Indiana, Massachusetts, Michigan, Minnesota, Missouri, New York, North Carolina, Pennsylvania, and Virginia to achieve goals unique to each community and to reduce racial disparities by at least 20 percent.[38] Imagine the changes we could make in reforming prosecution if every city, county, and state prosecutor had alliances with this type of program.

A community-based program in Savannah, Georgia, called Show Us Your Guns was born out of collaboration with the Motion for Justice initiative, and through that program, mostly young Black men charged with gun possession were diverted from the criminal justice system and connected with another community organization that provided services instead of traditional prosecution.[39] The district attorney for Chatham County, Georgia, Shelena Cook, a Black woman, partnered with Carl Gilliard, a Georgia state legislator and founder of Savannah Feed the Hungry, to offer each member of the program from age sixteen to twenty-five an opportunity outside of the courthouse and jailhouse that included job training and support, educational support, housing support, health resources, and conflict resolution training. These diversions were done without any guilty pleas, unlike so many other programs that offer diversion after a person's criminal record is already blemished.

BLACK WOMEN PROSECUTOR INITIATIVE

In recognition of the unique challenges that Black women elected prosecutors face in their efforts to reform our justice system, the Vera Institute for Justice's Reshaping Prosecution initiative created the Black Women Lead project to support Black women chief district attorneys and state's attorneys and to work with a coalition of organizations to support Black women prosecutors in their fight to transform a carceral prosecution system. The overwhelming number of chief prosecutors (progressive, traditional, or conservative) are white men. As of 2019, 95 percent of all elected prosecutors were white prosecutors. Women of color represented 1 percent of elected prosecutors in 2015 and increased to 2 percent in 2019, according to a report from the Reflective Democracy Campaign. Overall, Black women lawyers represent 2.8 percent of all lawyers in the United States.[40] Early in my career, I joined the Alliance of Black Women Attorneys of Maryland to enhance my professional development and gain support as a Black woman prosecutor and trial attorney. As a line prosecutor, I faced implicit racial bias from coworkers and white police officers. Black women lawyers and prosecutors face unique challenges, including racist attacks, implicit racial bias, and vicious attacks for doing the same job that their white colleagues do and using the same prosecutorial discretion that their white colleagues use. White progressive prosecutors face attacks, but those attacks are not based on race or gender.

PARTNERSHIP WITH FAIR AND JUST PROSECUTION

Reformist prosecutors often face resistance from various groups and negative attacks from the media for their efforts to transform the prosecutorial process. Reform prosecutors need organizations to defend them from coordinated attacks from antireform organizations, lawmakers, and individuals. In addition, district attorneys and state's attorneys committed to reform need organizations to help amplify their voices in the media. Fair and Just Prosecution, founded by former federal prosecutor Miriam Aroni Krinsky, is one of many national organizations tasked with this role.

Fair and Just Prosecution maintains an informal membership of elected reform prosecutors and defends and supports progressive prosecutors in various ways, including publishing newspaper opinion pieces, writing position papers on reforms, and offering training sessions for member prosecutors. The group's "21 Principles for the 21st Century Prosecutor" makes recommendations for ways that reformist prosecutors can reduce incarceration and increase fairness to achieve racial equity.[41] The twenty-one recommendations include using restorative justice practices and diversion, providing treatment for mental illness and drug addiction, treating kids like kids, addressing racial equity, holding police accountable, and ending the death penalty.

Fair and Just Prosecution also works with elected local and state prosecutors to assist prosecutors to move beyond incarceration and build a system rooted in fairness and racial equity. It connects prosecutors to other local and national organizations, academic institutions, and expert resources. The organization also supports police accountability through, among other things, a national database of police misconduct to inform the public and, eventually, strengthen public safety and public trust that the prosecutorial system works for everyone.[42] In its efforts to create alliances, Fair and Just Prosecution connects reform prosecutors with the tools necessary to support prosecutorial reform.

ALLIANCES FOR VIOLENT CRIME INITIATIVES

In discussions about progressive coalitions, alliances, and reform organizations, one important point is often overlooked—how to address violent crimes. Most reform prosecutors and many organizations focus on nonviolent crimes, and they avoid addressing the issue of violent crime for fear of triggering backlash and accusations that they are increasing violent crime rates. They therefore limit reform programs to the three N's—nonviolent, nonserious, and nonsexual.

Roughly half of state prisoners are incarcerated due to violent crimes.[43] The combined jail and prison population holds almost 40 percent violent offenders.[44] Black people are imprisoned at five times the rate of white people in state prisons.[45] Many violent offenders are serving long sentences, life sentences, habitual offender sentences, and mandatory minimum sentences, some for crimes committed as adolescents decades earlier. When prosecutors exclude all violent crime from pretrial intervention, diversion, or restorative justice programs, they fail to recognize that violent offenders are not a monolithic group. Many adolescents and young people overwhelmingly come from communities that are suffering deeply. These youth are greatly impacted by community trauma and other personal trauma, and this trauma contributes to their poor decisions that lead to criminal activity. This does not mean that prosecutors should not hold them accountable, but it means that prosecutors should look at violent cases on an individual basis, take a deep look at the underlying trauma to find ways to treat it, *and* hold an individual accountable. Accountability does not always need to take a punitive form. Prosecutors cannot treat every case as "One jail size fits all."

Many Americans believe that violent crime is out of control and must be brought under control through the carceral system. But the public perception that violent crime is raging uncontrollably is not supported by data. According to the Federal Bureau of Investigation, from 1993 to 2019, violent crime rates in the United States fell 49 percent, with murder and nonnegligent manslaughter falling 47 percent, aggravated assault falling 43 percent, and robbery rates dropping 68 percent.[46] (In the same time period, property crimes also dropped, with rates of burglary decreasing 69 percent, motor vehicle theft dropping 64 percent, and larceny and theft dropping almost 50 percent.)[47] Despite recent upticks in homicide rates, murder rates across the United States have plummeted since the 1990s. Prosecutors and alliances must work toward a cultural shift in the mindset of many Americans away from the "Lock everyone (disproportionately Black men) up" mentality of the 1990s.

For substantive reforms to occur, prosecutors and alliances need to change the prosecutorial culture and its systemic structure. They will also need to change the rules that prosecutors play by that rely on convictions and instead offer new diversion and restorative justice programs that include violent crimes—pre- and postconviction.

Partnerships of violence-prevention strategies could help curb violent crime before it occurs. In 2015, the Office of the Attorney General for the

District of Columbia was concerned about the rising rates of homicide, assault with intent to kill, assault with a deadly weapon, and retaliatory conduct that occurred after a killing. It launched a program called Cure the Streets. It identified credible messengers, individuals who were known and respected in the community and often had spent time in jail. Those credible messengers then identified potential victims and potential wrongdoers, and the program then provided those identified with services that might reduce retaliation and violence. The program's one site has expanded to ten, and according to a former DC attorney general, Karl Racine, in communities with Cure the Streets sites, the incidence of serious assaults and homicides is lower than in other communities without Cure the Street sites, as the program acts as a violence interrupter. In the collaboration, Cure the Streets employs roughly a hundred people in the community.[48]

Equal Justice USA is another organization that builds on community-based solutions to violence outside of the criminal justice system. Equal Justice USA defines justice as "safety, healing and accountability that repairs"[49] through a racial justice lens. The group builds its coalition work by organizing and advocating for state resources to address violent crime. The anti–death penalty movement is also a large part of its work. Through its state partnerships, Equal Justice USA has helped to end the death penalty in nine states.[50]

Until reformist prosecutors and alliances start involving violent offenders in pretrial intervention, diversion, restorative justice, public safety reentry programs, and other violence-prevention strategies, they will not be up to the task of ending (or even lessening) mass incarceration. Bold change requires bold actions.

Despite conversations about the need for public safety, prosecutors, including progressive ones, overwhelmingly go after millions of low-level misdemeanors yearly. These crimes do not increase danger to the public. Felony cases do not make up the bulk of the work that prosecutors do day in and day out. In the fight for prosecutorial reform, prosecutors punch down at the lowest-hanging fruit, meaning nonviolent misdemeanors. I would like to see prosecutors with support of state and local alliances punch up and spend more time on crimes that really make us unsafe.

RETHINKING PUBLIC SAFETY

The most dangerous threat to public safety comes from mass shootings, white supremacy groups, and paramilitary groups that cause domestic terrorism. Using Congress's definition of a mass shooting as a shooting where three or more persons are murdered, white people committed 55 percent of mass shootings and Black people committed 18 percent as of February 2020.[51] Despite the misperception that Black people are more prone to violence, historically white people have committed the largest massacres in the nation, dating back to Tulsa Oklahoma in 1920 and even earlier. I would like to see prosecutors in partnership with local and state law enforcement alliances spend more time investigating people who are prone to commit mass crimes and hate crimes. Hate crimes have become an epidemic, with one hate crime being committed every hour.[52] In the last twenty years, hate groups have grown by 100 percent.[53] At a time when FBI Director Charles Wray has said that the greatest domestic terrorist threat is white supremacists, prosecutors must do more to fight hate crimes.[54] In the 1990s, when the federal government stated that the use of crack cocaine was an epidemic, the federal Violent Crime Control and Law Enforcement Act of 1994 (the 1994 Crime Bill) and similar state laws were passed with broad bipartisan support. After these laws were passed, mass incarceration increased to an all-time high, with many Black people disproportionately incarcerated with mandatory sentences for possession of small amounts of drugs. With the new epidemic of hate crimes, we need broad-based coalitions with lawmakers, prosecutors, and the community to work aggressively to address hate crimes.

Americans feel increasingly unsafe in churches, synagogues, movie theaters, schools, grocery stores, night clubs, and just about everywhere else. If prosecutors joined forces with law enforcement, interstate and intrastate prosecutors, and other groups to investigate white supremacy groups, domestic terrorists, and paramilitary groups and to monitor the internet for crimes in the same way police and prosecutors scrutinize poor Black neighborhoods in Baltimore and other cities, as a society we would be safer. A joint task force could be established among prosecutors and their alliances to investigate and aggressively prosecute individuals and hate groups for hate crimes.

In the summer of 2022, Maryland initiated the Emmett Till alert system, a hate alert system that warns residents when credible threats are made and then transmits notices to Black elected officials in Maryland, national racial justice organizations, clergy, and other community leaders.[55] This action followed bomb threats at three Maryland historically Black colleges and universities, vandalism at a Black church, and other hate incidents. Beyond warning residents of threats or acts of hate, prosecutors must join forces to review these threats and vigorously investigate and prosecute any crimes. Like the "change oil" light on a car's dashboard, an alert warning will do little to improve safety until the requisite actions are taken.

ALLIANCES ON ECONOMIC CRIMES

Another example of punching up involves economic crimes. Even though most prosecutor offices, like my former office in Baltimore, maintain an economic crimes unit, their main focus remains with low-level crimes. The NAACP has long fought for decades to address racial inequities that allow Black people with lower incomes to be penalized by prosecutors while wealthy people escape prosecution.[56] I recommend that prosecutors align with state and local agencies to pursue cases against wealthy individuals who commit economic crimes for which all taxpayers pay a price. These alliances will be far more beneficial to the public than going after someone who steals a bag of oranges from a grocery store. I and many other prosecutors have prosecuted thefts from grocery stores that required several store employees to be present in court to prosecute a simple shoplifting case, which ended up costing the store more money than the theft itself. What if instead of pursuing these low-level crimes, we started punching up and spent more time prosecuting wealthy individuals and businesses that commit economic crimes, such as labor and wage fraud, illegal predatory businesses in low-income Black neighborhoods, illegal financial schemes that prey on the elderly and low-income people, and other serious economic crimes? I've seen too few prosecutions of economic crimes, and when the perpetrators are prosecuted, they receive only a slap on the wrist at sentencing—unlike so many Black defendants charged with lesser crimes.

Stability helps to keep us safe, and prosecuting unemployed or working people for minor economic crimes often destabilizes individuals and does nothing to maintain public safety. Prosecutors need to change their perception of crime and safety and then partner with organizations to help make us safer by taking a more equitable approach to prosecution.

YOUTH COALITIONS

The most vulnerable people who are in need of broad coalitions with prosecutors to protect them from prosecutorial overreaching are youth and people who suffer with mental illness and substance abuse issues. Prosecutors need to work with youth advocacy groups and mental health organizations and professionals to develop alternatives to jail for adolescents and establish a minimum age of eighteen or, preferably, twenty-five for prosecution as an adult (twenty-five is the age at which the frontal cortex is fully developed). Troubled youth who commit crimes due to socioeconomic and sociopsychological reasons deserve to have adults, as members of a democratic society, consider options that facilitate reform and not penalize young, often Black people for challenges they cannot control.

In 2016, the Office of the Attorney General for the District of Columbia led by Karl Racine entered a partnership with the DC Department of Human Services, which had a youth diversion program called Alternatives to the Criminal Experience. The program focused on understanding the underlying reasons that young people entered the criminal justice system for low-level offenses and then tailored services to address their underlying trauma or other reasons. The program offered mental health services, counseling, mentoring, substance abuse, and tutoring for school. According to Racine, the program had a 75 percent to 83 percent rate of success—meaning the young people did not recidivate and commit another crime within two years of the first crime and the treatment they received.[57] Enhancing public safety by using evidence-based approaches in partnerships that differ from a traditional tough-on-crime approach actually reduces the likelihood that a person will commit another wrong.

I would like to see mental health organizations and youth advocacy groups join forces with reform-minded prosecutors to show how the effects of poverty harm many Black youth. In the infamous 2013 case of Ethan Couch, the sixteen-year-old white Texas teenager had a blood alcohol level that was three times the legal limit[58] when he crashed his truck and killed four people and injured nine others, including one woman who was left paralyzed. Couch was charged with four counts of manslaughter at his trial, and a defense witness, psychologist Dick Miller, testified that Couch's irresponsible actions were caused by his family's wealth and their irresponsibility: they never taught him rules.[59] The defense became known in media circles as the "affluenza" defense. Although the prosecutor recommended incarceration, in 2014, a judge sentenced Ethan Couch to ten years' probation, which included a stay at a rehabilitation facility, ultimately costing the state of Texas almost $200,000 when his parents failed to pay.[60] (Couch later violated his probation and was sentenced to prison.) If we want to learn how to treat crime differently with Black people, all we need to do is look at how we treat a white child who has committed harm.

Fair and Just Prosecution's "21 Principles for the 21st Century Prosecutor," which were coauthored in partnership with Emily Bazelon, the Justice Collaborative and the Brennan Center for Justice, recommends that even after conviction or adjudication of a juvenile, prosecutors should seek treatment as alternatives to incarceration.[61] Incarceration of adolescents is detrimental to their mental health and emotional development. We need strong alliances to work with prosecutors to help to give Black adolescents the same grace and mercy that are shown to white adolescents charged with a crime. In order to address racial disparities, prosecutors must be willing to align with community leaders, juvenile justice advocates, faith-based organizations, mental health, and drug abuse organizations as well as family support groups to provide alternatives to detention and incarceration for youth. For over twenty-five years, the Annie E. Casey Foundation's Juvenile Detention Alternative Initiative has worked with juvenile justice advocates and practitioners to create a more racially equitable system. The initiative has worked to see the possibilities beyond juvenile detention and reduced the disproportionate number of Black youth in detention centers.[62]

Mental health and substance abuse issues affect many of the criminal defendants that I see in court. While prosecutors can take steps to help these individuals find treatment, we still do not have the resources to treat everyone who needs assistance. A coordinated effort between activists, progressive prosecutors, politicians, and community organizations can secure more government and private funding for rehabilitation programs. We should pair these initiatives with significant reentry reforms that invest in returning citizens to society to prevent recidivism. We need mental health and substance abuse organizations, juvenile counseling services, and social work organizations to support prosecutors as they pivot from a carceral approach.

GRASSROOTS ORGANIZATIONS AND POLITICAL ACTION COMMITTEES

Before the term *mass incarceration* was first used, US Attorney General Robert Jackson said that "the prosecutor has more control over life, liberty, and reputation than any other person in America."[63] His words were spoken in 1940, but they ring just as clearly and truly today. The fact remains that in many counties, conservative and traditional prosecutors wield their significant power against criminal justice reform. Just as some prosecutors use their office for justice and fairness, others view justice only as punishment. Still others use their power in unlawful or unconstitutional ways to obtain a conviction. In order to combat these practices, we need strong grassroots organizations, political action committees (PACs), and others aligned with reform candidates in order to elect more reformist prosecutors and keep them in office. As opposing organizations and PACs raise millions of dollars to either defeat or oust reform prosecutors such as Chesa Boudin, we need resources to expand the small cadre of progressive prosecutors. Money is necessary to political campaigns, but it does not always win an election. Grassroots community alignments are vital. In 2022, Maryland attorney Robbie Leonard was a candidate for state's attorney for Baltimore County and was backed by the Maryland Justice & Public Safety PAC funded by billionaire George Soros, but he narrowly lost in his bid to unseat the incumbent, Scott Schellenberger, a four-term conservative Democratic prosecutor. Money doesn't vote. People vote.

Under the protection of the law, prosecutors have committed wrongs against African Americans for hundreds of years. We need to remember the deliberate systemic wrongs of the past to significantly alter the course of our future. Now awakened, America must choose to reform a system built on the backs of Black people. As the African proverb says, "If you want to go fast, go alone. If you want to go far, go together." To create a just system, we need a broad alliance of elected officials, community organizations, corporations, nonprofits, health professionals, business leaders, juvenile justice, and mental health advocacy groups—citizens all working to alter America's carceral prosecutorial policy and achieve racial equity.

CONCLUSION

Hope and fear cannot occupy the same space. Invite one to stay.
—Maya Angelou

My mother always believed in hope. In all things, she always said, "You've got to have hope." And so, to honor my mother, Naomi, I want to end on a hopeful note. While it may not always feel like it, there are many reasons for hope as we work to radically transform a prosecutorial system that was built to incarcerate Black individuals and ruin the lives of many Black people.

First, people like you are reading this book. You are looking for ways to reform the prosecutorial system of about 2,400 state and local prosecutors, and you will do so by learning more from other books, research materials, organizations, activists, allies, and like-minded people in the process. Several years ago, there were few elected progressive prosecutors. Now, the number continues to grow. The exact number of reform prosecutors varies as there is no uniform definition (typically, these prosecutors are self-described as progressive or reform minded), and elections come and go. Fair and Just Prosecution's network of reform prosecutors grew from more than a dozen in 2017 to over seventy elected prosecutors within five years.[1] State prosecutorial reforms have been implemented in bail reform, reduction in prosecutions for certain misdemeanors, diversion for mental health and substance abuse, restorative justice measures, conviction and sentencing reviews, and juvenile justice reforms. Protests helped to fuel these prosecutors' actions and brought and secured prosecution and conviction of Derek Chauvin for George Floyd's murder in Minneapolis, Minnesota, in 2020 and the swift charges against the five Black police officers who killed Tyre Nichols in Memphis, Tennessee, in 2023. The efforts of activists have pushed prosecutors toward change.

There is reason to hope, but much more work is left to do.

As reform-minded prosecutors number only a few of the more than 2,400 state elected prosecutors, the real work must be done by people in the trenches—including you. Prosecutors have power, but their power is not limitless. The people also have power to push the pendulum to swing toward justice and transform a carceral system currently aimed at Black people.

And so I firmly believe that with committed effort, we will be able to change the prediction that one of every three Black boys born in 2001 will be incarcerated at some time in their lifetime.[2] Armed with the knowledge of how the prosecutor's office works, I hope readers will participate in the concerted and sustained effort to transform the criminal justice system.

Part of that effort involves continuing our education. I receive daily Google and publication alerts on prosecutors, cases, and laws in criminal justice, particularly in relation to Black people and racial disparities. I look for new developments and for areas where I might best be a part of change. Like a knife's blade, I want to continue to sharpen my own knowledge.

I highly recommend that readers visit local courts to see how prosecutors work. Many courts still have ongoing virtual hearings with links online, but whether virtual or live, observing prosecutors in action will help people to understand the process. As an attorney, I still watch parts of high-profile jury trials in person for my own trial education.

The best education also comes from meeting with people who have encountered the prosecutorial system or are still incarcerated. Check online for secular and nonsecular organizations that have prison connections to learn from those most impacted by prosecutors and most in need of reforms during and after incarceration. These connections will provide a human personal touch that will go far beyond the words on any page.

While individual learning is good, there is strength in collective numbers. I strongly urge reform-minded individuals to join racial justice organizations, which will allow them to broaden their knowledge base and become involved in large-scale community activities. It will also help to refine where readers can be most useful, given their interests, skills, and time commitments. Start where you are, and work from there. However you choose to become involved, begin to do the work. Change will occur in the US prosecutorial system as individuals work individually and collectively toward reforms. This can start by sharing what you know. For years, many people have been fed the false narrative that the United States needs to lock up people (mostly Black people) to keep our streets safe. Educate friends, family members, coworkers, and acquaintances about the information contained in this book.

Over time, through racial equity and justice reform organizations, our collective efforts to educate the public on the punitive effects of long prison sentences and the decimation of the Black community will become successful. When we educate others, show up, denounce tough-on-crime prosecutors and initiatives, and work toward transformative reforms—whether through protests, legislative hearings, communications with politicians, community efforts, or racial justice organizations—we make a difference.

I'm often asked how reform prosecutors and activists' actions can change the footprint of the carceral prosecution system. My answer is this: when and if the recommendations in this book are accomplished, the numbers of people in US jails and prisons will be greatly reduced. We can start by supporting diversion, restorative justice, and community-based programs that address the racial trauma caused by overpolicing and overprosecution, mental health issues, and substantive abuse issues. We also can decline to prosecute many of the thirteen million misdemeanor cases brought annually (misdemeanors make up 80 percent of criminal cases prosecuted in state courts in the United States). The reality is that if we took even this small step, the US carceral footprint would be mostly eliminated. But we can't stop at misdemeanors and look the other way when it comes to felonies. By providing adequate resources—through restorative justice, community programs, and diversion—the number of felonies committed will reduce. By treating substance abuse, mental health needs, racial trauma, and economic issues, we can help people meet challenges without punitive measures. The agenda for a broad coalition must include bail reforms, juvenile justice, inclusion of diversion programs, and restorative justice. It must eliminate mandatory minimums, enhanced sentencing, and the death penalty. It must insist on sentencing and conviction reviews as well as police oversight.

I recommend that activists work toward significantly lowering prison funding and applying the funds formerly allocated for prisons and jails to providing the tools that people need to be successful in life. As prosecutors are forced to move away from convictions and incarceration for African Americans and toward diversionary efforts, restorative justice, and community programs, justice reinvestment will take root. Justice reinvestment would take state and local budget money that is earmarked to house Black people in jails and prisons and instead reinvest the money in Black communities in ways that are life-affirming for Black people. If this is done in Maryland, the nearly $300 million the state spends annually to house 7,795 Baltimore City prisoners and the almost $1 billion it spends to house 20,000 Maryland prisoners will be largely eliminated, and that money could instead fund social services for mental health and substance abuse and for other needs.[3] The trauma and needs of Black children (who are twice as likely as white children to experience a parent in prison) can be addressed through justice funds reallocation.[4]

But to do all of this, we need sustainable hope. It will not be an easy task. It will take steady, relentless effort, and it will take all of us. My hope is that this book will provide a pathway for people to overhaul and turn the systemically racial prosecutorial system upside down. The rewards will benefit all of us. The failing prosecutorial system fails everyone because the racial disproportionality in the criminal justice system that devastates Black lives costs all Americans. Successful racial equity approaches in prosecutorial reforms that are targeted toward Black people will improve the entire justice system and will uplift all people. Taxpayers shoulder the burden of high prosecutorial and policing budgets, probation, incarceration, and parole costs. When we reduce incarceration and lower recidivism rates by reinvesting funds in the Black community, society collectively benefits. And, setting aside monetary concerns, we are all injured when we dehumanize the people with whom we share our lives and country. Societal racism serves no one and harms everyone.

One constant throughout American history has been Black devaluation, but we can—and will—change that. Keep working, and keep hoping.

Acknowledgments

Whenever someone embarks on a major task like writing a book, many people are owed a debt of gratitude. I will not be able to name every person who lent a helping hand or gave a word of encouragement, but please know that I hold each of your names dearly in my heart. To all the individuals who allowed me to interview you to obtain different perspectives for *Get Off My Neck*—including defense attorneys, public defenders, prosecutors, former prosecutors, community activists, law professors, lawmakers, racial justice leaders, sociologists, and families of formerly incarcerated individuals and others—I thank you from the bottom of my heart. This book would not have been possible without my alliances with the people who work every day to make the prosecutorial system fair and just for everyone.

I have a few friends who are more like sisters. I've known Dianne Timmons-Himes since childhood, as our mothers were good friends. As adults and throughout the writing of this book, Dianne has been one of my strongest advocates, lifting me daily with supportive texts, calls, prayers, cards, and visits. I can't thank her enough for the love she has shown toward me at high times, low moments, and everything in between. I am blessed to call her my sister-friend. And I give a special thanks to my longtime friend Simona Farrise Best, who has been a kindred spirit and sister from another mother. Simona has supported me in my book effort from the beginning, even when I had doubts. I thank the members of my entire sister circle, named and unnamed, who through words of encouragement, acts of kindness, and prayers kept my spirits lifted throughout the publishing process.

A sincere thanks to Sharon Sochil Washington, who helped me to organize my thoughts in an orderly fashion to put them into a book proposal. Whenever I doubted if I would find a publisher who shared my vision for *Get Off My Neck*, your spirituality, emails, and positive spirit kept me lifted up. For that, I am eternally grateful beyond words.

I give thanks to my acquisitions editor, Matt Browne, and members of the MIT Press publicity and marketing team, who saw and believed in my vision before I wrote the first words on a page. Your support has allowed me to write the best book that I could write.

To my amazing agent, Jenny Stephens at Sterling Lord Literistic, thanks for your calmness in answering all of my many first-time author questions and getting me to the finish line with a published book. No words can fully express what your support has meant to me. From our first Zoom meeting, just before Henry was born, during the pandemic in 2021, I felt a special bond between the two of us. Your unwavering support of *Get Off My Neck* from the beginning has been invaluable to me. And I am deeply grateful for your support and honored to call you my literary agent.

A book on this topic is not possible without researchers. Thank you to Rory Fleming and Kalani Browne for your research assistance.

My brother, Emery, was my biggest cheerleader throughout my life. I miss him dearly. I wrote much of *Get Off My Neck* at my computer on his desk as I sat in Em's chair to feel a connection to his spirit.

And most important, I give thanks for a loving and supportive mother, Naomi, who has gone to be with the ancestors. My mother left me with her DNA, and it runs deeply through my veins, providing me with resilience in her earthly absence. In writing this book, I felt her spirit guiding and encouraging me. As always, I want to make my mother proud, and I hope this book has accomplished that goal.

Notes

INTRODUCTION

1. "Report to the United Nations on Racial Disparities in the U.S. Criminal Justice System," The Sentencing Project, April 19, 2018, https://www.sentencingproject.org/publications /un-report-on-racial-disparities.

2. "Report to the United Nations."

3. "Report to the United Nations."

4. Wendy Sawyer, "How Race Impacts Who Is Detained Pretrial," Prison Policy Initiative, October 9, 2019, https://www.prisonpolicy.org/blog/2019/10/09/pretrial_race; "QuickFacts," US Census Bureau, https://www.census.gov/quickfacts.

5. Pierre Thomas, John Kelly, and Tonya Simpson, "ABC News Analysis of Police Arrests Nationwide Reveals Stark Racial Disparity," ABC News, June 11, 2020, https://abcnews .go.com/us/abc-news-analysis-police-arrests-nationwide-reveals-stark/story?id=71188546.

6. Radley Balko, "Another 'Excuse' for Police Bias Bites the Dust," *Washington Post*, June 4, 2019, https://www.washingtonpost.com/opinions/2019/06/04/another-excuse-police -bias-bites-dust.

7. Balko, "Another 'Excuse' for Police Bias."

8. Matt Ford, "Racism and the Execution Chamber," *The Atlantic*, June 23, 2014, https:// www.theatlantic.com/politics/archive/2014/06/race-and-the-death-penalty/373081.

9. John Gramlich, "Only 2% of Federal Criminal Defendants Go to Trial, and Most Who Do Are Found Guilty," Pew Research Center, June 11, 2019, https://www.pewresearch.org /fact-tank/2019/06/11/only-2-of-federal-criminal-defendants-go-to-trial-and-most-who -do-are-found-guilty; "America's Massive Misdemeanor System Deepens Inequality," Equal Justice Initiative, January 9, 2019, https://eji.org/news/americas-massive-misdemeanor -system-deepens-inequality/.

10. "Tipping the Scales: Challengers Take On the Old Boys Club of Elected Prosecutors," Reflective Democracy Campaign, October 2019, https://wholeads.us/research /tipping-the-scales-elected-prosecutors.

11. James Baldwin, *The Price of the Ticket: Collected Nonfiction: 1948–1985* (Boston: Beacon Press, 1985 [2021]).

12. "Reverend Al Sharpton Eulogy Transcript at George Floyd's Memorial Service," @rev, June 4, 2020, https://www.rev.com/blog/transcripts/reverend-al-sharpton-eulogy-transcript-at-george-floyd-memorial-service.

13. "ABA Survey Finds 1.3M Lawyers in the U.S.," American Bar Association, June 20, 2022, https://www.americanbar.org/news/abanews/aba-news-archives/2022/06/aba-lawyers-survey.

CHAPTER 1

1. Annette Gordon-Reed, "Thomas Jefferson's Vision of Equality Was Not All-Inclusive. But It Was Transformative," *Time*, February 20, 2020, https://time.com/5783989/thomas-jefferson-all-men-created-equal.

2. "Report to the United Nations on Racial Disparities in the U.S. Criminal Justice System," The Sentencing Project, April 19, 2018, https://www.sentencingproject.org/publications/un-report-on-racial-disparities.

3. "Youth Arrests by Offense and Race, 2018," Office of Juvenile Justice and Delinquency Prevention, Office of Justice Programs, US Department of Justice.

4. "Report to the United Nations on Racial Disparities."

5. "Report to the United Nations on Racial Disparities."

6. Carol Anderson, *White Rage: The Unspoken Truth of Our Racial Divide* (New York: Bloomsbury, 2016).

7. Anderson, *White Rage*.

8. History.com editors, "Black Codes," History.com, updated March 29, 2023, https://www.history.com/topics/black-history/black-codes.

9. J. E. Hansan, "Jim Crow Laws and Racial Segregation," Social Welfare History Project, Virginia Commonwealth University, 2011, https://socialwelfare.library.vcu.edu/eras/civil-war-reconstruction/jim-crow-laws-andracial-segregation.

10. Richard North Patterson, "'History Doesn't Repeat Itself, But It Often Rhymes'—Mark Twain," *Magazine of Ohio Wesleyan University*, Fall 2018, https://www.owu.edu/alumni-and-friends/owu-magazine/fall-2018/history-doesnt-repeat-itself-but-it-often-rhymes.

11. Cindy Wu and Prue Brady, "Private Companies Producing with US Prison Labor in 2020: Prison Labor in the US, Part II," Corporate Accountability Lab, August 5, 2020, https://corpaccountabilitylab.org/calblog/2020/8/5/private-companies-producing-with-us-prison-labor-in-2020-prison-labor-in-the-us-part-ii.

12. Daniele Selby, "How the 13th Amendment Kept Slavery Alive: Perspectives from the Prison Where Slavery Never Ended," Innocence Project, September 17, 2021, https://innocenceproject.org/13th-amendment-slavery-prison-labor-angola-louisiana.

13. Aaron Morrison, "Slavery, Involuntary Servitude Rejected by 4 States' Voters," AP News, November 9, 2022, https://apnews.com/article/2022-midterm-elections-slavery-on -ballot-561268e344f17d8562939cde301d2cbf.

14. Emily Widra and Tiana Herring, "States of Incarceration: The Global Context 2021," Prison Policy Initiative, September 2021, https://www.prisonpolicy.org/global/2021.html.

15. Kimberlee Kruesi, "Slavery Is on the Ballot for Voters in 5 US States," AP News, October 22, 2022, https://apnews.com/article/2022-midterms-13th-amendment-slavery-4a0341cf82 fa33942bda6a5d17ac4348.

16. Dana Ford, "Was Freddie Gray's Knife Legal?," CNN, May 6, 2015, https://www.cnn .com/2015/05/06/us/freddie-gray-knife/index.html.

17. Wyatt Massey and Kevin Rector, "Under DOJ Scrutiny, Baltimore Police Practice of 'Clearing Corners' Draws Ire and Praise," *Baltimore Sun*, August 13, 2016, https://www.baltimoresun .com/news/crime/bs-md-police-clearing-corner-20160813-story.html.

18. Massey and Rector, "Under DOJ Scrutiny."

19. Wendy Sawyer and Peter Wagner, "Mass Incarceration: The Whole Pie 2022," Prison Policy Initiative, March 14, 2022, https://www.prisonpolicy.org/reports/pie2022.html.

20. Wendy Sawyer, "How Race Impacts Who Is Detained Pretrial," Prison Policy Initiative, October 9, 2019, https://www.prisonpolicy.org/blog/2019/10/09/pretrial_race; "QuickFacts," US Census Bureau, https://www.census.gov/quickfacts.

21. Peter Eisler, Linda So, Jason Szep, Grant Smith, and Ned Parker, "Death Sentence: Why 4,998 Died in U.S. Jails without Getting Their Day in Court," Reuters Investigates, October 16, 2020, https://www.reuters.com/investigates/special-report/usa-jails-deaths.

22. Eisler et al., "Death Sentence."

23. Estate of Larry Eugene Price, Jr. v. Turn Key Health Clinics, Sebastian County, Arkansas et al., case no. 2:23-cv-02008-PKH, US District Court for the Western District of Arkansas, Fort Smith Division, filed January 13, 2023, Justia, https://dockets.justia.com/docket /arkansas/arwdce/2:2023cv02008/67638.

24. Eisler et al., "Death Sentence."

25. Alexis de Tocqueville, *Democracy in America*, ed. and trans. Harvey C. Mansfield and Delba Winthrop (Chicago: The University of Chicago Press, 2000).

26. Melissa Block, "What Changed after DC Ended Cash Bail," NPR, September 2, 2018, https://www.npr.org/2018/09/02/644085158/what-changed-after-d-c-ended-cash-bail.

27. Matthew Hendrickson and Andy Grimm, "Illinois Set to Be First State to End Cash Bail after State Supreme Court Ruling," updated July 18, 2023, https://chicago.suntimes.com /politics/2023/7/18/23759583/safe-t-act-bail-illinois-court-decision-reform.

28. Nick Chrastil, "Fair Wayne Bryant, Man Sentenced to Life in Prison for Attempting to Steal Hedge Clippers in 1997, Granted New Parole Hearing," The Lens, August 12, 2020,

https://thelensnola.org/2020/08/12/fair-wayne-bryant-man-sentenced-to-life-in-prison-for
-attempting-to-steal-hedge-clippers-in-1997-granted-new-parole-hearing.

29. Laurel Wamsley, "Louisiana Supreme Court Won't Review Life Sentence for Man Who Stole Hedge Clippers," NPR, August 5, 2020, https://www.npr.org/2020/08/05/899525589 /louisiana-supreme-court-wont-review-lifesentence-for-man-who-stole-hedge-clippe.

30. "Written Submission of the American Civil Liberties Union on Racial Disparities in Sentencing," ACLU, October 27, 2014, https://www.aclu.org/sites/default/files/assets/141027 _iachr_racial_disparities_aclu_submission_0.pdf.

31. "Race and Ethnicity: 'Three Strikes' Laws," Law Library: American Law and Legal Information, accessed February 6, 2021, https://law.jrank.org/pages/12136/Race-Ethnicity--Three -Strikes-Laws.html.

32. "Lynching in America: Confronting the Legacy of Racial Terror," 3rd ed. (Montgomery, AL: Equal Justice Initiative, 2017), 39.

33. Anderson, *White Rage*.

34. "Lynching in America: Outside the South," Equal Justice Initiative, accessed August 8, 2023, https://eji.org/issues/lynching-in-america-outside-the-south; "Lynching in America: Confronting the Legacy of Racial Terror," 44.

35. Sherrilyn A. Ifill, *On the Courthouse Lawn: Confronting the Legacy of Lynching in the 21st Century* (Boston: Beacon, 2007), 58; "Public Spectacle Lynchings," Equal Justice Initiative, February 14, 2018, https://eji.org/news/history-racial-injustice-public-spectacle-lynchings.

36. "More Than a Century after It Was First Proposed, President Biden Signs Historic Law Making Lynching a Federal Crime," Death Penalty Information Center, March 31, 2022, https://deathpenaltyinfo.org/news/more-than-a-century-after-it-was-first-proposed-president -biden-signs-historic-law-making-lynching-a-federal-crime.

37. "New Report: U.S. Death Penalty Is Rooted in Lynching Past," Innocence Project, February 20, 2015, https://innocenceproject.org/new-report-u-s-death-penalty-is-rooted-in -lynching-past.

38. Matt Ford, "Racism and the Execution Chamber," *The Atlantic*, June 23, 2014, https://www .theatlantic.com/politics/archive/2014/06/race-and-the-death-penalty/373081.

39. Sandra E. Garcia, "DNA Evidence Exonerates a Man of Murder after 20 Years in Prison," *New York Times*, October 16, 2018, https://www.nytimes.com/2018/10/16/us/20-years -exonerated-dna-prison.html.

40. Edwin Grimsley, "What Wrongful Convictions Teach Us about Racial Inequality," Innocence Project, September 26, 2012, https://innocenceproject.org/what-wrongful-convictions -teach-us-about-racial-inequality.

41. "State by State," Death Penalty Information Center, accessed April 7, 2022, https:// deathpenaltyinfo.org/state-and-federal-info/state-by-state.

42. Rob Arthur, "New Data Shows Police Use More Force against Black Citizens Even Though Whites Resist More," Slate, May 30, 2019, https://slate.com/news-and-politics/2019/05 /chicago-police-department-consent-decree-black-lives-matter-resistance.html.

CHAPTER 2

1. A. Leon Higginbotham, Jr., *In the Matter of Color: Race and the American Legal Process: The Colonial Period* (New York: Oxford University Press, 1980); A. Leon Higginbotham, Jr., "Virginia Led the Way in Legal Oppression," *Washington Post*, May 21, 1978, https://www .washingtonpost.com/archive/opinions/1978/05/21/virginia-led-the-way-in-legal-oppression /664bcdf4-8aaf-475f-8ea7-eb597aee7ecd.

2. "Slave Patrols: An Early Form of American Policing," National Law Enforcement Officers Memorial Fund, July 10, 2019, https://nleomf.org/slave-patrols-an-early-form-of-american -policing.

3. Thomas D. Morris, "Slaves and the Rule of Evidence in Criminal Trials," *Chicago-Kent Law Review*, June 1993, https://scholarship.kentlaw.iit.edu/cgi/viewcontent.cgi?referer =&httpsredir=1&article=2907&context=cklawreview.

4. "1921 Tulsa Race Massacre: The Attack on Greenwood," Tulsa Historical Society and Museum, https://www.tulsahistory.org/exhibit/1921-tulsa-race-massacre/#flexible-content.

5. "A New York Professor and Tulsa DA Helped Clear Records of Black Men Accused of Wrongdoing in Race Massacre," *Tulsa World*, May 31, 2021, https://tulsaworld.com/news /local/racemassacre/a-new-york-professor-and-tulsa-da-helped-clear-records-of-black-men -accused-of/article_2e5b0336-bc25-11eb-8b26-2f3208adf713.html.

6. Randi Richardson, "Tulsa Race Massacre, 100 Years Later: Why It Happened and Why It's Still Relevant Today," NBC News, May 28, 2021, https://www.nbcnews.com/news/nbcblk /tulsa-race-massacre-100-years-later-why-it-happened-why-n1268877.

7. Gene Demby, "I'm from Philly. 30 Years Later, I'm Still Trying to Make Sense of the MOVE Bombing," NPR, May 13, 2015, https://www.npr.org/sections/codeswitch/2015 /05/13/406243272/im-from-philly-30-years-later-im-still-trying-to-make-sense-of-the -move-bombing#:~:text=m%20From%20Philly.-,30%20Years%20Later%2C%20I'm%20 Still%20Trying%20To%20Make%20Sense,make%20sense%20of%20it%20all.

8. Lindsey Norward, "The Day Philadelphia Bombed Its Own People," Vox, August 15, 2019, https://www.vox.com/the-highlight/2019/8/8/20747198/philadelphia-bombing -1985-move.

9. Demby, "I'm From Philly."

10. Heather Ann Thompson, "Saying Her Name," *The New Yorker*, May 16, 2021, https://www .newyorker.com/news/essay/saying-her-name.

11. Norward, "The Day Philadelphia Bombed Its Own People."

12. Norward, "The Day Philadelphia Bombed Its Own People."

13. Ed Pilkington, "The Day Police Bombed a City Street: Can Scars of 1985 MOVE Atrocity Be Healed?," *The Guardian*, May 10, 2020, https://www.theguardian.com/us-news/2020/may/10/move-1985-bombing-reconciliation-philadelphia.

14. Justin Fenton, "'No Heroes Here': Exhaustive Report Lays Out Two Decades of Baltimore Police and City Failure That Led to GTTF Scandal," *Baltimore Sun*, January 13, 2022, https://www.baltimoresun.com/news/crime/bs-md-ci-cr-gttf-bromwich-report-20220113-jku765zjbrd6fggcjashvdtmgi-story.html.

15. Carrie Heard and Eyder Peralta, "Justice Department Issues Scathing Report on Baltimore Police Department," NPR, August 9, 2016, https://www.npr.org/sections/thetwo-way/2016/08/09/489372162/justice-department-to-issue-critical-report-on-baltimore-police-department.

16. Brady v. Maryland, 373 U.S. 83 (1963), Justia, https://supreme.justia.com/cases/federal/us/373/83.

17. Dakin Andone, Hollie Silverman, and Melissa Alonso, "The Minneapolis Police Officer Who Knelt on George Floyd's Neck Had 18 Previous Complaints against Him, Police Department Says," CNN, May 29, 2020, https://www.cnn.com/2020/05/28/us/minneapolis-officer-complaints-george-floyd/index.html.

18. Jared Goyette, "2 New Lawsuits Allege Excessive Force, Discrimination by Derek Chauvin," Fox9, May 31, 2022, https://www.fox9.com/news/john-pope-zoya-code-derek-chauvin-police-brutality-lawsuits-minneapolis.

19. Goyette, "2 New Lawsuits Allege Excessive Force."

20. Jay Michaelson, "95% of Prosecutors Are White and They Treat Blacks Worse," Daily Beast, updated July 12, 2017, https://www.thedailybeast.com/95-of-prosecutors-are-white-and-they-treat-blacks-worse.

21. Megan Crepeau, "Dozens of Convictions Vacated in Final Push to Drop Cases Connected to Convicted Former Chicago Police Sergeant," *Chicago Tribune*, April 22, 2022, https://www.chicagotribune.com/news/criminal-justice/ct-ronald-watts-convictions-dismissed-20220422-jqhry6dhkbfkndk52dsjqdaeqi-story.html.

22. Kerri O'Brien, "146 Virginia Police Officers Decertified, New Law Expands to Include Excessive Force and Lying," ABC 8 News, updated February 18, 2022, https://www.wric.com/news/taking-action/146-virginia-police-officers-decertified-new-law-expands-to-include-excessive-force-and-lying.

23. Tom Jackman, "Fairfax Seeks to Dismiss 400 Convictions in Cases Brought by One Officer," *Washington Post*, April 16, 2021, https://www.washingtonpost.com/dc-md-va/2021/04/16/convictions-dismiss-jonathan-freitag-fairfax.

24. Alessandro Marazzi Sassoon, "Brevard County Sheriff's Deputy Fired after Past Misconduct Revealed by *Washington Post*," *Florida Today*, April 19, 2021, https://www.floridatoday.com/story/news/2021/04/19/brevard-florida-sheriffs-deputy-fired-after-misconduct-history-virginia-revealed/7287865002.

25. Philip Matthew Stinson, *The Henry A. Wallace Police Crime Database*, database v.012122.0842, Bowling Green State University, 2022, https://policecrime.bgsu.edu.

26. "Departments and Programs," Bowling Green State University, https://www.bgsu.edu/health-and-human-services/programs.html.

27. Jobina Fortson, "UMES Law Enforcement Accused of Over-Policing," 47 ABC WMDT, November 24, 2015, https://www.wmdt.com/2015/11/umes-law-enforcement-accused-of-over-policing.

28. "EJI Joins Community to Memorialize Lynching Victims on Maryland's Eastern Shore," Equal Justice Initiative, November 4, 2017, https://eji.org/news/community-memorializes-terror-lynchings-in-maryland/.

29. Justin Fenton, "Three Men Exonerated in Notorious 1983 Murder of Baltimore Student File Federal Lawsuit against Police Officers," *Baltimore Sun*, August 13, 2020, https://www.baltimoresun.com/news/crime/bs-md-ci-cr-harlem-park-three-sue-20200813-xmz2nl265fastgglxixc5mm7wa-story.html.

30. Fenton, "Three Men Exonerated."

31. Lara Bazelon, "David Simon Made Baltimore Detectives Famous. Now Their Cases Are Falling Apart. Has Reality Caught Up to the 'Murder Police'?," *Intelligencer*, January 12, 2022, https://nymag.com/intelligencer/2022/01/did-david-simon-glorify-baltimores-detectives.html.

32. "DPIC Adds Eleven Cases to Innocence List, Bringing National Death-Row Exoneration Total to 185," Death Penalty Information Center, February 18, 2021, https://deathpenaltyinfo.org/news/dpic-adds-eleven-cases-to-innocence-list-bringing-national-death-row-exoneration-total-to-185.

33. "DPIC Adds Eleven Cases."

34. Samuel R. Gross, Maurice J. Possley, Kaitlin Jackson Roll, and Klara Huber Stephens, "Government Misconduct and Convicting the Innocent: The Role of Prosecutors, Police and Other Law Enforcement," National Registry of Exonerations, September 1, 2020, https://www.law.umich.edu/special/exoneration/Documents/Government_Misconduct_and_Convicting_the_Innocent.pdf.

35. Emma Zack, "Why Holding Prosecutors Accountable Is So Difficult," Innocence Project, April 23, 2020, https://innocenceproject.org/why-holding-prosecutors-accountable-is-so-difficult.

36. Alexa Ura, "Anderson to Serve 9 Days in Jail, Give Up Law License as Part of Deal," *Texas Tribune*, November 8, 2013, https://www.texastribune.org/2013/11/08/ken-anderson-serve-jail-time-give-law-license.

37. Zack, "Why Holding Prosecutors Accountable Is So Difficult."

38. Associated Press, "Ex-Prosecutor Accused of Interfering with Investigation into Ahmaud Arbery's Killing," NPR, September 2, 2021, https://www.npr.org/2021/09/02/1033809949/ahmaud-arbery-former-prosecutor-indicted-misconduct-georgia.

39. Jessica Savage, "AG Prosecutors Detail Their Case against Former Brunswick DA," WTOC 11, May 5, 2022, https://www.wtoc.com/2022/05/05/ag-prosecutors-detail-their-case-against-former-brunswick-da.

40. Sam Levin, "White Supremacists and Militias Have Infiltrated Police across the US, Report Says," *The Guardian*, August 27, 2020, https://www.theguardian.com/us-news/2020/aug/27/white-supremacists-militias-infiltrate-us-police-report.

41. Vida B. Johnson, "KKK in the PD: White Supremacist Police and What to Do about It," Race, Racism and the Law, June 29, 2019, https://racism.org/articles/law-and-justice/criminal-justice-and-racism/134-police-brutality-and-lynchings/3010-kkk-in-the-pd-white-supremacist.

42. Jonathan Bandler, "Police Officer Suspended over Baboon Facebook Post," *USA Today*, May 4, 2015, https://www.usatoday.com/story/news/nation/2015/05/04/police-officer-suspended-facebook-post/26876041/.

43. Michaelson, "95% of Prosecutors Are White."

44. "Black People More Than Three Times as Likely as White People to Be Killed during a Police Encounter," Harvard T. H. Chan School of Public Health, accessed February 6, 2021, https://www.hsph.harvard.edu/news/hsph-in-the-news/blacks-whites-police-deaths-disparity.

45. Danielle Haynes, "Study: Black Americans 3 Times More Likely to Be Killed by Police," UPI, June 24, 2020, https://www.upi.com/top_news/us/2020/06/24/study-black-americans-3-times-more-likely-to-be-killed-by-police/6121592949925.

46. Max Nesterak, "Judge Removes County Prosecutors in George Floyd Case," *Minnesota Reformer*, September 11, 2020, https://minnesotareformer.com/briefs/judge-removes-county-prosecutors-in-george-floyd-case.

47. "Fatal Force: 1,066 People Have Been Shot and Killed by Police in the Past 12 Months," *Washington Post*, updated April 10, 2023, https://www.washingtonpost.com/graphics/investigations/police-shootings-database.

48. Erik Ortiz, "More Officers Were Charged in Fatal Police Shootings in 2021. Not Everyone Sees Progress," NBC News, January 22, 2022, https://www.nbcnews.com/news/us-news/officers-charged-fatal-police-shootings-2021-not-everyone-sees-progres-rcna12799.

49. Ortiz, "More Officers Were Charged."

50. Shaila Dewan, "Few Police Officers Who Cause Deaths Charged or Convicted," *New York Times*, September 24, 2020, https://www.nytimes.com/2020/09/24/us/police-killings-prosecution-charges.html.

51. Rose Hackman, "'It's Like We're Seen as Animals': Black Men on Their Vulnerability and Resilience," *The Guardian*, July 12, 2016, https://www.theguardian.com/world/2016/jul/12/black-men-america-violence-vulnerable-detroit.

CHAPTER 3

1. "America's Massive Misdemeanor System Deepens Inequality," Equal Justice Initiative, January 9, 2019, https://eji.org/news/americas-massive-misdemeanor-system-deepens-inequality.

2. "What Prosecution Costs," Vera Institute of Justice, https://www.vera.org/publications/what-prosecution-costs.

3. Sam McCann, "In Virginia, Money—Not Justice—Drives Prosecution," Vera Institute of Justice, June 14, 2022, https://www.vera.org/news/in-virginia-money-not-justice-drives-prosecution.

4. Adam M. Gershowitz and Laura R. Killinger, "The State (Never) Rests: How Excessive Prosecutorial Caseloads Harm Criminal Defendants," *Northwestern University Law Review* 105 (2015): 261, https://scholarlycommons.law.northwestern.edu/nulr/vol105/iss1/5.

5. Gershowitz and Killinger, "The State (Never) Rests."

6. Clark Neily, "Prisons Are Packed Because Prosecutors Are Coercing Plea Deals. And, Yes, It's Totally Legal," NBC News Think, August 8, 2019, https://www.nbcnews.com/think/opinion/prisons-are-packed-because-prosecutors-are-coercing-plea-deals-yes-ncna1034201; Emily Yoffe, "Innocence Is Irrelevant," *The Atlantic*, September 2017, https://www.theatlantic.com/magazine/archive/2017/09/innocence-is-irrelevant/534171/.

7. Dan Canon, "On TV Every Defendant Gets a Trial. But in Real Life, Trials Are Rare," *Washington Post*, March 17, 2022, https://www.washingtonpost.com/outlook/2022/03/17/tv-every-defendant-gets-trial-real-life-trials-are-rare.

8. Bordenkircher v. Hayes, 434 U.S. 357 (1978).

9. Paul Butler, "The Prosecutor Problem," Brennan Center for Justice, August 23, 2021, https://www.brennancenter.org/our-work/analysis-opinion/prosecutor-problem.

10. "Research Finds Evidence of Racial Bias in Plea Deals," Equal Justice Initiative, October 26, 2017, https://eji.org/news/research-finds-racial-disparities-in-plea-deals; Carlos Berdejó, "Criminalizing Race: Racial Disparities in Plea Bargaining," *Boston College Law Review* 59, no. 4 (2018): 1187–1250.

11. "Research Finds Evidence of Racial Bias in Plea Deals"; Berdejó, "Criminalizing Race."

12. Besiki Kutateladze, Whitney Tymas, and Mary Crowley, "Race and Prosecution in Manhattan," research summary, Vera Institute of Justice, July 2014, https://www.vera.org/publications/race-and-prosecution-in-manhattan.

13. Gene Demby, "Study Reveals Worse Outcomes for Black and Latino Defendants," NPR, July 17, 2014, https://www.npr.org/sections/codeswitch/2014/07/17/332075947/study-reveals-worse-outcomes-for-black-and-latino-defendants.

14. Berdejó, "Criminalizing Race."

15. US Department of Justice, Civil Rights Division, *Investigation of the Baltimore City Police Department*, August 10, 2016, https://s3.documentcloud.org/documents/3009376/BPD -Findings-Report-FINAL.pdf.

16. David A. Graham, "The Horror of the Baltimore Police Department," *The Atlantic*, August 10, 2016, https://www.theatlantic.com/news/archive/2016/08/the-horror-of-the -baltimore-police-department/495329.

17. "QuickFacts, Baltimore City, Maryland," US Census Bureau, https://www.census.gov /quickfacts/baltimorecitymaryland; US Department of Justice, *Investigation of the Baltimore City Police Department*.

18. US Department of Justice, *Investigation of the Baltimore City Police Department*.

19. "Rates of Drug Use and Sales, by Race; Rates of Drug Related Criminal Justice Measures, by Race" (chart), The Hamilton Project, October 21, 2016, https://www.hamiltonproject.org /charts/rates_of_drug_use_and_sales_by_race_rates_of_drug_related_criminal_justice.

20. Gershowitz and Killinger, "The State (Never) Rests."

21. Tushar Kansal, "Racial Disparity in Sentencing," Open Society Foundations, January 2005, https://www.opensocietyfoundations.org/publications/racial-disparity-sentencing.

22. Kansal, "Racial Disparity in Sentencing."

23. Ashley Nellis, "The Color of Justice: Racial and Ethnic Disparity in State Prisons," The Sentencing Project, October 13, 2021, https://www.sentencingproject.org/publications /color-of-justice-racial-and-ethnic-disparity-in-state-prisons.

24. Nellis, "The Color of Justice."

25. Berdejó, "Criminalizing Race."

26. Brian D. Johnson, *Final Report on Racial Justice in Prosecution in Baltimore*, University of Maryland, February 2022, https://content.govdelivery.com/attachments/mdbaltimo resao/2022/03/16/file_attachments/2104881/final_report_on_racial_disparity_feb _2022.pdf.

27. US Department of Justice, Civil Rights Division, *Investigation of the Ferguson Police Department*, March 4, 2015, https://www.justice.gov/sites/default/files/opa/press-releases /attachments/2015/03/04/ferguson_police_department_report.pdf.

28. US Department of Justice, *Investigation of the Ferguson Police Department*.

29. US Department of Justice, *Investigation of the Ferguson Police Department*.

30. Josh McGhee, "Blacks Make Up a Larger Share of Defendants in Cook County," *U.S. News and World Report*, December 11, 2021, https://www.usnews.com/news/best-states/illinois /articles/2021-12-11/blacks-make-up-a-larger-share-of-defendants-in-cook-county.

31. "Incarceration Trends: Alameda County, CA," Vera Institute of Justice, updated February 14, 2023, https://trends.vera.org/state/CA/county/alameda_county.

32. Jerry Iannelli, "Miami's Justice System Widely Discriminates against Blacks, ACLU Report Warns," *Miami New Times*, July 19, 2018, https://www.miaminewtimes.com/news/miami -justice-system-discriminates-against-blacks-aclu-data-shows-10540037.

33. Iannelli, "Miami's Justice System"; Nick Petersen and Marisa Omori with Roberto Cancio, Oshea Johnson, Rachel Lautenschlager, and Brandon Martinez, "Unequal Treatment: Racial and Ethnic Disparities in Miami-Dade Criminal Justice," ACLU Florida Greater Miami, July 2018, https://www.aclufl.org/en/publications/unequal-treatment-racial-and-ethnic -disparities-miami-dade-criminal-justice.

34. "Racial Disparities Revealed in Maricopa County Prosecution Practices," ACLU Arizona, July 16, 2020, https://www.acluaz.org/en/press-releases/racial-disparities-revealed -maricopa-county-prosecution-practices.

CHAPTER 4

1. Wendy Sawyer, "Youth Confinement: The Whole Pie 2019," Prison Policy Initiative, December 19, 2019, https://www.prisonpolicy.org/reports/youth2019.html.

2. Sawyer, "Youth Confinement."

3. "Despite Improvements, an Ineffective and Biased System Remains," *The State of America's Children 2020: Youth Justice*, Children's Defense Fund, accessed February 6, 2021, https:// www.childrensdefense.org/policy/resources/soac-2020-youth-justice.

4. Phil Davis, "Maryland's Highest Court Opens Door for Juveniles Who Can Be Rehabilitated to Avoid Adult Prison System," *Baltimore Sun*, August 4, 2021, https://www.baltimoresun .com/news/crime/bs-md-co-cr-appeals-court-juvenile-ruling-20210804-jfbr3t6ukjgetprd 26fgjagtby-story.html.

5. Hannah Gaskill, "Amid Juvenile Justice Reform Push, Commission Examines Maryland's High Rate of Trying Young People as Adults," Maryland Matters, July 21, 2021, https:// www.marylandmatters.org/2021/07/21/amid-juvenile-justice-reform-push-commission -examines-marylands-high-rate-of-trying-young-people-as-adults.

6. Gaskill, "Amid Juvenile Justice Reform Push."

7. Hannah Gaskill, "Reform Council Recommends Ending Policy of Automatically Charging Some Youth as Adults," Maryland Matters, September 9, 2021, https://www.maryland matters.org/2021/09/09/reform-council-recommends-ending-policy-of-automatically -charging-some-youth-as-adults.

8. "QuickFacts Maryland," US Census Bureau, https://www.census.gov/quickfacts/fact/table /MD/BZA115220.

9. Capital News Service, "Juvenile Detention Declined, Yet Black Children Detained at High Rate," Maryland Matters, January 2, 2021, https://www.marylandmatters.org/2021/01/02 /juvenile-detention-declined-yet-black-children-detained-at-high-rate.

10. Julie O'Donoghue, "Juvenile Justice Official Suggests Louisiana Prosecutors Should Charge More Minors as Adults," *Louisiana Illuminator*, August 9, 2022, https://lailluminator .com/2022/08/09/juvenile-justice-official-suggests-louisiana-prosecutors-should-charge -more-minors-as-adults.

11. "Despite Improvements, an Ineffective and Biased System Remains."

12. Capital News Service, "Juvenile Detention Declined."

13. Sawyer, "Youth Confinement"; "Despite Improvements, an Ineffective and Biased System Remains."

14. Nicole Scialabba, "Should Juveniles Be Charged as Adults in the Criminal Justice System?," American Bar Association, October 3, 2016, https://www.americanbar.org/groups/litigation /committees/childrens-rights/articles/2016/should-juveniles-be-charged-as-adults.

15. Joshua Rovner, "Black Disparities in Youth Incarceration," The Sentencing Project, July 15, 2021, https://www.sentencingproject.org/publications/black-disparities-youth -incarceration.

16. Erica L. Green, "Lost Girls: Young Women Face Harsher Punishment in Maryland's Juvenile Justice System," *Baltimore Sun*, December 16, 2016, https://www.baltimoresun.com/news /investigations/bal-juvenile-justice-gender-gap-20161216-story.html.

17. Rovner, "Black Disparities in Youth Incarceration."

18. Lauren Gill, "Easy Money: How Counties Are Funneling Covid Relief Funds into New Jails," *The Nation*, July 26, 2022, https://www.thenation.com/article/society/covid-relief-jail -prison.

19. Rovner, "Black Disparities in Youth Incarceration."

20. "Black Children Five Times More Likely Than White Youth to Be Incarcerated," Equal Justice Initiative, September 14, 2017, https://eji.org/news/black-children-five-times-more-likely -than-whites-to-be-incarcerated.

21. Jacob Brogan, "How Does a Public Defender Work?," Slate, May 8, 2017, https://slate.com /business/2017/05/working-how-does-a-baltimore-public-defender-work.html.

22. Carroll Bogert and LynNell Hancock, "Analysis: How the Media Created a 'Superpredator' Myth That Harmed a Generation of Black Youth," NBC News, November 20, 2020, https:// www.nbcnews.com/news/us-news/analysis-how-media-created-superpredator-myth -harmed-generation-black-youth-n1248101.

23. Nicky Zizaza, "'A Literal Mug Shot of a 6-Year-Old Girl': Grandmother Outraged over Child's Arrest," ClickOrlando.com, September 23, 2019, https://www.clickorlando.com /2019/09/23/a-literal-mug-shot-of-a-6-year-old-girl-grandmother-outraged-over-childs-arrest.

24. P. R. Lockhart, "The Parkland Shooting Fueled Calls for More School Police. Civil Rights Groups Want Them Removed," Vox, September 20, 2018, https://www.vox.com /identities/2018/9/20/17856416/school-discipline-policing-black-students-report.

25. "Maryland Enacts Sweeping Youth Justice Reforms," Annie E. Casey Foundation, June 21, 2022, https://www.aecf.org/blog/maryland-enacts-sweeping-youth-justice-reforms.

26. Donna St. George, "As Activists Try to Get Police out of Schools, Maryland Arrest Data Shows Racial Gap," *Washington Post*, June 24, 2020, https://www.washingtonpost.com/local/education/as-activists-try-to-get-police-out-of-schools-maryland-arrest-data-shows-racial-gap/2020/06/24/8056414e-b598-11ea-a8da-693df3d7674a_story.html.

27. Evie Blad and Alex Harsin, "Analysis Reveals Racial Disparities in School Arrests," PBS, February 27, 2017, https://www.pbs.org/newshour/education/analysis-reveals-racial-disparities-school-arrests.

28. Rebecca Tan, "For First Time in 19 Years, Montgomery County Schools Set to Reopen without Police," *Washington Post*, August 25, 2021, https://www.washingtonpost.com/local/md-politics/montgomery-schools-police-officer-program/2021/08/25/99fe70d2-058b-11ec-a654-900a78538242_story.html.

29. "End Juvenile Life without Parole," ACLU, June 25, 2009, https://www.aclu.org/end-juvenile-life-without-parole.

30. Shirley L. Smith, "Mississippi Man's Case Could Affect Fate of Hundreds of Juvenile Lifers," Mississippi Center for Investigative Reporting, October 20, 2020, https://www.mississippicir.org/news/mississippi-mans-case-could-affect-fate-of-hundreds-of-juvenile-lifers.

31. Ronnie K. Stephens, "Jones v. Mississippi Upholds Life without Parole for Children," Interrogating Justice, May 20, 2021, https://interrogatingjustice.org/ending-mass-incarceration/jones-v-mississippi-upholds-life-without-parole-for-children.

32. Miller v. Alabama, 567 U.S. 460 (2012), Justia, https://supreme.justia.com/cases/federal/us/567/460/.

33. Jones v. Mississippi, 593 U.S. —, 141 S. Ct. 1307 (2021), Legal Information Institute, https://www.law.cornell.edu/supremecourt/text/18-1259.

34. Joshua Rovner, "Juvenile Life without Parole: An Overview," The Sentencing Project, April 27, 2023, https://www.sentencingproject.org/policy-brief/juvenile-life-without-parole-an-overview.

35. "Maryland Bans Life without Parole for Children," Equal Justice Initiative, April 12, 2021, https://eji.org/news/maryland-bans-life-without-parole-for-children.

36. "The Teen Brain: 7 Things to Know," National Institute of Mental Health, https://www.nimh.nih.gov/health/publications/the-teen-brain-7-things-to-know; Stephen Johnson, "Why Is 18 the Age of Adulthood If the Brain Can Take 30 Years to Mature?," Big Think, January 31, 2022, https://bigthink.com/neuropsych/adult-brain.

37. Commonwealth v. Ligon, 314 A.2d (Pa. 1973), Casetext, https://casetext.com/case/commonwealth-v-ligon.

38. Swaminathan Natarajan and Lauren Potts, "Joe Ligon: America's 'Longest Juvenile Lifer' on 68 Years in Prison," BBC News, May 9, 2021, https://www.bbc.com/news/world-us-canada-57022924.

39. Bogert and Hancock, "Analysis: How the Media Created a 'Superpredator' Myth."

40. Samuel R. Sommers, "On Racial Diversity and Group Decision Making: Identifying Multiple Effects of Racial Composition on Jury Deliberations," *Journal of Personality and Social Psychology* 90, no. 4 (2006): 597–612, https://www.apa.org/pubs/journals/releases/psp-904597.pdf; Emmanuel Felton, "Many Juries in America Remain Mostly White, Prompting States to Take Action to Eliminate Racial Discrimination in Their Selection," *Washington Post*, December 23, 2021, https://www.washingtonpost.com/national/racial-discrimination-jury-selection/2021/12/18/2b6ec690-5382-11ec-8ad5-b5c50c1fb4d9_story.html.

41. Peters v. Kiff, 407 U.S. 493 (1972), Justia, https://supreme.justia.com/cases/federal/us/407/493.

42. Ginger Jackson-Gleich, "Rigging the Jury: How Each State Reduces Jury Diversity by Excluding People with Criminal Records," American Bar Association, May 2, 2022, https://www.americanbar.org/groups/judicial/publications/judges_journal/2022/spring/rigging-jury-how-each-state-reduces-jury-diversity.

43. Batson v. Kentucky, 476 U.S. 79 (1986), Casetext, https://casetext.com/case/batson-v-kentucky.

44. Miller v. Alabama, 567 U.S. 479.

CHAPTER 5

1. Anthony Izaguirre, "Timeline: The Saga of Meek Mill and How He Ended Up in Jail," AP News, December 2, 2017, Associated Press, https://www.ksl.com/article/46209600.

2. Izaguirre, "Timeline: The Sage of Meek Mill."

3. Izaguirre, "Timeline: The Saga of Meek Mill."

4. Bobby Allyn, "Meek Mill Pleads Guilty to Misdemeanor Gun Charge, Ends 12-Year Legal Case," NPR, August 27, 2019, https://www.npr.org/2019/08/27/754769378/meek-mill-pleads-guilty-to-misdemeanor-gun-charge-ends-12-year-legal-case; Melissa Chan, "How Meek Mill Became the Face of Criminal Justice Reform," *Time*, April 27, 2018, https://time.com/5256757/meek-mill-symbol-prison/.

5. Joe Coscarelli, "Meek Mill's Criminal Case Ends with a Misdemeanor Guilty Plea," *New York Times*, August 27, 2019, https://www.nytimes.com/2019/08/27/arts/music/meek-mill-free.html.

6. Allyn, "Meek Mill Pleads Guilty."

7. Coscarelli, "Meek Mill's Criminal Case Ends."

8. Coscarelli, "Meek Mill's Criminal Case Ends."

9. Kory Grow, "Meek Mill's Legal Troubles: A History," *Rolling Stone*, March 14, 2018, https://www.rollingstone.com/music/music-news/meek-mills-legal-troubles-a-history-117981.

10. Jesse Jannetta, Justin Breaux, Helen Ho, and Jeremy Porter, "Examining Racial and Ethnic Disparities in Probation Revocation," Urban Institute, April 2014, https://www.urban.org/sites/default/files/publication/22746/413174-examining-racial-and-ethnic-disparities-in-probation-revocation.pdf; Wendy Sawyer and Peter Wagner, "Mass Incarceration: The Whole Pie 2022," Prison Policy Initiative, March 14, 2022, https://www.prisonpolicy.org/reports/pie2022.html; Chan, "How Meek Mill Became the Face."

11. "Limiting Incarceration for Technical Violations of Probation and Parole," National Conference of State Legislatures, updated February 6, 2023, https://www.ncsl.org/research/civil-and-criminal-justice/limiting-incarceration-for-technical-violations-of-probation-and-parole.aspx.

12. "Probation and Parole Systems Marked by High Stakes, Missed Opportunities," Pew, September 25, 2018, https://www.pewtrusts.org/en/research-and-analysis/issue-briefs/2018/09/probation-and-parole-systems-marked-by-high-stakes-missed-opportunities.

13. Chan, "How Meek Mill Became the Face."

14. "Probation and Parole Systems Marked by High Stakes."

15. Jannetta et al., "Examining Racial and Ethnic Disparities."

16. Jannetta et al., "Examining Racial and Ethnic Disparities."

17. Jannetta et al., "Examining Racial and Ethnic Disparities."

18. "Probation and Parole Driving Mass Incarceration," Equal Justice Initiative, November 25, 2020, https://eji.org/news/probation-and-parole-driving-mass-incarceration.

19. "A Tale of Two Countries: Racially Targeted Arrests in the Era of Marijuana Reform," ACLU, 2020, https://www.aclu.org/report/tale-two-countries-racially-targeted-arrests-era-marijuana-reform.

20. "A Tale of Two Countries."

21. Pierre Thomas, Yun Choi, Jasmine Brown, and Pete Madden, "Driving While Black: ABC News Analysis of Traffic Stops Reveals Racial Disparities in Several US Cities," ABC News, September 9, 2020, https://abcnews.go.com/US/driving-black-abc-news-analysis-traffic-stops-reveals/story?id=72891419.

22. Ryan Gorman, "Cops Charged in Freddie Gray's Death Have Lower Bails Than Teen Who Turned Himself in for Rioting," Insider, May 1, 2015, https://www.businessinsider.com/cops-charged-in-fredie-grays-death-had-lower-bail-than-teenager-2015-5.

23. Caitlin Goldblatt, "Baltimore Teen Hit with $500,000 Bail: 'It Hurt' to See Freddie Gray Videos," *The Guardian*, May 12, 2015, https://www.theguardian.com/us-news/2015/may/12/baltimore-teen-allen-bullock-freddie-gray-death-protests.

24. Jon Swaine, Oliver Laughland, Paul Lewis, and Mae Ryan, "Baltimore Rioter Turned Himself in—But Family Can't Afford $500,000 Bail," *The Guardian*, April 30, 2015, https://www.theguardian.com/us-news/2015/apr/30/baltimore-rioters-parents-500000-bail-allen-bullock.

25. Luke Broadwater and Jessica Anderson, "Teen Charged with Rioting at Freddie Gray March Released on $500,000 Bail," *Baltimore Sun*, May 8, 2015, https://www.baltimoresun.com/news/crime/bal-teen-charged-with-rioting-released-on-500000-bail-20150508-story.html; Goldblatt, "Baltimore Teen Hit with $500,000 Bail."

26. Hal Riedl, "Remember Allen Bullock, the Face of Rioting in Baltimore? Here's What Happened to Him," *Baltimore Sun*, April 29, 2017, https://www.baltimoresun.com/opinion/op-ed/bs-ed-bullock-today-20170429-story.html.

27. Jessica Anderson, "Teen Who Smashed Traffic Cone through Car Window during 2015 Unrest Returns to Prison for Violating Probation," *Baltimore Sun*, July 14, 2017, https://www.baltimoresun.com/news/crime/bs-md-ci-bullock-sentencing-20170712-story.html.

28. "Rethinking Approaches to Over Incarceration of Black Young Adults in Maryland," Justice Policy Institute, November 6, 2019, https://justicepolicy.org/research/policy-briefs-2019-rethinking-approaches-to-over-incarceration-of-black-young-adults-in-maryland.

29. "Rethinking Approaches to Over Incarceration."

30. "Rethinking Approaches to Over Incarceration."

31. "Rethinking Approaches to Over Incarceration."

32. "White Cop Justin Craven Charged with Felony in Ernest Satterwhite Case," NBC News, April 8, 2015, https://www.nbcnews.com/storyline/walter-scott-shooting/white-cop-justin-craven-charged-felony-ernest-satterwhite-case-n337681.

33. Tony Bartelme and Andrews Knapp, "Ex-Officer Pleads Guilty in Shooting, No Prison Term in Black Driver's Death, an SC Case That Put Deadly Force in Spotlight," *Post and Courier*, April 10, 2016, https://www.postandcourier.com/archives/ex-officer-pleads-guilty-in-shooting-no-prison-term-in-elderly-black-driver-s-death/article_c7de43e8-ffdc-53c1-adbf-6c249073d625.html.

34. Reuters Staff, "Ex-South Carolina Officer Gets Probation over Black Man's Slaying: Media," Reuters, April 11, 2016, https://www.reuters.com/article/us-usa-police-south-carolina/ex-south-carolina-officer-gets-probation-over-black-mans-slaying-media-idUSKCN0X9066.

35. Laura Wagner, "Prosecutors Won't Seek Jail Time for Ex-NYPD Officer Who Killed Unarmed Man," NPR, March 23, 2016, https://www.npr.org/sections/thetwo-way/2016/03/23/471637806/prosecutors-wont-seek-jail-time-for-ex-nypd-officer-who-killed-unarmed-man.

36. Laura Wagner, "Former NYPD Officer Peter Liang Gets Probation for Fatal Shooting," NPR, April 19, 2016, https://www.npr.org/sections/thetwo-way/2016/04/19/474846986/former-nypd-officer-peter-liang-gets-house-arrest-probation-for-fatal-shooting.

37. Michelle Suzanne Phelps, "Why Ending Mass Probation Is Crucial to U.S. Criminal Justice Reform," Scholars Strategy Network, September 14, 2018, https://scholars.org/contribution/why-ending-mass-probation-crucial-us-criminal.

38. Michelle S. Phelps, "Mass Probation and Inequality, Race, Class and Gender Disparities in Supervision and Revocation," in *Handbook on Punishment Decisions Locations of Disparity*, ed. J. Ulmer and M. Bradley (New York: Routledge, 2018), 43–63.

39. World Population Review, "La Plata, Maryland Population 2023," https://worldpopulationreview.com/us-cities/la-plata-md-population.

40. Phelps, "Mass Probation and Inequality."

41. Phelps, "Mass Probation and Inequality."

CHAPTER 6

1. "Officer Charged in Freddie Gray Case Gets Promoted," AP News, August 6, 2022, https://apnews.com/article/arrests-maryland-baltimore-marilyn-mosby-db67bf56d0030ffd331b7492de90ed8a.

2. Eli Hager, "Cops Win Another Round Pursuing the Prosecutor Who Pursued Them," The Marshall Project, March 20, 2017, https://www.themarshallproject.org/2017/03/20/cops-win-another-round-pursuing-the-prosecutor-who-pursued-them.

3. Safia Samee Ali, "Officers in Freddie Gray Case Suing Marilyn Mosby," NBC News, July 28, 2016, https://www.nbcnews.com/storyline/baltimore-unrest/officers-freddie-gray-case-suing-marilyn-mosby-n618966.

4. Sean Yoes, "Supreme Court Rules for Mosby in Freddie Gray Officers Lawsuit," Afro News, November 14, 2018, https://afro.com/supreme-court-rules-for-mosby-in-freddie-gray-officers-lawsuit.

5. "Fatal Force: 1,066 People Have Been Shot and Killed by Police in the Past 12 Months," *Washington Post*, updated April 10, 2023, https://www.washingtonpost.com/graphics/investigations/police-shootings-database; Brian Howey, Wesley Lowery, and Steven Rich, "The Unseen Toll of Nonfatal Police Shootings," *Washington Post*, October 21, 2022, https://www.washingtonpost.com/investigations/interactive/2022/police-shootings-non-fatal.

6. Mapping Police Violence Database, https://mappingpoliceviolence.us.

7. Barry Sims, "Teen Apologizes for Destruction during April Unrest," WBAL-TV 11, March 1, 2016, https://www.wbaltv.com/article/teen-apologizes-for-destruction-during-april-unrest/7099227#.

8. Jennifer Gonnerman, "Larry Krasner's Campaign to End Mass Incarceration," *The New Yorker*, October 22, 2018; Alan Feuer, "He Sued Police 75 Times. Democrats Want Him as Philadelphia's Top Prosecutor," *New York Times*, June 17, 2017, https://www.nytimes.com/2017/06/17/us/philadelphia-krasner-district-attorney-police.html.

9. Charles Abraham, "MOVE: Philadelphia's Forgotten Bombing," *James Madison Undergraduate Research Journal* 7, no. 1 (2020): 27–36, http://commons.lib.jmu.edu/jmurj/vol7/iss1/3.

10. Joe Holden, Kerri Corrado, and Wakisha Bailey, "Former Philadelphia Police Officer Eric Ruch Found Guilty of Voluntary Manslaughter in Fatal Shooting of Dennis Plowden," CBS News Philadelphia, updated September 21, 2022, https://www.cbsnews.com/philadelphia/news/eric-ruch-guilty-voluntary-manslaughter-dennis-plowden.

11. CBS3 Staff, "DA Larry Krasner Calls Judge Ordering Former Philly Police Officer to Stand on Trial Historic Moment," CBS News Philadelphia, updated October 5, 2022, https://www.cbsnews.com/philadelphia/news/larry-krasner-philadelphia-shooting-edsaul-mendoza-thomas-siderio.

12. Katie Meyer, "Philly DA Larry Krasner Cruises to Reelection Victory," WHYY, updated November 2, 2021, https://whyy.org/articles/philly-da-larry-krasner-cruises-to-reelection-victory.

13. José Garza, Zoom interview with author, October 11, 2022.

14. Garza, Zoom interview.

15. Jessica Anderson, "In Maryland, Police No Longer Investigate Themselves after Deadly Shootings. Here's How Cases Are Being Handled," *Baltimore Sun*, October 15, 2021, https://www.baltimoresun.com/news/crime/bs-md-cr-ag-investigative-unit-first-cases-20211015-neuuephmujduxdegl5bokd4kuy-story.html; "Deaths Involving a Law Enforcement Officer," Fifth Report to the State of Maryland, Governor's Office of Crime Prevention, Youth, and Victim Services, http://goccp.maryland.gov/crime-statistics/law-enforcement-reports/deaths-involving-law-enforcement.

16. Conviction Review/Integrity Units Resource Center, Penn Carey Law, University of Pennsylvania, https://www.law.upenn.edu/institutes/quattronecenter/conviction-integrity-units-resource-center.php.

17. "Maryland 2017," The National Registry of Exonerations, updated June 2, 2022, https://exonerations.newkirkcenter.uci.edu/groups/group-exonerations/maryland-2017.

18. Elliot Weld, "Manhattan DA to Toss Nearly 200 Tainted Convictions," Law360, November 17, 2022, https://www.law360.com/trials/articles/1550660?nl_pk=4d46eb1c-95d9-4592-b67c-10f3e35cedc2&utm_source=newsletter&utm_medium=email&utm_campaign=trials&utm_content=2022-11-18&read_more=1&nlsidx=0&nlaidx=7.

19. Jamila Hodge, Zoom interview with author, October 24, 2022.

20. Matt Nadel and Charlie Lee, "Prosecutors in These States Can Review Sentences They Deem Extreme. Few Do," The Marshall Project, November 11, 2022, https://www.themarshallproject.org/2022/11/11/prosecutors-in-these-states-can-review-sentences-they-deem-extreme-few-do-it.

21. Christina Maxouris, "Michael Thompson Is Free after Decades in Prison. Now He Wants to Be an Advocate for Criminal Justice Reform," CNN, updated January 29, 2021, https://www.cnn.com/2021/01/29/us/michael-thompson-michigan-release/index.html.

22. Angie Jackson, "Gov. Whitmer Grants Clemency to Four Michigan Prisoners," *Detroit Free Press*, December 22, 2020, https://www.freep.com/story/news/local/michigan/2020/12/22/michigan-prisoner-commutations-clemency-whitmer/4005236001.

23. *The Sentence of Michael Thompson*, directed by Kyle Thrash and Haley Elizabeth Anderson (New York: MSNBC Films, 2022), https://www.docnyc.net/film/mtpff-program-changing-the-system/the-sentence-of-michael-thompson.

24. Michael Thomas, "Michigan Man Released from Prison after Spending Decades behind Bars," WLNS6.com, updated January 28, 2021, https://www.wlns.com/6-news-now/michigan-man-released-from-prison-after-serving-decades-behind-bars.

25. Nadel and Lee, "Prosecutors in These States Can Review Sentences."

26. Tim Prudente, "Hopkins Researchers Find No Uptick in Crime, Complaints after Marilyn Mosby Stops Prosecuting Drug Possession," *Baltimore Sun*, October 19, 2021, https://www.baltimoresun.com/news/crime/bs-md-ci-cr-hopkins-study-mosby-drug-policy-20211019-3agerxsorbfpbotuy7a2p3m54e-story.html?s=03.

27. "Baltimore's No-Prosecution Policy for Low-Level Drug Possession and Prostitution Finds Almost No Rearrests for Serious Offenses," Johns Hopkins Bloomberg School of Public Health, October 19, 2021, https://publichealth.jhu.edu/2021/baltimores-no-prosecution-policy-for-low-level-drug-possession-and-prostitution-finds-almost-no-rearrests-for-serious-offenses; Saba Rouhani, Catherine Tomko, Noelle P. Weicker, and Susan G. Sherman, "Evaluation of Prosecutorial Policy Reforms Eliminating Criminal Penalties for Drug Possession and Sex Work in Baltimore, Maryland," Johns Hopkins Bloomberg School of Public Health, 2021, https://publichealth.jhu.edu/sites/default/files/2021-10/prosecutorial-policy-evaluation-report-20211019.pdf.

28. Noah Goldberg, "Brooklyn District Attorney Will Stop Prosecuting Low-Level Crimes during Coronavirus Outbreak," *New York Daily News*, March 17, 2020, https://www.nydailynews.com/coronavirus/ny-coronavirus-brooklyn-district-attorney-outbreak-low-level-crimes-20200317-tq6d5ckvxjhpjaqitzkenl67pi-story.html; ABC7.com Staff, "New DA Gascon to Decline Prosecution on Range of Low-Level Crimes," ABC7, December 10, 2020, https://abc7.com/george-gascon-los-angeles-district-attorney-lada-misdemeanor-crimes/8674095/; Nazish Dholakia, Insha Rahman, and Aaron Stagoff-Belfort, "Four Ways the Pandemic Made Us Rethink Our Criminal Legal System," Vera Institute of Justice, June 9, 2021, https://www.vera.org/news/four-ways-the-pandemic-made-us-rethink-our-criminal-legal-system.

29. Times Editorial Board, "Editorial: The Empire Strikes Back—against Progressive Prosecutors," *Los Angeles Times*, October 31, 2022, https://www.latimes.com/opinion/story/2022-10-31/progressive-prosecutors-attacked; Amanda Agan, Jennifer L. Doleac, and Anna Harvey, "Misdemeanor Prosecution," National Bureau of Economic Research, March 22, 2021, revised August 2022, https://www.nber.org/system/files/working_papers/w28600/w28600.pdf.

30. Garza, Zoom interview.

31. Rebecca Beitsch, "States Consider Restorative Justice as Alternative to Mass Incarceration," PBS, July 20, 2016, https://www.pbs.org/newshour/nation/states-consider-restorative-justice-alternative-mass-incarceration.

32. *Brooklyn District Attorney Eric Gonzalez: Annual Report 2018*, District Attorney Kings County, http://brooklynda.org/wp-content/uploads/2019/10/Annual-Report-2019-Single-Page-Format.pdf; "Our Work," Common Justice, https://www.commonjustice.org/our_work.

33. "Is Prison the Answer to Violence?," The Marshall Project, Common Justice, https://www.commonjustice.org/is_prison_the_answer_to_violence.

34. David Howard King, "'We Can Do Both' District Attorneys Weigh In on Fighting for Racial Justice and against Gun Violence," New York State Bar Association, January 26, 2022, https://nysba.org/we-can-do-both-district-attorneys-weigh-in-on-fighting-for-racial-justice-and-against-gun-violence.

35. Danielle Sered, "Accounting for Violence: How to Increase Safety and Break Our Failed Reliance on Mass Incarceration," Vera Institute of Justice, 2017, https://www.vera.org/downloads/publications/accounting-for-violence.pdf.

36. Sered, "Accounting for Violence."

37. "Restorative Justice Program," Office of the Attorney General for the District of Columbia, https://oag.dc.gov/public-safety/restorative-justice-program.

38. Karl Racine, Zoom interview with author, December 30, 2022.

39. Racine, Zoom interview.

40. "Policy: Neighborhood Courts," San Francisco District Attorney, https://www.sfdistrictattorney.org/policy/restorative-justice/neighborhood-courts.

41. "Policy: Neighborhood Courts."

42. Christi Yoder, "Restorative Justice: Reintegrating Offenders and Healing the Community," *Longmont Observer*, July 15, 2017, https://www.longmontleader.com/local-news/restorative-justice-reintegrating-offenders-healing-community-2380788.

43. Reese Frederickson, Alissa Marque Heydari, and Chloe Marmet, "Restorative Justice: A Best Practice Guide for Prosecutors in Smaller Jurisdictions," Institute for Innovation in Prosecution at John Jay College, January 2022, https://static1.squarespace.com/static/5c4fbee5697a9849dae88a23/t/61f18ead2f9f040ed03aa1f1/1643220659137/FINAL+Restorative+Justice+Paper+2022.pdf; David Belden, "Controversies around Restorative Justice," Tikkun, January 9, 2012, https://www.tikkun.org/controversies-around-restorative-justice.

44. Justice Policy Institute and the Prison Policy Initiative, "Introduction: Mapping Baltimore's Corrections and Community Challenges," Prison Policy Initiative, February 2015, https://www.prisonpolicy.org/origin/md/report.html.

45. Rachel Eisenberg and Allie Preston, "Progressive Prosecutors Are Not Tied to the Rise in Violent Crime," Center for American Progress, October 26, 2022, https://www.american progress.org/article/progressive-prosecutors-are-not-tied-to-the-rise-in-violent-crime; Todd Foglesong et al, "Violent Crime and Public Prosecution," Munk School of Global Affairs and Public Policy, October 20, 2022, https://munkschool.utoronto.ca/research/violent -crime-and-public-prosecution.

46. Jessica Brand and Jessica Pishko, "Bail Reform: Explained," The Appeal, June 14, 2018, https://theappeal.org/bail-reform-explained-4abb73dd2e8a.

47. Wendy Sawyer and Peter Wagner, "Mass Incarceration: The Whole Pie 2022," Prison Policy Initiative, March 14, 2022, https://www.prisonpolicy.org/reports/pie2022.html.

48. Tiana Herring, "Releasing People Pretrial Doesn't Harm Public Safety," Prison Policy Initiative, November 17, 2020, https://www.prisonpolicy.org/blog/2020/11/17/pretrial -releases.

49. Michael Hardy, "How Houston Is Leading the Way on Keeping Poor Defendants out of Jail," *Texas Monthly*, December 5, 2019, https://www.texasmonthly.com/news-politics /how-houston-leading-way-keeping-poor-defendants-out-jail.

50. Allie Preston and Rachael Eisenberg, "Cash Bail Reform Is Not a Threat to Public Safety," Center for American Progress, September 19, 2022, https://www.americanprogress.org /article/cash-bail-reform-is-not-a-threat-to-public-safety; Office of the New York City Comptroller Brad Lander, "NYC Bail Trends since 2019," 2022, https://comptroller.nyc.gov /wp-content/uploads/documents/NYC_Bail_Trends_Since_2019.pdf.

51. Don Stemen and David Olson, "Dollars and Sense in Cook County: Examining the Impact of General Order 18.8A on Felony Bond Court Decisions, Pretrial Release, and Crime," Safety and Justice Challenge, 2020, https://safetyandjusticechallenge.org/resources /dollars-and-sense-in-cook-county.

52. Brandon L. Garrett, Sandra Guerra Thompson, Dottie Carmichael, Iftekhairul Islam, Andrea Seasock, and Songman Kang, "Monitoring Pretrial Reform in Harris County: Fourth Report of the Court-Appointed Monitor," Harris County, Texas, Independent Monitor for the O'Donnell v. Harris County Decree, 2022, April 18, 2022, https://jad.harriscountytx.gov /Portals/70/documents/ODonnell-Monitor-Fourth-Report-Final.pdf.

53. Herring, "Releasing People Pretrial."

54. Herring, "Releasing People Pretrial."

55. "America's Massive Misdemeanor System Deepens Inequality," Equal Justice Initiative, January 9, 2019, https://eji.org/news/americas-massive-misdemeanor-system-deepens-inequality.

56. Miriam Becker-Cohen and KiDeuk Kim, "The Revolving Door: Mental Illness, Incarceration, Inadequate Care, and Inadequate Evidence," Urban Wire, April 7, 2015, https://www .urban.org/urban-wire/revolving-door-mental-illness-incarceration-inadequate-care-and -inadequate-evidence.

57. US Census Bureau, "QuickFacts Stafford County, Virginia," accessed April 14, 2023, https://www.census.gov/quickfacts/staffordcountyvirginia.

58. Theresa Vargas, "Neli Latson Is—Finally—Free. It Only Took 11 Years, Two Governors and a National Conversation about Race and Disability," *Washington Post*, June 23, 2021, https://www.washingtonpost.com/local/neli-latson-black-autistic-free/2021/06/23/1024d4e4-d446-11eb-a53a-3b5450fdca7a_story.html.

59. Garza, Zoom interview.

60. Kristin Henning, Zoom interview with author, October 19, 2022.

61. Henning, Zoom interview.

62. "Former Philadelphia District Attorney Rufus Seth Williams Sentenced to Five Years in Prison for Federal Bribery Charge," US Attorney's Office, District of New Jersey, October 24, 2017, https://www.justice.gov/usao-nj/pr/former-philadelphia-district-attorney-rufus-seth-williams-sentenced-five-years-prison.

63. Vida Johnson, Zoom interview with author, October 12, 2022.

64. "Police Disciplinary Records by State," WYNC.org, accessed August 8, 2023, https://project.wnyc.org/disciplinary-records.

65. Lee O. Sanderlin and Jessica Anderson, "After Court Battle, Marilyn Mosby Releases List of 305 Baltimore Police Officers with Credibility Issues," *Baltimore Sun*, May 26, 2022, https://www.baltimoresun.com/news/crime/bs-md-ci-cr-marilyn-mosby-list-cops-credibility-issues-20220525-n5kab6xio5cpjjgio7acoehaiu-story.html.

66. Eli Hager and Justin George, "One Way to Deal with Cops Who Lie? Blacklist Them, Some DAs Say," The Marshall Project, January 17, 2019, https://www.themarshallproject.org/2019/01/17/one-way-to-deal-with-cops-who-lie-blacklist-them-some-das-say.

67. "Criminal Justice Standards for the Prosecution Function," sec. 3-1.2(b), American Bar Association, 2018.

CHAPTER 7

1. Stephanie Daniel, "Misidentification, Arrest of Black Teen Leads to New Colorado Law Changing a Police Eyewitness Procedure," KUNC, January 14, 2022, https://www.kunc.org/news/2022-01-14/misidentification-arrest-of-black-teen-leads-to-new-colorado-law-changing-a-police-eyewitness-procedure.

2. Daniel, "Misidentification, Arrest."

3. Edwin Grimsley, "What Wrongful Convictions Teach Us about Racial Inequality," Innocence Project, September 26, 2012, https://innocenceproject.org/what-wrongful-convictions-teach-us-about-racial-inequality.

4. Daniel, "Misidentification, Arrest."

5. Daniel, "Misidentification, Arrest."

6. Jemima Denham, "Georgetown Law Professors Weigh In on DC Council Rewrite of Criminal Code," *The Hoya*, November 11, 2021, https://thehoya.com/georgetown-law -professors-weigh-in-on-d-c-council-rewrite-of-criminal-code.

7. Denham, "Georgetown Law Professors."

8. "New Poll: DC Residents Overwhelmingly Support Revised Criminal Code Act of 2021, a Groundbreaking Criminal Justice Reform Measure," fwd.us, June 14, 2022, https://www .fwd.us/news/new-poll-dc-residents-overwhelmingly-support-revised-criminal-code-act-of -2021-a-groundbreaking-criminal-justice-reform-measure.

9. Susan Davis, "Congress Overturns DC Crime Bill with President Biden's Help," NPR, March 8, 2023, https://www.npr.org/2023/03/08/1161902691/d-c-crime-bill-biden-overturn.

10. Rebekah Bastian, "What We Can Learn from Ruth Bader Ginsburg about Bringing Others Along in Discussions of Equality," *Forbes*, September 19, 2020, https://www.forbes.com /sites/rebekahbastian/2020/09/19/what-we-can-learn-from-ruth-bader-ginsburg/?sh =7a2a31cc1fe8.

11. Katie Mettler, "Once Jailed, These Women Now Hold Courts Accountable—with Help from Students, Retirees and Fiona Apple," *Washington Post*, April 9, 2021, https://www .washingtonpost.com/local/public-safety/courtwatch-prince-georges/2021/04/08/dc63e064 -2e96-11eb-bae0-50bb17126614_story.html.

12. Bryce Covert, "The Court Watch Movement Wants to Expose the 'House of Cards,'" *The Appeal*, July 16, 2018, https://theappeal.org/court-watch-accountability-movement.

13. Covert, "The Court Watch Movement."

14. Daniel A. Medina, "The Progressive Prosecutors Blazing a New Path for the US Justice System," *The Guardian*, July 23, 2019, https://www.theguardian.com/us-news/2019/jul/23 /us-justice-system-progressive-prosecutors-mass-incarceration-death-penalty.

15. "ABA Court Watching," American Bar Association, May 2021, https://www.americanbar .org/groups/legal_aid_indigent_defense/indigent_defense_systems_improvement/court -watching0/aba-court-watching.

16. "ABA Court Watching."

17. "About Us," CourtWatch PG, accessed August 8, 2023, https://courtwatchpg.com.

18. "Qiana Johnson, Founder, CourtWatch," Lifeafterrelease.org, accessed August 8, 2023, https://mailchi.mp/lifeafterrelease/qiana-johnson.

19. Johnson v. State, No. 1042–2021 (Md. Ct. Spec. App. Apr. 25, 2022), Justia, https://law .justia.com/cases/maryland/court-of-appeals/2022/11-21.html.

20. "Qiana Johnson, Founder, CourtWatch."

21. "Carmen Johnson Sentenced for Two Separate Residential Mortgage Fraud Schemes," US Attorney's Office, District of Maryland, June 4, 2015, https://www.justice.gov/usao-md/pr /carmen-johnson-sentenced-two-separate-residential-mortgage-fraud-schemes.

22. "Dr. Carmen Johnson, Director, CourtWatch," Lifeafterrelease.org, accessed August 8, 2023, https://mailchi.mp/lifeafterrelease/dr-carmen-johnson.

23. Katie Mettler, "Court Watchers, with Fiona Apple's Help, Are Fighting to Keep Virtual Access beyond the Pandemic," *Washington Post*, March 18, 2022, https://www.washingtonpost.com /dc-md-va/2022/03/18/virtual-court-access.

24. Mettler, "Court Watchers."

25. Elliot Williams, "Fiona Apple Ditched the Grammys to Shout Out This PG County Court-watching Group," NPR, March 31, 2021, https://www.npr.org/local/305/2021/03/31 /983046391/fiona-apple-ditched-the-grammys-to-shout-out-this-p-g-county-courtwatch ing-group.

26. Katie Mettler, "Senior Judge Urges Md. Courts to Keep Virtual Access beyond Pandemic," *Washington Post*, April 7, 2022, https://www.washingtonpost.com/dc-md-va/2022/04/07 /maryland-court-virtual.

27. DeRay McKesson, Zoom interview with author, October 28, 2022.

28. Ashish S. Joshi and Christina T. Kline, "Lack of Jury Diversity: A National Problem with Individual Consequences," American Bar Association, September 1, 2015, https:// www.americanbar.org/groups/litigation/committees/diversity-inclusion/articles/2015 /lack-of-jury-diversity-national-problem-individual-consequences.

29. Russell Contreras, "Courts May See Spike in People Wanting to Serve on Juries," Axios, July 5, 2021, https://www.axios.com/2021/07/05/courts-spike-people-serve-juries-george-floyd.

30. Rita Omokha, "Since 'Ferguson': Life for Students after Michael Brown," *The Hechinger Report*, August 4, 2022, https://hechingerreport.org/since-ferguson-life-for-students-after -michael-brown.

31. Omokha, "Since 'Ferguson.'"

32. Josh Sanburn, "All the Ways Darren Wilson Described Being Afraid of Michael Brown," *Time*, November 25, 2014, https://time.com/3605346/darren-wilson-michael-brown-demon.

33. Sanburn, "All the Ways Darren Wilson Described."

34. Gabriella Nuñez and Erin Dobrzyn, "Protesting Is Part of American History, These Historic Demonstrations Led to Changes in US Policy," ClickOrlando.com, updated June 12, 2020, https://www.clickorlando.com/features/2020/06/10/protesting-is-part-of-american-history -these-historic-demonstrations-led-to-changes-in-us-policy.

35. Nuñez and Dobrzyn, "Protesting Is Part of American History."

36. Sarah Frostenson, "The Women's Marches May Have Been the Largest Demonstration in US History," Vox, January 31, 2017, https://www.vox.com/2017/1/22/14350808 /womens-marches-largest-demonstration-us-history-map.

37. Leanna Garfield and Zoë Ettinger, "14 of the Biggest Marches and Protests in American History," Insider, June 1, 2020, https://www.businessinsider.com/largest-marches-us

-history-2017-1#an-anti-vietnam-war-protest-in-washington-dc-happened-on-november
-15-1969-2.

38. Garfield and Ettinger, "14 Biggest Marches."

39. Frostenson, "The Women's Marches."

40. "2018 Person of the Year: The Wesley Bell Coalition," *St. Louis American*, December 27, 2018, https://www.stlamerican.com/news/editorials/2018-person-of-the-year-the-wesley -bell-coalition/article_2823de6a-0981-11e9-90a4-0b47e1ef0e3d.html.

41. "Meet Wesley," Wesley Bell U.S. Senate, accessed August 8, 2023, https://www.votewesley bell.com/meet-wesley.

42. Maurice Possley, "Keith Davis, Jr.: Other Maryland Exonerations," National Registry of Exonerations, updated February 15, 2023, https://www.law.umich.edu/special/exoneration /Pages/casedetail.aspx?caseid=6543.

43. Tim Prudente, "Activist DeRay McKesson's Nonprofit Takes Up Defense of Keith Davis Jr., Unveils Website Faulting State's Case," *Baltimore Sun*, July 21, 2021, https://www .baltimoresun.com/news/crime/bs-md-ci-cr-campaign-zero-keith-davis-jr-20210721-oa2c jygd2ngi7kq5c3fsraqmue-story.html.

44. Prudente, "Activist DeRay McKesson's Nonprofit."

45. Ron Cassie, "The Many Trials of Keith Davis Jr.," Baltimore, November 2021, https://www .baltimoremagazine.com/section/historypolitics/the-many-trials-of-keith-davis-jr-remains -incarcerated-wife-fights-for-his-freedom.

46. Kelly Davis, Zoom interview with author, February 3, 2023.

47. Chao Xiong and Paul Walsh, "Ex-Police Officer Derek Chauvin Charged with Murder, Manslaughter in George Floyd Death," *Star Tribune*, May 30, 2020, https://www.startribune .com/protests-build-anew-after-fired-officer-charged-jailed/570869672.

48. Jane C. Timm, "Most States Disenfranchise Felons. Maine and Vermont Allow Inmates to Vote from Prison," NBC News, February 24, 2018, https://www.nbcnews.com /politics/politics-news/states-rethink-prisoner-voting-rights-incarceration-rates-rise -n850406.

49. Jason Lemon, "Can Prisoners Vote in Other Countries? Bernie Sanders Wants Felons to Cast Ballots While Incarcerated," *Newsweek*, April 24, 2019, https://www.newsweek.com /which-countries-felons-vote-1405142.

50. Sam Levine, "Iowa Ends Lifetime Voting Ban on People with Felony Convictions," *The Guardian*, August 5, 2020, https://www.theguardian.com/us-news/2020/aug/05/iowa -voting-felony-lifetime-ban-ended.

51. Malia Brink, "Fines Fees, and the Right to Vote," *Human Rights Magazine* 45, no. 1, American Bar Association, February 9, 2020, https://www.americanbar.org/groups/crsj/publications /human_rights_magazine_home/voting-rights/fines--fees--and-the-right-to-vote.

52. Courtney Connley, "Why Restoring Voting Rights to Former Felons Is 'One of the Key Civil Right Issues of Our Time,'" CNBC Make It, updated October 21, 2020, https://www.cnbc.com/2020/10/20/restoring-voting-rights-to-former-felons-is-one-of-the-key-civil-right-issues-of-our-time.html.

53. German Lopez, "5.2 Million People Can't Vote Due to Their Felony Record, according to a New Report," Vox, October 14, 2020, https://www.vox.com/2020/10/14/21515850/voting-rights-sentencing-project-felon-disenfranchisement.

54. Christopher Uggen, Ryan Larson, and Sarah Shannon, with Arleth Pulido-Nava, "Locked Out 2020: Estimates of People Denied Voting Rights Due to a Felony Conviction," The Sentencing Project, 2020, https://www.sentencingproject.org/app/uploads/2022/08/Locked-Out-2020.pdf.

55. "UN Committee Says U.S. Bans on Former Prisoner Voting Violate International Law," ACLU.org, accessed February 6, 2021, https://www.aclu.org/other/un-committee-says-us-bans-former-prisoner-voting-violate-international-law.

56. Amita Kelly, "Does It Matter That 95 Percent of Elected Prosecutors Are White?," NPR, July 8, 2015, https://www.npr.org/sections/itsallpolitics/2015/07/08/420913118/does-it-matter-that-95-of-elected-prosecutors-are-white.

57. Christina Carrega, "For the Few Black Women Prosecutors, Hate and 'Misogynoir' Are Part of Life," ABC News, March 21, 2020, https://abcnews.go.com/US/black-women-prosecutors-hate-misogynoir-part-life/story?id=68961291.

58. Cheryl Corley, "Newly Elected DAs Vow to Continue Reforms, End Policies Deemed Unfair," NPR, November 26, 2020, https://www.npr.org/2020/11/26/938425725/newly-elected-das-vow-to-continue-reforms-end-policies-deemed-unfair.

59. Angela J. Davis, "The Carceral Force of Prosecutor Associations, Explained," The Appeal, February 26, 2021, https://theappeal.org/the-lab/explainers/the-carceral-force-of-prosecutor-associations-explained.

60. bell hooks, *Feminism Is for Everybody: Passionate Politics* (New York: Routledge, 2015), 110.

CHAPTER 8

1. Gabriella Nunez, "Prosecutors Map Out Ahmaud Arbery's Jog before Resting Its Case in Trial," 11 Alive, updated November 16, 2021, https://www.11alive.com/article/news/crime/ahmaud-arbery/mapping-ahmaud-arberys-run-how-2-mile-jog-turned-into-evidence/85-0b472389-3fd3-4119-a85e-91d56781504b.

2. Amy Harmon and Sabrina Tavernise, "One Big Difference about George Floyd Protests: Many White Faces," *New York Times*, updated June 17, 2020, https://www.nytimes.com/2020/06/12/us/george-floyd-white-protesters.html.

3. Fabriola Cineas, "How Portland's Wall of Moms Collapsed—and Was Reborn under Black Leadership," Vox, August 4, 2020, https://www.vox.com/21353939/portland-wall-of-moms-collapses-to-form-moms-united-for-black-lives.

4. Cineas, "How Portland's Wall of Moms Collapsed."

5. Jenny Singer, "Don't Watch 'The Help' . . . or These Other White-Savior Movies," *Glamour*, June 11, 2020, https://www.glamour.com/story/the-help-white-savior-movies.

6. James Baldwin, "On Being White and Other Lies," in *Black on White, Black Writers on What It Means to Be White*, ed. David R. Roediger (New York: Schocken Books, 1998).

7. Baldwin, "On Being White and Other Lies," 178.

8. Baldwin, "On Being White and Other Lies," 180.

9. "Abolitionism," *Africans in America*, PBS, accessed February 6, 2021, https://www.pbs.org/wgbh/aia/part4/4narr2.html.

10. Linton Weeks, "How Black Abolitionists Changed a Nation," NPR History Dept., February 26, 2015, https://www.npr.org/sections/npr-history-dept/2015/02/26/388993874/how-black-abolitionists-changed-a-nation.

11. "About NAACP," NAACP, accessed February 6, 2021, https://naacp.org/nations-premier-civil-rights-organization; "Our History: Our Founders," NAACP, accessed February 6, 2021, https://naacp.org/about/our-history.

12. Anthony Siracusa, "A Century Ago, James Weldon Johnson Became the First Black Person to Head the NAACP," *The Conversation*, November 24, 2020. https://theconversation.com/a-century-ago-james-weldon-johnson-became-the-first-black-person-to-head-the-naacp-149513.

13. "Congress of Racial Equality (CORE)," *King Encyclopedia*, The Martin Luther King, Jr. Research and Education Institute, Stanford University, accessed February 6, 2021, https://kinginstitute.stanford.edu/encyclopedia/congress-racial-equality-core.

14. Martin Luther King Jr., "Letter from Birmingham Jail," in *Why We Can't Wait* (New York: Berkley, 2000), 85–112.

15. "Ralph Emerson McGill," International Civil Rights Walk of Fame, National Park Service, accessed February 6, 2021, https://www.nps.gov/features/malu/feat0002/wof/Ralph_McGill.htm.

16. King, "Letter from Birmingham Jail."

17. Krissah Thompson, "In March on Washington, White Activists Were Largely Overlooked but Strategically Essential," *Washington Post*, August 25, 2013, https://www.washingtonpost.com/lifestyle/style/in-march-on-washington-white-activists-were-largely-overlooked-but-strategically-essential/2013/08/25/f2738c2a-eb27-11e2-8023-b7f07811d98e_story.html.

18. Thompson, "In March on Washington."

19. Judy Lubin, Zoom interview with author, December 3, 2022.

20. George Lipsitz, *The Possessive Investment in Whiteness* (Philadelphia: Temple University Press, 2018).

21. Lipsitz, *The Possessive Investment in Whiteness*.

22. Lipsitz, *The Possessive Investment in Whiteness*, chap. 6, paraphrasing from Toni Cade Bambara's novel, *The Salt Eaters*.

23. Paulo Freire, *Pedagogy of the Oppressed*: 30th anniversary ed. (New York: Continuum, 2000).

24. King, "Letter from Birmingham Jail."

25. Brian Schaffner, "White Republicans and Independents Are Starting to Acknowledge Their Privilege, But Will It Last?," Data for Progress, June 15, 2020, https://www.dataforprogress .org/blog/2020/6/15/white-republicans-and-independents-are-starting-to-acknowledge -their-privilege-but-will-it-last.

26. Rory Fleming, Zoom interview with author, December 31, 2022.

27. Peggy McIntosh, "White Privilege: Unpacking the Invisible Knapsack," Peace and Freedom, July/August 1989, https://psychology.umbc.edu/files/2016/10/White-Privilege_McIntosh -1989.pdf.

28. Melissa DePino, "Why I Tweeted the Starbucks Arrest Video," CNN, April 16, 2018, https:// www.cnn.com/2018/04/16/opinions/philadelphia-starbucks-why-i-tweeted-the-video -depino-opnion/index.html.

29. Renée Graham, "Use Your White Privilege to Fight Racism," *Boston Globe*, April 24, 2018, https://www.bostonglobe.com/opinion/2018/04/24/use-your-white-privilege-fight-racism /l3kE21EFsMpTF6uboe72pI/story.html.

30. DePino, "Why I Tweeted the Starbucks Arrest Video."

31. Errin Haines Whack, "Black Men Arrested at Starbucks Settle with the Company," AP News, May 2, 2018, https://apnews.com/article/774de094bff34421af4cb250a20475dc.

32. Whack, "Black Men Arrested at Starbucks."

33. Nicholas Turner and Sam McCann, "Chesa Boudin's Recall Isn't about Crime, It's about Gentrification," Vera Institute of Justice, July 26, 2022, https://www.vera.org/news/chesa -boudins-recall-isnt-about-crime-its-about-gentrification.

34. Turner and McCann, "Chesa Boudin's Recall Isn't about Crime."

35. California Constitution, article II, clause B, section 14 (June 8, 1976).

36. Bigad Shaban and Robert Campos, "83,000 Signatures Submitted to Force SF District Attorney Chesa Boudin into Recall Election," NBC Bay Area, updated October 29, 2021, https://www.nbcbayarea.com/investigations/83000-signatures-submitted-to-force-sf-district -attorney-chesa-boudin-into-recall-election/2697663.

37. Rose Aguilar and Bee Soll, "San Francisco Ousts DA Chesa Boudin with 25.8% Voter Turnout," KALW, June 8, 2022, https://www.kalw.org/show/your-call/2022-06-08/san -francisco-ousts-da-chesa-boudin.

38. Turner and McCann, "Chesa Boudin's Recall Isn't about Crime."

39. "QuickFacts, San Francisco County, California," US Census Bureau, https://www.census .gov/quickfacts/sanfranciscocountycalifornia; Nami Sumida, "San Francisco May Be Small,

But It's among America's Most Densely Populated Cities," *San Francisco Chronicle*, November 29, 2021, https://www.sfchronicle.com/sf/article/San-Francisco-may-be-small-but-it-s-among-16650575.php.

40. "QuickFacts, Philadelphia County, Pennsylvania," US Census Bureau, https://www.census.gov/quickfacts/fact/table/philadelphiacountypennsylvania/AGE775221.

41. 6ABC Digital Staff, "Philadelphia DA Larry Krasner Wins Reelection for Second Term, AP Reports," 6ABC, November 3, 2021, https://6abc.com/2021-election-philadelphia-results-philly-da-larry-krasner-charles-peruto/11191301.

42. Emily Owens, Erin Kerrison, and Bernardo Santos Da Silveira, "Examining Racial Disparities in Criminal Case Outcomes among Indigent Defendants in San Francisco," Quattrone Center, Penn Law, May 2017, https://www.law.upenn.edu/live/files/6791-examining-racial-disparities-may-2017combinedpdf.

CHAPTER 9

1. Ned Oliver, "Virginia Lawmakers Vote to Reform 224-Year-Old Jury Sentencing Law," *Virginia Mercury*, October 17, 2020, https://www.virginiamercury.com/2020/10/17/a-revolutionary-change-va-lawmakers-vote-to-reform-224-year-old-jury-sentencing-law.

2. Danielle Musselman, "Virginia Joins the Majority of the Nation and Ends Jury Sentencing," *Interrogating Justice*, July 12, 2021, https://interrogatingjustice.org/uncategorized/fairness-in-sentencing/virginia-joins-the-majority-of-the-nation-and-ends-jury-sentencing.

3. Andrew Van Dam, "Algorithms Were Supposed to Make Virginia Judges Fairer. What Happened Was Far More Complicated," *Washington Post*, November 19, 2019, https://www.washingtonpost.com/business/2019/11/19/algorithms-were-supposed-make-virginia-judges-more-fair-what-actually-happened-was-far-more-complicated.

4. Oliver, "Virginia Lawmakers Vote to Reform."

5. "Virginia Profile," Prison Policy Initiative, accessed August 8, 2023, https://www.prisonpolicy.org/profiles/va.html.

6. Jenny Gathright, "Jury Sentencing Reform Brings Virginia 'out of the Ice Age,' Proponents Say," DCist, December 17, 2020, https://dcist.com/story/20/12/17/jury-sentencing-reform-brings-virginia-out-ice-age.

7. Oliver, "Virginia Lawmakers Vote to Reform."

8. Amy Ashworth, Anton Bell, Buta Biberaj, Parisa Dehghani-Tafti, Steve Descano, Howard Gwynn, James M. Hingeley, et al., "Virginia Progressive Prosecutors for Justice," March 8, 2021, https://www.charlottesville.gov/DocumentCenter/View/5184/Virginia-Progressive-Prosecutors-for-Justice-letter-to-General-Assembly-382021.

9. Samantha O'Connell, "Virginia Becomes First Southern State to Abolish the Death Penalty," American Bar Association, March 24, 2021, https://www.americanbar.org

/groups/committees/death_penalty_representation/publications/project_blog/virginia
-death-penalty-repeal.

10. Colleen Long, "Report: Death Penalty Cases Show History of Racial Disparity," AP News, September 15, 2020, https://apnews.com/article/united-states-lifestyle-race-and-ethnicity -discrimination-racial-injustice-ded1f517a0fd64bf1d55c448a06acccc.

11. "State by State," Death Penalty Information Center, accessed April 7, 2022, https:// deathpenaltyinfo.org/state-and-federal-info/state-by-state; Diana Velayos, "What States Still Have Execution? Which One Has the Most?," AS, November 4, 2021, https://en.as.com /en/2021/11/04/latest_news/1636033758_438314.html.

12. "Join the Movement for Criminal Justice Reform in Virginia," Justice Forward, https:// justiceforwardva.com/about.

13. "Home Page," Maryland Alliance for Justice Reform, accessed August 8, 2023, https://www .ma4jr.org.

14. "Felony Murder Rule," Maryland Alliance for Justice Reform, accessed August 8, 2023, https://www.ma4jr.org/felony-murder-rule.

15. Nazgol Ghandnoosh, Emma Stammen, and Connie Budaci, "Felony Murder, An On Ramp for Extreme Sentencing," The Sentencing Project, March 31, 2022, https://www.sentencing project.org/reports/felony-murder-an-on-ramp-for-extreme-sentencing.

16. Ghandnoosh, Stammen, and Budaci, "Felony Murder."

17. "Florida Prisoner Executed after 10-Year Fight for Life," *St. Petersburg Times*, August 29, 1987; "Executed But Did Not Directly Kill Victim," Executions Overview, Death Penalty Information Center, https://deathpenaltyinfo.org/executions/executions-overview /executed-but-did-not-directly-kill-victim.

18. Editorial Advisory Board, "Editorial Advisory Board: It's Time to Abolish Felony Murder in Md.," *The Daily Record*, June 30, 2022, https://thedailyrecord.com/2022/06/30/ editorial-advisory-board-its-time-to-abolish-felony-murder-in-md.

19. "Felony Murder Explained: What Is Felony Murder?," Felony Murder Law Reform, https:// fmlr.org/felony-murder-explained.

20. Ghandnoosh, Stammen, and Budaci, "Felony Murder."

21. Ghandnoosh, Stammen, and Budaci, "Felony Murder."

22. Akhi Johnson, Zoom interview with author, October 18, 2022.

23. Vera Institute of Justice, "Reshaping Prosecution Initiative: A Safer and More Equitable Approach," accessed 8/7/2023, https://www.vera.org/ending-mass-incarceration /criminalization-racial-disparities/prosecution-reform/reshaping-prosecution-initiative.

24. Johnson, Zoom interview.

25. Johnson, Zoom interview.

26. Richard Luscombe, "'Unjust Practices': US Prosecutor Takes Stand against Minor Police Traffic Stops," *The Guardian*, September 9, 2021, https://www.theguardian.com/us-news/2021/sep/09/minnesota-prosecutor-philando-castile-cases-minor-traffic-violations.

27. Dana Thiede, "Officer Charged in Philando Castile Shooting," KVUE, November 17, 2016, https://www.kvue.com/article/news/local/officer-charged-in-philando-castile-shooting/89-352780092.

28. Emma Brown, "'He Knew the Kids and They Loved Him': Minn. Shooting Victim Was an Adored School Cafeteria Manager," *Washington Post*, July 7, 2016, https://www.washingtonpost.com/news/education/wp/2016/07/07/he-knew-the-kids-and-they-loved-him-minnesota-shooting-victim-was-an-adored-school-cafeteria-manager.

29. Sarah Horner, "One Year On, Prosecutor Discusses Cop's 'Unreasonable Panic' in Castile Killing," Pioneer Press, updated December 17, 2017, https://www.twincities.com/2017/12/16/one-year-on-prosecutor-discusses-cops-unreasonable-panic-in-castile-killing.

30. Horner, "One Year On, Prosecutor Discusses."

31. Luscombe, "'Unjust Practices'"; "Research Shows Black Drivers More Likely to Be Stopped by Police," New York University, May 5, 2020, https://www.nyu.edu/about/news-publications/news/2020/may/black-drivers-more-likely-to-be-stopped-by-police.html.

32. Emma Pierson, Camelia Simoiu, Jan Overgoor, Sam Corbett-Davies, Daniel Jenson, Amy Shoemaker, Vignesh Ramachandran, et al., "A Large-Scale Analysis of Racial Disparities in Police Stops across the United States," *Nature Human Behavior*, May 4, 2020, https://www.nature.com/articles/s41562-020-0858-1.

33. Mara H. Gottfried, "Ramsey County Attorney Says He Won't Prosecute Most Felonies That Result from Pretextual Traffic Stops," TwinCities.com Pioneer Press, updated October 22, 2021, https://www.twincities.com/2021/09/08/ramsey-county-attorney-says-he-wont-prosecute-felonies-that-result-from-pretextual-traffic-stops.

34. "Reshaping Prosecution: A Safer and More Equitable Approach," Vera Institute of Justice, https://www.vera.org/ending-mass-incarceration/criminalization-racial-disparities/prosecution-reform/reshaping-prosecution-initiative.

35. Akhi Johnson, Zoom interview with author, October 18, 2022.

36. *Motion for Justice*, Vera Institute of Justice, video, accessed August 8, 2023, https://motionforjustice.vera.org.

37. Jamila Hodge, Zoom interview with author, October 24, 2022.

38. "Vera Institute Partners with Eight New Prosecutors' Offices to Reduce Racial Disparities in Prosecution by 20 Percent," Vera Institute of Justice, https://www.vera.org/newsroom/vera-institute-partners-with-eight-new-prosecutors-offices-to-reduce-racial-disparities-in-prosecution-by-20-percent.

39. Johnson, Zoom interview.

40. "Tipping the Scales: Challengers Take On the Old Boys Club of Elected Prosecutors," Reflective Democracy Campaign, October 2019, https://wholeads.us/research/tipping-the-scales-elected-prosecutors.

41. "Issues: A New Vision for the Justice System," Fair and Just Prosecution, accessed August 16, 2023, https://fairandjustprosecution.org/issues/a-new-vision-for-the-justice-system.

42. "Issues: A New Vision for the Justice System."

43. Alexi Jones, "Reform without Results: Why States Should Stop Excluding Violent Offenses from Criminal Justice Reforms," Prison Policy Initiative, April 2020, https://www.prison policy.org/reports/violence.html.

44. Jones, "Reform without Results."

45. Ashley Nellis, "The Color of Justice: Racial and Ethnic Disparity in State Prisons," The Sentencing Project, October 13, 2021, https://www.sentencingproject.org/publications /color-of-justice-racial-and-ethnic-disparity-in-state-prisons.

46. John Gramlich, "What the Data Says (and Doesn't Say) about Crime in the United States," Pew Research Center, accessed November 20, 2020, https://www.pewresearch.org /fact-tank/2020/11/20/facts-about-crime-in-the-u-s.

47. Gramlich, "What the Data Says."

48. Karl Racine, Zoom interview with author, December 30, 2022.

49. Hodge, Zoom interview; "Home Page: The EJUSA Difference," Equal Justice USA, accessed August 8, 2023, https://ejusa.org.

50. "About Us: Accomplishments," Equal Justice USA, accessed August 14, 2023, https://ejusa .org/about-us/accomplishments.

51. "Mass Shootings in the U.S. by Shooter's by Race/Ethnicity as of Feb 2020," Statista, January 5, 2021, https://www.statista.com/statistics/476456/mass-shootings-in-the-us-by -shooter-s-race.

52. Rashawn Ray, "Preventing Racial Hate Crimes Means Tackling White Supremacist Ideology," Brookings, May 17, 2022, https://www.brookings.edu/blog/how-we-rise/2022/05/17 /preventing-racial-hate-crimes-means-tackling-white-supremacist-ideology.

53. Ray, "Preventing Racial Hate Crimes."

54. Jonathan Franklin, "A New System to Flag Racist Incidents and Acts of Hate Is Named after Emmett Till," NPR, August 23, 2022, https://www.npr.org/2022/08/23/1118969209 /emmett-till-alert-system-maryland-hate-crimes.

55. Franklin, "A New System to Flag Racist Incidents."

56. "Race & Justice: The Challenge," NAACP, accessed August 8, 2023, https://naacp.org/issues /race-justice.

57. Racine, Zoom interview with author.

58. "Man Who Used 'Affluenza' Defense for Killing 4 People in DUI Crash Is Jailed in Texas," CBS News, January 3, 2020, https://www.cbsnews.com/news/ethan-couch-affluenza-defense-killing-4-people-dui-crash-jailed-fort-worth-texas-probation-today-2020-01-03.

59. Caila Klass and Alexa Valiente, "'Affluenza' DUI Case: What Happened the Night of the Accident That Left 4 People Dead," ABC News, December 31, 2015, https://abcnews.go.com/US/affluenza-dui-case-happened-night-accident-left-people/story?id=34481444.

60. Meg Wagner, "'Affluenza' Teen's Rehab Cost Taxpayers Nearly $200,000 after Wealthy Parents Found 'Financially Unable to Pay,'" Daily News, April 13, 2016, https://www.nydailynews.com/news/national/affluenza-teen-parents-paid-fraction-200k-rehab-bill-article-1.2598964.

61. "Issues: A New Vision for the Justice System."

62. "Juvenile Detention Alternatives Initiative (JDAI)," Annie E. Casey Foundation, accessed August 8, 2023, https://www.aecf.org/work/juvenile-justice/jdai.

63. Robert H. Jackson, US Attorney General, "The Federal Prosecutor," address delivered at the Second Annual Conference of United States Attorneys, April 1, 1940, *Journal of the American Judicature Society* 24 (1940): 18–20; Benjamin Levin, "Imagining the Progressive Prosecutor," *Minnesota Law Review* 105 (2021): 1415–1451.

CONCLUSION

1. Miriam Aroni Krinsky, *Change from Within: Reimaging the 21st-Century Prosecutor* (New York: The New Press, 2022), xi.

2. "Report to the United Nations on Racial Disparities in the U.S. Criminal Justice System," The Sentencing Project, April 19, 2018, https://www.sentencingproject.org/publications/un-report-on-racial-disparities.

3. Justice Policy Institute and the Prison Policy Initiative, "The Right Investment?: Corrections Spending in Baltimore City," Prison Policy Initiative, February 2015, https://www.prisonpolicy.org/origin/md/report.html.

4. Liz Komar, Ashley Nellis, and Kristen M. Budd, "Counting Down: Paths to a 20-Year Maximum Prison Sentence," The Sentencing Project, February 15, 2023, https://www.sentencingproject.org/reports/counting-down-paths-to-a-20-year-maximum-prison-sentence.

Index